Cicero

For David Daube

I have resolved to take
wisdom for my playmate;
for I know she will be a good
counsellor and a comforter to me
in trouble and in sorrow

The Wisdom of Solomon 8, 9

CICERO

AND THE ROMAN REPUBLIC

Manfred Fuhrmann

Translated by
W.E. Yuill

BLACKWELL
Oxford UK & Cambridge USA

Copyright © Artemis Verlag, 1990
English translation © Basil Blackwell Ltd, 1992

First published 1990
English translation first published 1992

Blackwell Publishers
108 Cowley Road
Oxford   OX4 1JF
UK

Three Cambridge Center
Cambridge, Massachusetts 02142
USA

British Library Cataloguing in Publication Data

A CIP catalogue record for this book is available from the British Library.

Library of Congress Cataloging-in-Publication Data

Fuhrmann, Manfred.
    [Cicero und die römische Republik.   English]
    Cicero and the Roman Republic/Manfred Fuhrmann; translated by
W. E. Yuill.
        p.   cm.
    Translation of: Cicero und die römische Republik.
    Includes bibliographical references and index.
    ISBN 0–631–17879–1 (acid-free paper)
    1. Cicero, Marcus Tullius.   2. Rome – Politics and
government – 265–30 BC   3. Statesmen – Rome – Biography.   4. Orators –
Rome – Biography.   I. Title.
DG260.C5F8413   1992
937'.05'092 – dc20
[B]   91–41486
                                                                      CIP

Typeset in 10 on 12 pt Sabon
by Graphicraft Typesetters Ltd, Hong Kong
Printed in Great Britain by TJ Press (Padstow) Ltd; Padstow, Cornwall

This book is printed on acid-free paper

Contents

Preface

A biography which takes as its subject a personality from the ancient world generally suffers from the dearth of sources. As far as statemen are concerned, the motives for their actions tend to remain in the dark, while little is known of their private lives. In the case of writers and philosophers, as a rule, the biographer has to make do with a sketchy pattern of isolated facts; otherwise he or she has to resort to a reconstruction of the general historical and cultural background and to an analysis of surviving works.

In this respect Cicero forms one of the rare exceptions. For all three dimensions of his life – political events in late Republican Rome, his literary works and his career – evidence is available on an uncommonly large scale, his own and that of others, from contemporary and from later sources. As regards Cicero's own evidence, the forensic and political speeches naturally assume great significance. But the abundance of private letters is quite remarkable and unparalleled – some 900 in total, including about 100 items from Cicero's correspondents. In the letters to his friend Atticus in particular, the author's thoughts, motives and moods are directly revealed as with no other individual from the ancient world. In the case of Cicero, therefore, the biographer can and indeed must select and, by the very fact of this selection, adopt a point of view, as is otherwise only possible and necessary with personalities from more recent centuries. Cicero belongs to those few figures who admit a considerable degree of freedom in any account of their lives and who are at the same time subject to arbitrary judgements – and no such account can presume to come anywhere near exhausting its subject.

The present undertaking stands in a long line of Cicero biographies. It may be justified by its particular purpose: I am concerned above all to present Cicero's life to those readers who do not possess extensive previous knowledge of the subject and to whom ancient languages and the history and culture of the ancient world are relatively unfamiliar. I have consequently aimed at a clear and generally comprehensible style of presentation which pays due regard not only to Cicero's life but also to the relevant premises of Cicero's thought and actions, to the Roman state and its history, as well as to contemporary cultural factors, particularly Greek rhetoric and philosophy. Whatever is here stated as fact is vouched for by sources and, wherever possible, Cicero is allowed to speak for himself.

Amongst the works to which I am particularly indebted, the history of Roman literature (*Scriptorum illustrium Latinae linguae libri XVIII*), completed about 1437 by Sicco Polentone, town clerk of Padua, takes pride of place. Books 10–16 contain an account of Cicero's life which is not only vivid and true to the sources, but which is also concerned to deal with those general factors which the reader needs to know about. Apart from this major source, work on the present biography entailed constant reference to that product of Christoph Martin Wieland's old age – his chronologically arranged translation into German of all Cicero's letters (7 volumes, Zurich 1808–21). Wieland's commentaries furnish a range of insights into Cicero's personal relationships that have not been matched even now, while the style of his translation aimed at a lucidity of expression which served as a guideline for the quotations from Cicero reproduced here. Finally, there is the biography produced by the ancient historian Matthias Gelzer which first appeared in 1939 in Pauly's *Realencyclopädie der classischen Altertumswissenchaft* and was subsequently published separately in 1969. This work helped me to find my way through a mass of evidence. Particularly helpful was the book's cautiously judicious assessment of Cicero, especially when it was a matter of judging his shortcomings as a politician which have so often been deprecated.

1

Cicero's Antecedents and Youth

It was under the consuls Quintus Servilius Caepio and Gaius Atilius Serranus that Marcus Tullius Cicero was born, on the third day before the nones of January, that is on 3 January 106 BC. He was the same age as Pompey and six years older than Caesar. His mother gave birth painlessly, while his nurse, so it was said, had been informed in a prophetic vision that she would nurture great good fortune for Rome.[1]

Cicero's birthplace was Arpinum, now called Arpino, a small town on Volscian territory about 60 miles south-east of Rome. It lies in hilly country on the slopes of the Liri valley and is fortified by a well-preserved polygonal rampart, a so-called Cyclopean wall.

Arpinum is first mentioned as a bone of contention in the Second Samnite War: according to Livy it had been recaptured by the Romans in 305 BC.[2] Not long afterwards, in 303, its inhabitants were granted Roman citizenship, not initially as full citizens, but merely the *civitas sine suffragio*, i.e. lacking the vote and other political rights. Nevertheless, they were henceforth on an equal footing with Romans as regards the civil law. They might contract valid Roman marriages, litigate in the Roman courts and so on. Arpinum was initially a *praefectura*; it was run by a *praefectus* from Rome and had little say in the management of its own affairs. In 188 BC a law was passed conferring full citizenship on its inhabitants: only then were they eligible to take part in elections in Rome and, moreover, to stand for election. Later on, we do not know when exactly (probably in the course of the second century BC), Arpinum became a proper *municipium*, an Italic country town with full autonomy.

The history of Arpinum reflects the features typical of that period – the fourth and third centuries BC – when Rome was gaining control of central and southern Italy. Throughout the area there were urban communities which had formed more or less stable alliances on the basis of ethnic affinities and which devoted their energies to feuding with each other at every point. The Volscians were one of the smaller tribes, neighbours of the Latins in the west and the Samnites in the east; they were assailed on both sides and ultimately suffered the usual fate, subservience to Rome. The dominant power, for its part, had no thought of depriving its subject territories of every vestige of their autonomy. It preferred to adhere to the ancient principle of the communal or city state: the dependent communities were simply no longer permitted to pursue an independent foreign policy. Otherwise they could manage their own affairs according to the treaty they had been granted, and their inhabitants had in gradually increasing measure access to the Roman citizenship that was generally sought after.

At the time of Cicero's birth, therefore, the map of central and southern Italy still presented an extremely motley appearance. It was not a territorial state divided into a number of administrative districts that Rome ruled over, but a conglomerate consisting of numerous small territories with a highly diverse legal status. Thus, apart from the municipia and the praefecturae already referred to, there were so-called colonies or settlements, under either Roman or Latin jurisdiction; in the former case they were outposts of Rome, a part of Rome itself. The inhabitants of the municipia, however, were reckoned to be no more than allies, Latins (since what had once been an ethnic feature had become a kind of legal status), or Romans without the suffrage – which was customarily a preliminary step towards full Roman citizenship. The allies, who had played a major part in the creation of the Empire, all wished ultimately to become Roman citizens. When Cicero was a young man a bitter conflict between them and Rome was to arise over this very issue.

Cicero has paid a handsome tribute to his home town, which was also the home of the celebrated Marius. The dialogue *De Legibus* – a conversation involving Cicero himself, his brother Quintus and his friend Atticus – takes place on the estate near Arpinum which he had inherited from his father, and the introduction to the second book in particular deals affectionately with the setting. The speakers have set off for a walk and make their way to a small island round which the Fibrenus flows before entering the Liri. Atticus, in Arpinum for the first time, had expected nothing but crags and mountains; he is surprised by the charm of the countryside. Cicero says he is attracted by the landscape, not only because it is beautiful and peaceful, but also because he regards Arpinum as his own, and his brother's, proper home (*patria*). This is where they come from, as members of a very old family. This is where their ancestors had left so many traces. The villa which Atticus sees there in front of him had been renovated on a grand scale by Cicero's father, who, being of a frail constitution, had spent his life there pursuing his studies. Cicero had been born in a smaller house while his grandfather was still alive.

Atticus asks how Cicero's statement that Arpinum was his proper home is to be understood: do he and his brother have two homes? Cicero declares yes – everyone who came from a municipium had two homes, a *patria loci* and a *patria juris* – his place of origin was his home in the sense of his natural setting, Rome was his home by virtue of the legal status it conferred. The greater fatherland, for which one must be prepared to lay down one's life, was the more important, but one nevertheless felt hardly less drawn to that fatherland where one had grown up. The brief exchange shows that, during Cicero's youth and long afterwards, an attitude existed among Romans living outside Rome which corresponded precisely to the constitutional situation of Italy, a kind of federative system.

Cicero's family name, Tullius, was evidently an ancient one: Rome's legendary sixth king Servius is said to have borne it, and the leader of the Volscians, familiar to us from the Coriolanus legend, was called Attius Tullus. It is only from the time of Cicero onwards, however, that the name crops up with relative frequency; it appears at that time among a number of families who were not apparently related. Thus, in 72 BC or a little later, Cicero represented a certain Marcus Tullius, who is otherwise unknown. And a Tullius Rufus who had been a *quaestor* and had fought on Caesar's side in the civil war between Caesar and Pompey had been slain by his own followers because they thought he was a traitor. In the ancient world Cicero's cognomen was derived from *cicer*, a chick-pea: an ancestor who was given this nickname was said to have had a wart resembling a pea on the end of his nose.[3] Hence, a nickname of the Roman kind, as in their portraits, which were anything but flattering. Such nicknames often corresponded to the 'Distinguishing Marks' entry in contemporary passports as, for instance, Naevius from *naevus*, a birthmark, Verrucosus from *verruca*, a wart, and so on.

Cicero claims to have been descended from a very old family, but, in fact, records go no further back than his paternal grandfather. He was also called Marcus Tullius Cicero, like his son and his grandson, and what is known of him suggests that he was actively involved in the rivalries and conflicts that culminated in the Gracchian crisis. He evidently sided with those who wished things to be kept as they were and who refused to countenance any change. During his lifetime Greek civilization, the most advanced of its day, with all its achievements – from pottery to poetry and scholarship – was penetrating to every corner of Italy, and not only Rome itself but the entire surrounding area was filled with Greek products and luxuries, Greek tradesmen, craftsmen, cooks and doctors. It is no wonder that it became fashionable, and not merely among the upper classes, for people to use the Greek language as a lingua franca. 'Our people', grandfather Cicero is said to have remarked, 'are like Syrian slaves: the better they speak Greek, the more shiftless they are.'[4]

In Rome certain minor changes took place before the reforms of the Gracchi. Thus, supporters of the reform group – *Populares*, as they were later dubbed – contrived to have the secret ballot introduced for elections and judicial verdicts (in 139 and 137 BC): the electorate was no longer to be controlled and cajoled by the wealthy and influential. When an argument then arose in Arpinum as well, as to whether a secret ballot by means of tokens might be introduced, grandfather Cicero opposed the suggestion as long as he lived. This placed him in the intriguing position of being at loggerheads with Marcus Gratidius, his wife's brother. There was hence ample precedent in the family for his grandson's conservative political stance.

The Gratidii came from Arpinum and were no doubt on friendly terms with the Marii, who were also from there. In *Brutus*, Cicero reports that his great-uncle Marcus Gratidius was an educated man, widely read in Greek literature, a close friend of the famous orator Marcus Antonius (one of the principal participants in the dialogue *De Oratore*) and himself an eloquent speaker.[5] He had served as an officer under Antonius, who was *praetor* at the time, and had been killed in action against Cilician pirates (in 102 BC). He was the husband of Maria, a sister of the celebrated Marius; his son Marcus was adopted by Marcus Marius, another brother of Maria, and was henceforward known as Marcus Marius Gratidianus. In the civil war of the eighties he belonged, as people's tribune and then as praetor, to Cinna's party – Sulla's victorious followers murdered him in November 82 in an exceptionally brutal manner, with the subsequent revolutionary leader Cataline taking part in the deed.

As can be seen, Cicero's relatives were everywhere involved in those turbulent times, and the two main trends that dominated public life and ultimately shook the very foundations of the Roman state were mirrored in miniature in his family: the conservatives, who were fighting to retain intact the traditional rule of the aristocracy, and the innovators who were committed to Greek culture and opposed to the supremacy of the aristocracy.

Cicero's paternal grandfather had two sons. In addition to Cicero's father, there was a younger son by the name of Lucius, who likewise belonged to the 'progressive' party: he was, as Cicero writes, *humanissimus homo*, a highly cultured individual.[6] He, too, accompanied Antonius to Cilicia, perhaps through the mediation of Gratidius and probably died soon after his return from there. He left a son, also called Lucius, who was thus a cousin of Cicero, as well as a daughter, who married Lucius Aelius Tubero, the famous lawyer. Quintus Aelius Tubero was a son of this marriage. In 46 BC this latter Tubero conducted the prosecution's case against Ligarius. In his speech for the defence, the second Caesar speech, which has come down to us, Cicero was able to secure Ligarius's acquittal.

Almost all the information we have about Cicero's father, who, as already mentioned, was also called Marcus Tullius Cicero, comes from his famous son. He was a Roman *eques*, or knight, and being, as his son writes, in poor health, mostly lived a retired life on his estate in Arpinum, taking no part in public affairs.[7] Wicked tongues asserted that he had been a fuller (*fullo*) by trade – and there is no reason to suppose that he did not carry on a business of this kind; there was nothing disreputable about that. He was married to a certain Helvia, and had two sons by her – Marcus Cicero and Quintus, younger by some four years. Helvia is not once referred to by her son Marcus in any of the surviving documents. But one anecdote has been handed down by Quintus which suggests that she was a prudent housewife:[8] she put her seal on all the empty wine jars so as to prevent jars being added which had been surreptitiously emptied behind her back. One of Helvia's sisters was married to an eques well versed in the law, Gaius Visellius Aculeo, a friend of the renowned orator Crassus. It seems Cicero's father already owned a house in Rome, like many members of the squirearchy; it was probably situated in the Carinae, on the western slope of the Esquiline Hill. His son Marcus handed it over to his younger brother after having purchased a splendid residence for himself at the foot of the Palatine Hill, on the north-east side (in 62 BC).

The introduction to the second book of *De Oratore* reveals that Cicero's father was a thoughtful man who carefully planned his sons' education. For him – as distinct from Cicero's grandfather – it went without saying that the future belonged to the education that had been imported from Greece, its literature, rhetoric and philosophy. This system, like Greek culture in general, was spreading throughout Italy at the time, and Cicero junior himself vouches for the fact that, in the period of peace between the Gracchian troubles and the civil wars of the eighties, Greek art and learning were enthusiastically cultivated, even outside Rome.[9] At the same time there was no lack of utilitarians who, in the bucolic fashion of ancient Rome, regarded all impractical knowledge and accomplishments as futile. They did their best to dissuade Cicero's father, as well as his sons, from an educational scheme that provided for a broad curriculum on the new pattern: such aspirations were pointless and foolish. Cicero and his brother, however, sided with their father, being guided mainly by two outstanding examples: the orators Crassus and Antonius, with whom they had close personal ties. For Crassus was actually a friend of their uncle Aculeo, while their connection with Antonius reached back as far as their great-uncle, Gratidius. It was obvious that Crassus and Antonius had both made a thorough study of Greek literature and philosophy, although they had attempted more or less to conceal the fact from their Roman acquaintances.

No doubt we may assume that the place where their training took place, apart from the preliminary stages, was Rome, with Crassus acting as their advisor. Young Cicero studied in the company of his brother and his cousins, Aculeo's sons (one of whom in fact achieved the rank of curule magistrate: Gaius Visellius Varro, died 58 BC). Marcus at once distinguished himself by his great talent and he made such a stir among his classmates that their fathers visited the school to marvel at this prodigy. His classmates were evidently not at all jealous: as a mark of distinction they used to accord him the central position as they walked to school.

'For, as far as my memory is able to look back into the past and revive the earliest impressions of my youth, whenever I cast my mind back that far, it is *he* whom I see before me as the one who first inspired me to take up and to pursue this calling (i.e. orator and advocate).'[10] Cicero wrote this in 62 BC – not about a teacher of rhetoric, but about the Greek poet Archias from Antioch in Syria who had found patrons in Rome and who probably was also granted Roman citizenship – so, at least, Cicero claimed when he defended his erstwhile teacher against the charge of having acquired Roman citizenship by false pretences. The lessons he had with Archias were certainly conducted in Greek, and the subject cannot have been anything other than Greek literature.

Do Cicero's first attempts at poetry derive from the teaching of Archias? They seem, it is true, to have been composed in Latin. Plutarch knew of a poem in tetrameters that was still extant in his day; it bore the title '*Pontius Glaucus*' ('The Sea-god Glaucus').[11] It deals, presumably in the ornate manner of the Hellenistic poets, with a Boeotian fisherman who eats a magic herb and is thereby transformed into an immortal maritime creature with the gift of prophecy. Cicero, who may have written this poem (of which nothing has survived) in 92 BC, when he was fourteen years old, was thus a precursor of Catullus and his circle, who formed the avant-garde of the age.

2

The Apprentice Years

Cicero concludes the dialogue *Brutus*, a historical account of Roman rhetoric, with an autobiographical sketch of his own career and his rise to become the most sought after advocate in Rome. Here, in connection with the journey he undertook in 79 BC (when he was twenty-seven years old) for purposes of study and recreation, he gives the following description of his appearance:

> At that time I suffered very much from emaciation and physical debility; I had a long, thin neck, a constitution and appearance which, it was believed, might jeopardize my life, were it to be subjected to physical strain and a major exertion of the lungs. And this worried those who were fond of me all the more, since I used to say everything without respite, without variation and with extreme exertion of my voice and body. Therefore, when my friends and the doctors advised me to give up my practice as an advocate, I thought I would prefer to run the risks, however great, rather than relinquish the hope of achieving fame as an orator.[1]

We would not be far wrong in supposing that the *sperata dicendi gloria* influenced the ideas and aspirations of the youthful Cicero from an early stage. His outstanding intellectual powers were obvious; they would have been manifested in the ease with which he learned things and in his extraordinary powers of expression. If Cicero had lived as a Greek among Greeks, he might have become a philosopher; in Rome, in spite of its receptiveness to Greek culture, there could be no question of any such profession. Since Cicero was not the scion of a house that belonged to the senatorial aristocracy, he was obliged to capitalize on his talents – and the only calling which Rome offered for these talents was that of a lawyer. Πολλὸν ἀριστεύειν καὶ ὑπείροχον ἔμμεναι ἄλλων – '[always] to be the first and distinguished before others.'[2] As a boy he once wrote to his brother that he had adopted this famous line from the *Iliad* as his motto.[3]

The lanky young man, threatened as much by his ambition as by his constitution, probably donned the toga of manhood in the year 91 or 90 on 17 March, as was the custom, on which day the Liberalia, a feast of Liber (Bacchus) was celebrated. Henceforth he was reckoned to be an adult and consequently might play his part in the public life of Rome, in meetings and debates at the forum. He was at once introduced by his father into the house of a famous and highly respected man, Quintus Mucius Scaevola, who was usually distinguished as 'the Augur' from a relative of the same name, 'the Pontifex'. This Scaevola, an eminent lawyer, had occupied the office of consul in 117, and at the time when Cicero made his acquaintance he was about eighty years old, but was still handing down legal opinions daily. Cicero's father reckoned that Cicero should not relinquish this man's company, unless he was forced to.[4] Cicero seems to have followed this advice, for he writes that he had firmly fixed in his mind many of Scaevola's sage pronouncements.[5] Besides, in the porch of Scaevola's house he was able to meet any number of leading figures who used to turn up there each morning, as was the custom with the upper class in Rome. Did his father originally mean to make a lawyer of his talented son, rather than an orator – in spite of his links with Crassus? Hardly. The legal lore which Scaevola imparted to him was probably meant from the start merely as an extra aid for the future orator.

At that time introduction to the *ius civile* was not effected by means of a systematic course of instruction, as it is today: that kind of legal training did not emerge until the Imperial period. Since the civil law as such had arisen and evolved from a welter of individual cases (Cicero was later to criticize the situation repeatedly and to demand that the law should be transformed into a systematic study[6]), there was no way open to budding lawyers other than to familiarize themselves with particular lawsuits or cases. The lawyers, the *iuris consulti*, used to draw up contracts and assess legal issues – they were questioned by the parties and the judges and then gave their opinion, their *responsum*. This normally took place in the forum or in the lawyer's home and anyone who wished could listen. Probably the lawyer then took the opportunity to explain the reasons for his decision to his pupils. It was somewhat in this manner that Cicero, then aged 16 or 17, was introduced to the Roman civil law by Scaevola.

The civil law was, of course, merely a small and relatively insignificant sector in the tradition of the Roman state. Cicero's principal goal during the years which followed his assumption of the adult toga was consequently of a different and much more comprehensive nature. His aim was to become familiar with this tradition as a whole, with its constitutional bodies, as well as with the complicated interplay of the strata which went to make up Roman society. In the first place, practically nothing was based on written statutes, well-nigh everything was governed by tradition. The stable edifice that constituted the Roman Republic in the second century BC and that was to be subjected during Cicero's lifetime to ever increasing stresses and strains had reached its prime in a lengthy process of evolution, advancing cautiously from one particular case to another.

Cicero thus had to master an intricate system that had been constructed in the course of many generations. For this purpose he undoubtedly had a number of literary works at his disposal – accounts of Roman history and the notable speeches of earlier politicians – but no treatises that would have introduced him systematically to the essential nature and evolution of the Roman state. The Romans were not capable of that degree of abstraction; it was only Cicero himself in his prime who was able to make statements of principle about the Roman constitution, thanks to the facility with which he could reduce complex structures to conceptual terms. The young Cicero, therefore, had to resort largely to his own powers of observation when he set out to identify the principles and regulations governing what went on in the forum. He took part in public meetings, listened to the lawyers' pleas and moved in circles frequented by those of his seniors who were prepared to answer questions put by their junior colleagues. What Cicero picked up in this manner, fitting one small stone to another to form a mosaic of the whole, was, reduced to its simplest terms, more or less the following.

In a formal sense, all authority in Republican Rome was derived from the people, from the assembly of its adult male citizens. This public assembly was organized in classes and it took important decisions according to this organization: it elected annually the senior civil servants, the magistrates; it ruled on proposed legislation; it passed judgement in the case of crimes against the state. However, it could neither conduct a debate nor launch any kind of initiative; it simply had to endorse or reject whatever matters its officers submitted to it.

The preponderance of power obviously lay with the magistrates, especially with those of the highest rank, the consuls and the praetors. All appointments were duplicated or filled by several officials; all officials of equal rank were entitled to intervene against each other, that is to prevent or to rescind the official measures taken by a colleague. Appointments were limited to one year and, as already mentioned, renewed annually by the assembly of the people. At the summit of the state stood the two consuls; their supreme authority, the *imperium* – a combination of civil and military powers – extended throughout the entire territory of the Empire. They were appointed primarily to represent the state in its relation to the gods, to foreign states and to the Romans, both collectively and as individual citizens. Their authority, originally boundless and including the power of life and death, was progressively curtailed by laws of appeal or *provocatio*, according to which measures that involved more than a certain sum of money had to be endorsed by the popular assembly. After the consuls came the praetors, who also exercised the unrestricted imperium and commanded armies in an emergency, but who as a rule presided over the judicial system. Apart from two further ranks in the civil service career, the *cursus honorum*, the *aediles* (four public officers who had change of streets, traffic, markets and public games) and quaestors, the Roman administrative structure included one other very remarkable institution: the people's tribunes. They had no clearly defined powers but were simply a controlling body; their right of prohibition, the celebrated veto, could annul any measure decreed by the magistrates, even by a consul.

The Roman Republic rested – apart from the popular assembly and the magistrates – on yet a third pillar: the council of elders, the Senate. Until the first century BC it consisted of three hundred; in Cicero's time, it had six hundred members appointed for life. Senate members were recruited from currently serving and former magistrates. The senators were ranked in classes according to the offices they had occupied. Standing orders regulated the procedures of debate and voting. The Senate held closed sessions in the Curia at the forum or in a temple. Young Cicero, who might take part in public meetings and listen to court hearings, did not have access to meetings of the Senate but had to content himself with watching these dignitaries, distinguished by the broad purple band on their togas, as they filed solemnly into their assembly chamber. The Senate, like the popular assembly, could only be convened by a magistrate; in constitutional terms it was merely an advisory body which gave the magistrates an opinion when asked. *De facto*, however, it behaved like a sovereign executive for the entire Roman state: it was here that all the threads came together; it was from this body that all the important decisions emerged; it was the Senate that guaranteed overall political continuity. And even though its recommendations, the *senatus consulta*, were not legally binding on the magistrates, the latter in fact usually acted as if they were implementing the will of the Senate. Here, in the Senate, if anywhere at all, it was revealed that Republican Rome was subject to aristocratic rule. For Cicero it was a foregone conclusion from the outset that he must do everything in his power to gain entrance to this illustrious body at the earliest date the law allowed, namely by being appointed to the first official grade, the office of quaestor.

Popular assembly, magistrates and Senate: these were the institutions of the Roman state, the bodies whose cooperation generated Roman policy. Behind these institutions stood Roman society: it was not organized into political parties, trade unions or other interest groups but was structured on corporate lines, integrated as a pattern of allegiances. The upper ranks were occupied by the members of the aristocracy, the senators and *equites* or knights. It was from these two classes that the officials came, and election to the office of magistrate, and hence to the Senate, was in practice restricted to them. In the hierarchy of Roman society, the knights were followed by the ordinary citizens, who were divided into classes with voting rights graded according to their means. Below them were the allies, the rest of the free population of the state, and the slave proletariate. Young Cicero did not have to visualize the hierarchy as an abstract scheme, as we do today. It was all there in the flesh before his very eyes, for strict regulations on dress made sure it was instantly obvious whether someone was a slave or a free man, a citizen or a foreigner, a senator or a knight. The whole scheme only held together, however, because it was integrated into a system of inherited social relationships. In the forefront were the various heads of the ruling aristocratic families; they were constantly concerned to preserve and extend their traditional authority according to the motto, 'do ut des' – 'I give in order that you may give', in this case offering protection and expecting services in return.

By virtue of this system Rome had achieved dominion over the entire Mediterranean area in the third and second century BC. Young Cicero was able to gather as much from the fairly banal chronicles that circulated, particularly in his day, giving an account of events year by year. The sequence of Roman successes had markedly adverse effects on the internal situation of Rome, on the structure of society and finally, during Cicero's lifetime, also on its institutional expression – the constitution. At about the year 90 BC Cicero could scarcely have had any clear notion of this process, either from reading or from first-hand observation; it had only just started, and its initial phases, separated by long intervals, must have struck the contemporary observer as isolated episodes. In short, essentially, it was really only the Roman upper class that profited from all the victories and conquests. The Roman yeomanry was largely deprived of its economic base by unremitting military service. The Italic allies, subject to the same burdens as Roman citizens, did not receive the same pay, and the crowds of prisoners of war were turned into hordes of slaves who cultivated the estates of the rich under wretched conditions. In this way a kind of social tinder was created which first caused individual flare-ups and then led to devastating conflagrations. Attempts by the Gracchi to provide Rome's uprooted citizens with farmsteads at the expense of the great estates were crushed with considerable bloodshed by the senatorial aristocracy. In Sicily, rebellions broke out among the slaves which Rome was able to suppress only through the large-scale deployment of troops. Fregellae, a town next door to Arpinum, was doomed to destruction, having risen in revolt because Rome could not make up its mind to give the Italic inhabitants Roman citizenship.

After the relatively tranquil period of the nineties, when Cicero was beginning to frequent the forum, a conflict was brewing from which the first great conflagration of the age of crisis was to issue, leading to the Social War, which was immediately succeeded by the civil war between Marius and Sulla. In more perceptive circles of the aristocracy it was realized that something had to be done, if they did not wish to drift into a catastrophe. The initiative was taken by Marcus Livius Drusus, a member of a most distinguished family, who endeavoured, as people's tribune, to eliminate the most dangerous trouble spots by means of a series of laws; the problem with the allies was also to be disposed of by granting them long overdue civic rights. This bold programme of reforms provoked resistance. In particular, the consul of the year 91, Lucius Marcius Philippus, opposed the policy of Drusus. Cicero was personally affected by these events. The orator Crassus, who took the part of Drusus, carried on a violent argument with Philippus in the Senate about the issue of the allies. In the course of the debate he became so heated that he contracted pneumonia and died a few days later. Marcus and Quintus Cicero, deeply affected by the sudden death of this brilliant man, at once went to the Curia to gaze at the spot where he had stood to utter his 'swansong' (as Cicero puts it).[7] Soon after, the Senate dropped its ambitious reform project and Drusus died by an assassin's hand – in that house on the Palatine Hill which was to come into Cicero's possession when he purchased it about a generation later.

The allies no longer believed in a peaceful solution; they took up arms against the supremacy of Rome. The war, the result of egregious short-sightedness on the part of the Romans, was in fact a paradox from the point of view of the rebellious allies (not all of whom took part in the war: the Latin colonies remained loyal to Rome and the Greek cities were not involved): they were bent on destroying Rome so as to force their admittance to the Roman state! Cicero, the budding orator and politician, was now more than ever dependent on his reading (we gather, for instance, that he learned by heart the emotional peroration of a famous speech for the defence).[8] A few second-rate tribunes, it is true, were still delivering speeches to meetings in the forum, but the business of the courts was at a standstill because of the war. There was only *one* tribunal that was indefatigably active: the court which a certain Quintus Varius had set up to try the followers of Drusus as the instigators of the Social War. As far as Cicero was concerned, these trials had the regrettable consequence that Gaius Aurelius Cotta, one of the most accomplished orators of his generation, was forced into exile.

In 89 BC Cicero served in the army under Gnaeus Pompeius Strabo, the father of Pompeius Magnus (Pompey). The Social War had by that time passed its climax: the Romans were forced to give way and offer citizenship to all those who were prepared to lay down their arms, so that the insurgents had achieved their war aim. Cicero, as eques, was a member of the *cohors praetoria*, the commander-in-chief's general staff. He made no comment on what he felt as he watched these events. He can scarcely have been filled with enthusiasm: he was no soldier, he detested violence and, as a native of Arpinum, he was bound to feel that the conflict with allies who had their principal town in Corfinium, not far from his own home, was somewhat pointless. What he tells us about that period of his life in one of his last orations, the Twelfth Philippic, is by way of being a moral lesson. He had witnessed the fruitless negotiations which the consul Pompeius and his brother had conducted with Publius Vettius Scato, one of the rebel commanders: at that time the parties had treated each other fairly and had not feared each other.[9] This is Cicero's conclusion from the point of view of one who had, in the interim, lived through forty-five years of civil war and dreadful atrocities.

Not long afterwards Cicero also served under Sulla, who was ruthlessly subjugating the intractable Samnites in southern Italy. From this period, too, he has recorded an event from his own experience, which occurred when Sulla was besieging the Samnite town of Nola. One day, while Sulla was making a sacrifice to the gods in front of his tent, a serpent appeared at the foot of the altar. The haruspex thereupon advised him to lead his army into battle at once; Sulla won the battle and captured the Samnite camp. Cicero, who narrates the incident in his treatise *On Soothsaying* (*De Divinatione*), remarks – sceptic that he was – that this success was no doubt due less to the perspicacity of the haruspex than to that of Sulla.[10]

With this campaign Cicero's military career ended before it had really begun. He never made any secret of his utterly unsoldierly nature – although this meant that he would never be able to pursue an independent policy or to play a really decisive role in an age of civil war and rebellious leaders (a fact of which he was never fully aware). Many people thought, he once wrote, that military triumphs were more important than success in domestic policies[11] – this was a view that ought to be corrected. Even as a boy he himself had thought that Marcus Aemilius Scaurus (the *princeps senatus* of Cicero's youth, a vigorous and successful defender of senatorial rights) was in no way inferior to Marius (the conqueror of the Cimbri and the Teutons). And in the course of his own political career he had held just as high an opinion of Quintus Lutatius Catulus (an incorruptible individual who opposed the sweeping powers granted to Pompey in the Third Mithridatic War and in the campaign against the pirates) as he had of Pompey himself: 'parvi enim sunt foris arma, nisi est consilium domi' – 'feats of arms in the field count for little, if the right decisions are not taken at home'.

It was from now on that the most intensive phase of Cicero's training began. In 88 BC the turmoil involving the factions of Marius and Sulla broke out, followed by the relatively tranquil years of Cinna's rule and, with Sulla's return from Asia Minor, a civil war culminating in the proscriptions, the legally sanctioned mass murder of his political opponents. Cicero's intellectual gifts were not much in demand in the 80s. He stayed in the background, preparing himself by rhetorical, legal and philosophical studies. In 88 BC he was still able to listen to the tribune Publius Sulpicius Rufus speaking in the forum, a man whose oratorical talents he rated as highly as those of Cotta. He was present when this speaker set in motion a momentous train of events. He observed how Rufus, by dint of strenuous efforts, forced through a law designed to give the new citizens, the former allies, a greater say in elections and other votes of the popular assembly. He saw how Rufus allied himself with Marius, the jejune hero of the Cimbrian war, who had squandered his political credit in suppressing a revolt in 100 BC, and how he finally persuaded the popular assembly to deprive the consul of the time, his worst enemy, Sulla, of the supreme command against Mithridates VI, King of Pontos, who had plunged all Greece and Asia Minor into turmoil. He saw how the command was transferred to Marius, but then events succeeded each other with breathtaking rapidity. In a surprise coup Sulla occupied Rome with troops he had standing by in the Campania; the decrees promulgated by Sulpicius Rufus were abrogated, Marius and his supporters were outlawed. Sulla had no time to consolidate his position in Rome, however, since the victorious advance of Mithridates called for rapid action. His departure for the East was followed by another reversal of fortune: Marius returned and, together with Lucius Cornelius Cinna, inaugurated a reign of terror. Numerous respected members of the senatorial aristocracy fell victim to the subsequent slaughter, among them – much to Cicero's dismay – the orator Antonius.

The process of ever more acute crises and upheavals had now entered a new phase. An idea of Marius, born in the emergency of the Cimbrian war, was the first step. Since there were not enough soldiers, destitute citizens, who spent their time loafing round the city and were not required to do military service, were recruited as mercenaries. Henceforth the basic pattern of Roman society, the system of allegiances, the client relationship, was militarized. The various commanders and their troops, bound together by mutual loyalties to their mutual advantage, bullied or dominated the civilian apparatus of the state – with the outbreak of the squabble between Marius and Sulla this became obvious. This was the price that had to be paid for the failure of the Gracchian agrarian reform: but for this failure there would have been enough citizens liable for military service. On the other hand, a proletariate largely alienated from the state would not have accumulated in the capital, ready to go to war for payment – even against their fellow-countrymen.

Cicero had a curious, almost uncanny attitude towards Marius, the most unbridled among the principal actors in this horrifying scene. At the time bizarre tales were told about this aged swashbuckler. Having been outlawed by Sulla, so Plutarch tells us, he escaped to Ostia and boarded a ship that was to take him to Africa.[12] Unfavourable winds forced the crew to land and Marius found himself in the marshy region at the mouth of the River Liri. He was discovered, captured and taken to the nearby town of Minturnae. There he was to be killed, but a Cimbrian refused to carry out the execution as ordered – whereupon the people of Minturnae set Marius free and he duly made his escape to Africa. Young Cicero was obviously deeply affected by the fate of his fellow-citizen from Arpinum. He composed a eulogy to Marius in hexameters, probably at a time when the events were still fresh in his mind. He makes a reference to it in the opening lines of *De Legibus*, which is set in Arpinum. Atticus remarks there, 'I recognise the grove and the oak tree of Arpinum that I read about so often in *Marius*', and Cicero's brother Quintus confirms their friend's conjecture, quoting a verse from the encomium: yes, this was indeed the oak from which once took flight 'the russet envoy of Jupiter, glimpsed in marvellous guise' 'nuntia fulvia Iovis, miranda visa figura'. In his *De Divinatione* Cicero even quotes a passage of thirteen hexameters describing an omen witnessed by Marius: the victorious battle of an eagle against a serpent. Marius had seen in this a prophecy of his rehabilitation and return home: 'faustaque signe laudis redutisque notavit'.[13] This poem, lost apart from one other line, therefore described the flight of Marius and probably also his return. Whether it dealt with his exploits in the Cimbrian campaign as well, or the war against Jugurtha, we do not know.

Even much later on Cicero still remembered Marius, after his own return from exile, and compared the latter's fate with his own. He dealt most fully with this theme in an address thanking the nation for his return home, which had been facilitated by a vote of the popular assembly. There he writes:

> I used to know a very gallant man, my compatriot Gaius Marius (like me, he had to battle not only against such as were determined to spare no one and nothing, but against fate itself, as though that had been ordained by some destiny) – I knew him when he was well advanced in years; at that time the magnitude of his misfortune had in no way broken his spirit, but fortified and restored it. I heard this man say, he had fared badly at the time when he was deprived of the fatherland he had saved from foreign conquest, when he heard that his enemies had seized and ransacked all his property, when he saw his young son sharing his misfortune, when, hiding in the marshes, he owed life and limb to the ready compassion of Minturnae's citizens, when, crossing to Africa in the frailest of skiffs, he approached as a destitute supplicant those on whom he had bestowed kingdoms. Now he had regained his *dignitas*, his standing, he would do everything in his power ... to implement his *virtus*, the vigour which he had never lost.[14]

Cicero's Marius cult is a remarkable phenomenon, in that he, the comprehensively cultured individual who owed what he was to his intellectual gifts, admired this rugged old warhorse, and, standing as he did in the moderate conservative camp, praised an inept member of the populist faction who put a fearful end to his career in senseless slaughter. Cicero cannot have had the complete Marius in mind: he created a model Marius who never existed in reality – the virtually immaculate saviour of Rome from the Cimbrian peril, who, moreover, came from Arpinum, as he himself did. Subsequently, when he was forced into exile, Cicero compared his own fate with that of a Marius stylized along similar lines. Cicero's capacity for wishful thinking, his yearning for the ideal, was apparently capable of encompassing not only the Roman Republic as a whole, which he was always prone to glorify, but also particular eminent personalities. Later on it was to be the younger Scipio whom he turned into a myth.

During the grim eighties Cicero applied himself diligently to his studies, particularly in rhetoric. In *Brutus* he states: 'I often used to practise declamation (as they say nowadays), together with Marcus Piso, Quintus Pompeius and others, day in, day out; I often did so in Latin, but even more frequently in Greek, because Greek, offering more in the way of embellishment, trained us to speak in the same manner in Latin, and because my eminent Greek teachers could teach and correct me only if I used Greek.'[15] Marcus Pupius Piso and Quintus Pompeius Bithynicus were older classmates of Cicero. Cicero's father entrusted him to the care of Piso, because the latter lived according to the strict moral code of his forefathers, and because he was highly educated, so that Piso assumed the role of mentor. In the customary fashion of the ancient world the historian Sallust turned this into a homosexual relationship in a lampoon aimed at Cicero: 'Or didn't you learn your unbridled loquacity from Marcus Piso at the cost of your virginity?'[16] Piso was later a follower of Pompey and achieved the consulship in 62 BC, two years after his schoolmate Cicero. One of the eminent Greek instructors for whose benefit Cicero declaimed in Greek was Apollonius Molon from Rhodes, equally accomplished as an orator and as a teacher of oratory. He appears to have been in Rome in 87 BC and to have visited the city a second time as ambassador of Rhodes (81 BC). Since he had no command of Latin, he was permitted to put his case to the Senate in Greek without an interpreter – the first Greek to do so. Cicero visited him later in Rhodes, during his grand tour, in order to have his enunciation improved.

What Cicero learned at that time can be fairly easily specified. Rhetoric, like all subjects of instruction in the ancient world, was created by the Greeks; the Romans dutifully adopted both its forms and its subject-matter, which had acquired their ultimate outlines in the

Hellenistic period. Reading and writing was followed, as a second stage, by an introduction to grammar and style that was based on an intensive study of literature. There then usually followed a number of years of instruction in rhetoric, that is, training in extempore public speaking, which formed the culmination of the course as a rule – although this was generally only the case with members of the upper social classes. During the second century BC the teaching of rhetoric had become firmly established and was provided not only by rhetoricians, but also by philosophers. It did not matter much that all teaching was conducted in Greek (the Greeks made very heavy weather of learning Latin). The Roman aristocracy had as good a command of Greek, the lingua franca of the time, as they had of their native tongue, and the techniques they acquired through the medium of Greek could readily be transferred to Roman practice. The violent domestic political conflicts unleashed by the Gracchi no doubt considerably increased the demand for rhetorical training. A few years later, as Cicero was growing up, a school of rhetoric in Latin was set up in Rome by a Roman (he was called Lucius Plotius Gallus). From then on Roman rhetoric was to be in a sense bilingual, i.e. the whole course was conducted for pupils between the ages of fifteen and twenty in Greek as well as in Latin.

While it was possible to familiarize oneself with the Roman tradition, the Roman state and its laws and military organization only by way of first-hand experience, since there was no theory and no body of knowledge recorded in the relevant literature, instruction in rhetoric, as an achievement of the Greeks, proceeded according to a strictly methodical system. The method was manifested in a clearly graduated scheme: it began with preliminary exercises similar to the present-day school essay. Rhetorical theory was dealt with in the greatest detail as an exemplary body of rules and devices which may be assigned to two main areas, style and the art of disputation. Practice was also provided in what Cicero described as declamation, a novel term at that time for speeches composed and delivered on typical issues, either imaginary or real. Literary sources for the theoretical part of the course, the sophisticated system of rhetorical rules, emerge in Greece in the age of Aristotle, in Rome in Cicero's time – principally, in fact, with Cicero's own rhetorical treatises. Examples of the preliminary exercises and declamations have been preserved only from the Imperial era.

'At the time when Philon, the head of the Academy, together with the aristocracy, had fled from Athens to Rome on account of the Mithridatic War, I formed the closest possible association with him, filled as I was with a marvellous passion for philosophy.'[17] – This is what Cicero writes about the beginning of his philosophical studies in 88 BC. This simple sentence enunciates nothing more nor less than a vocation unique in the Rome of that time: a summons to become one of the most versatile, elegant and humane philosophical authors of the ancient world. It was a sheer quirk of fate that the victorious advance of Mithridates drove from their homes the Greeks who were loyal to Rome, and that there should be among them Philon of Larissa, the head of the philosophical school founded by Plato. And it was a further stroke of fate that young Cicero instinctively grasped this chance and did not hesitate to absorb whatever Philon had to give him. By that time only implacable enemies of the Greeks were unable to see the advantages of rhetoric, a discipline that already enjoyed wide public support. Philosophy, on the other hand, the practical significance of which was not at all obvious, was still the preserve of a small intellectual élite, mostly of aristocratic descent. But even in this circle the sober Roman mind would hardly have expressed itself in such florid terms: 'I formed the closest possible association with him' [the text even says 'devoted myself'], 'filled as I was with a marvellous enthusiasm for philosophy.'

It was through these studies that Cicero first ventured into Greek territory proper: philosophy as an attempt at rational thinking, a rational mode of life and a view of the world founded on rational considerations was the cardinal invention of Greece. It achieved its climax there in the fourth century BC: bold, far-ranging speculation flourished alongside empirically based scientific research. The first two 'schools' – private foundations which survived miraculously until the end of the ancient period – made their appearance: the Academy of Plato and Aristotle's Peripatos, both situated in Athens, which had then become the centre of philosophical studies. Round about 300 BC two additional schools were opened: the one that took its name from Epicurus, and the Stoa, which was founded by Zeno. In the Hellenistic age their creative impulse faded and they were content to transmit the school's tradition, concentrating otherwise on ethical issues and offering practical assistance in difficult situations.

In Rome, philosophy – like rhetoric – became established in the course of the second century BC. The Stoic Panaetius lived for some time in the home of the younger Scipio Africanus, while other sages made their influence felt through lectures given in the course of briefer visits. But even if the Romans took an interest in philosophy, they were in no way inclined to speculation and abstract knowledge. They were able to accept only those things which fitted into their own world, whether private or political, and which seemed likely to prove beneficial. No doubt some Romans sensed a kind of force which cultivated the mind through the discussion of general problems, as practised in philosophy, and a number of them were indubitably fascinated by the pyrotechnics of argument. Basically, however, it was for them a question of finding their moral bearings, of establishing criteria for their own actions, of coping with issues which, as a small circle of far-sighted individuals realized, could not be settled solely with the aid of their own inherited traditions, religious or otherwise.

For this reason it was the Stoa which found a particularly ready response. This was the creed which least ran counter to traditional religious ideas. Above all – and this was most important for the political élite of the Roman state – it asserted more emphatically than any of the other schools that the individual's happiness and fulfilment depended on service to his fatherland and to mankind as a whole. As far as the Roman aristocracy was concerned, it was here that the justification for their total devotion to the exercise of power lay; conversely, this was where they deduced their obligation to use the power with which they had been entrusted solely for the good of the community. Unfortunately, as the outcome of the Gracchian turmoil and subsequent events were to show, only a minority of the ruling class availed themselves of the possibility of self-restraint offered by the Stoic ethical system. One result of this, again, was that soon afterwards, in the misery of the civil wars, the opposite philosophy to the Stoa, the teaching of Epicurus, acquired a considerable following. It claimed that human happiness depended on 'pleasure', on physical and intellectual enjoyments which could best be achieved in some remote retreat far removed from politics, that is, in an individualistic mode of existence.

Cicero subscribed neither to the socially committed Stoa nor to the individualistic teachings of Epicurus: following his own impulse rather than any model, he attached himself to Philon, the representative of the Academy. This implied the choice of a particularly scientific, particularly broadly based view of the world. It also meant that Cicero decided in favour of a basically critical attitude which was sceptical in regard to allegedly irrefutable truths. Philon represented a phase in the history of the Academy which professed a sceptical view and which operated with modestly cautious assumptions of probability. He was the last such representative – his successor reverted to dogma.

This choice was obviously not purely fortuitous; Cicero decided in favour of the approach which best matched his 'un-Roman' theoretical and intellectual attitude. A letter reveals that he had already met another philosopher before Philon, the Epicurean Phaedrus, whom he had acknowledged to be a competent representative of his school.[18] He became familiar with the Stoa, again, through meeting Diodotus, a philosopher of that persuasion, who introduced him to the dialectical method. He esteemed Diodotus subsequently throughout his life as a cultured, versatile individual and even took him into his household, thus making him his 'domestic philosopher', such as had existed in a number of aristocratic Roman families. (A notable example is the Epicurean Philodemus, who lived with Lucius Calpurnius Piso, the consul of the year 58 BC so detested by Cicero.) Diodotus went blind at an advanced age; he was not discouraged and devoted himself to philosophy even more keenly than before, took up geometry and played the lyre. About 60 BC he expired in the house of his patron, to whom he bequeathed his humble possessions. Otherwise, Cicero encountered the Stoic attitude in the person of Lucius Aelius Stilo, a philologist and antiquarian to whom he liked to listen at that time. As a Stoic, Philon decisively repudiated the arts of persuasion on moral grounds, and thus limited himself to composing speeches for others without himself performing as an orator.

Thus, already in the eighties, Cicero had become acquainted, not only with the teachings of the Academy, but also with those of the Stoa and of Epicurus. Indeed, we may assume that even the tradition of the Peripatos was not entirely unknown to him. Staseas of Naples, a philosopher of the Peripatetic school, was probably already living in the house of Cicero's fellow-student and mentor, Marcus Pupius Piso.

During the graveyard tranquillity of Cinna's tyrannical rule, therefore, Cicero acquired an encyclopaedic philosophical education from which none of the four great Athenian schools was excluded. His real teacher of philosophy, however, as he maintained throughout his life, was Philon of Larissa: it was he who moulded Cicero's thinking in a specially lasting way. It was to Philon in particular that he owed the sceptical attitude which he was to retain throughout his life. Even in his earliest surviving work, the rhetorical treatise, *On the Devising of Topics (De Inventione)*, he indicates that he did not care to commit himself to irrefutable verities, but preferred to operate with assumptions of probability which could be discarded, if they proved to be unworkable. The most important thing, he writes there, is 'that we do not recklessly and presumptuously assume something to be true' – 'ne cui rei temere atque arroganter assenserismus'.[19]

The treatise *De Inventione*, the first fruit that Cicero's rhetorical and philosophical studies bore for posterity, remained incomplete. It does not present the entire theoretical structure of rhetoric but only the first part, although this is the most important part – it outlines the rules for discovering appropriate material for any given theme. In the introduction to the first book of his major rhetorical work, *De Oratore*, Cicero tends to dissociate himself from this youthful essay – it was nothing but a set of rough notes – but posterity judges it in a more favourable light.[20] We sense even here that Cicero was not satisfied with the purely formal rules of academic rhetoric, but felt the need to underpin them with foundations built upon ethical and philosophical reflection. The most important evidence of this is the introduction to the first book: here, at the very outset, Cicero requires the true orator to combine formal competence with wisdom – an orator who does not aspire to reason and to moral principles corrupts both himself and his fatherland. Cicero observes quite rightly that the gift of eloquence in the free body politic is both indispensable and dangerous and, as a formal technique, needs some kind of outside control. He made a just assessment of rhetoric right from the start; the exposition at the beginning of *De Inventione* contains the germ of the programme which he was subsequently to deploy extensively in *De Oratore* under the phrase *orator perfectus*.

Cicero knew that translation is an appropriate method of enhancing the power of expression in one's native language. The earliest exercise of this kind that we know of is a version of a work by the versatile author Xenophon, who wrote in a simple, straightforward style. It is entitled *Oeconomicus* and deals with the art of household management. In the main section the owner of an estate describes his domestic circumstances and family life – the work offers some revealing glimpses into the life of Greek women. Cicero's translation was made round about 85 BC. Unlike the original, it has not survived – no more than a few fragments in the form of quotations have come down to us, mainly via the agricultural writer Columella. The translation strove to be accurate; a competent critic, the Church Father and translator of the Bible, St Jerome, thought it lacked the golden fluency of the Ciceronian style.[21] Cicero was still on the way towards his own fitting mode of expression.

The youthful Cicero ventured on a much more difficult task: he translated a Hellenistic didactic poem (in hexameters), the '*Phaenomena*' ('Celestial Apparitions') by Aratus, one of those works which attempt to conjure up poetic charms from a barren scientific subject. It deals with the constellations, the planets and (in the final third) with weather omens, and it enjoyed great success from the very beginning. Cicero's translation has been preserved, partly by way of quotations, but in part directly through certain manuscripts: as much as 480 lines in all. This is the most substantial segment of hexameter verse that has come down to us from any of the earlier Latin authors. The reproduction is more voluminous than the original, which is deliberately couched in a simple, matter-of-fact style; Cicero incorporated notes from various commentaries into his text. The main model in language and prosody was the early Roman poet Ennius. Lucretius seems to have known and used Cicero's rendering of Aratus. No Greek work was translated into Latin as frequently as the '*Phaenomena*'. The next to try his hand at it was Germanicus, the nephew of the Emperor Tiberius – he produced a free rendering, most of which has survived.

3

First Cases, a Crisis and
a Grand Tour

Sulla had defeated Mithridates in a series of battles and had forced him, by a hastily concluded peace treaty, to surrender his conquests. In the spring of 85 BC he returned from the East to Italy at the head of his formidable army. The followers of Marius were still on the rampage against the aristocracy, although they were already fighting for a lost cause. Amongst the victims of the massacre was Quintus Mucius Scaevola, known as the Pontifex, the most distinguished jurist of the Republic, with whom Cicero had pursued advanced legal studies after the death of Scaevola the Augur (87 BC). Once Sulla had made himself master of Italy after eighteen months of violent strife, he avenged himself on the adversaries of the senatorial aristocracy by the wholesale slaughter that has gone down in history under the terrible term 'proscriptions'. A total of 4,700 citizens, mostly equites (knights), are said to have been declared outlaws on published lists and to have been killed in consequence. Their property was forfeited to the state and auctioned off at throw-away prices. Sulla had himself elected dictator with authority to impose a constitution; his reactionary legislation endowed the senatorial aristocracy with the most sweeping powers imaginable.

Cicero steered clear of these conflicts, he remained unarmed, as he once said.[1] He would have much preferred to see the conflict resolved through a peaceful settlement, he claimed – a statement one can well believe of a man who hated any sort of violence.[2] Since this could not be achieved, he had committed himself to the party which actually won in the end. In his eyes the regime of Marius and his faction was illegitimate: Sulla had revived the laws and the courts and restored the state. But Cicero dissociated himself from the proscriptions right at the start: 'I cannot disapprove of the punishment of those who offered resistance with every possible means', he said with some asperity.[3] Later on he spoke of brutality: Sulla had gained a disreputable victory for a reputable cause.[4] In spite of his Marius cult, Cicero was a moderate conservative from the very beginning – even in the first of his surviving speeches he disapproved of the tyranny of Marius on the one hand, and the unlawful actions of Sulla's party on the other.[5]

In 81 BC he believed his hour had come; he was then twenty-five years old, a few years older than was usual for young people aiming at a political career. He had, it is true, many advantages over others of his kind: as he writes, unlike most others he did not have to learn his trade in the forum; when he appeared there to make his maiden speech, he had already completed his training as far as he was able.[6] He is no doubt referring here to the rhetorical, legal and philosophical education which he had acquired through years of study and diligent fostering of his many and various interests. All this provided him with the equipment which other beginners lacked.

The earliest surviving address is a speech on behalf of Publius Quinctius from 81 BC; it deals with a civil dispute. At the time he represented Quinctius, Cicero had already appeared as advocate on a number of occasions – we do not know what kind of cases they were. The case of Quinctius against a certain Naevius was complicated and had already been before the courts a number of times, but it was by no means sensational. Nevertheless, the young Cicero was faced by two illustrious personalities: the judge, Gaius Aquilius Gallus, and counsel for the opposing party, Quintus Hortensius Hortalus. Like Cicero, Aquilius Gallus had studied under Scaevola the Pontifex. Both of them achieved the praetorship in the same year. Cicero calls him his friend and extols the innovation through which Aquilius Gallus achieved immortality in the annals of Roman law: the prosecution of *dolus malus*, fraud.[7]

Cicero's works are the most fruitful source of information about Hortensius. During the years of Cicero's rise to prominence he was Rome's leading orator; Cicero had to outdo him, if he wished to take over this position. This he succeeded in doing, so that there is a suggestion of justifiable pride in the fact that *Brutus* concludes with a syncrisis, a comparison of the two rivals.[8] Hortensius was eight years older than Cicero and had already begun to appear in the forum in 95 BC, when he was nineteen. He was an aedile while Cicero was occupying his first public office, as praetor (75 BC), and he was made consul in the year in which Cicero was aedile (69 BC). He tried his hand at erotic poetry without much success; Catullus dedicated to him a verse epistle which accompanied his translation of a poem by Callimachus, 'The

Lock of Berenice' (*c.* 66–65 BC). Apart from this, Hortensius also composed 'Annals' of the Social War, probably in poetic form. As an orator Hortensius was the main proponent of a new fashionable style, the Asiatic style (because it derived from the rhetorical schools of Asia Minor), a floridly stilted mode of expression. Cicero praises his memory, his assiduity and the careful construction of his speeches – unfortunately, nothing by him survives, not a single fragment.

In the Verres trial (70 BC) Cicero and Hortensius were once more pitted against each other, Cicero for the prosecution, Hortensius for the defence. Cicero won, and after this Hortensius's fortunes began to decline. Cicero implies that he, for his part, had been assisted by his encyclopaedic knowledge and his philosophical training. Hortensius, on the other hand, would not have had any very high opinion of philosophy, since Cicero assigns to him the part of an opponent of philosophy in the fragmentary dialogue named after him, which is a tract in defence of philosophy. The same is true of another work, the *Academica Priora*. The decline of Hortensius in the sixties was also due – according to Cicero – to the fact that the ornate Asian style seemed insufferable in the mouth of the ageing speaker, and that, following his consulship, he failed to take the necessary care. Hortensius himself appears to have acknowledged the pre-eminence of his junior colleague: from 63 BC on he appeared for defendants together with Cicero in a number of cases. It was invariably Cicero who then made the final address. Cicero has paid extremely generous tribute to his erstwhile rival and ultimate political ally. Firstly, in the high praise accorded him at the end of Cicero's main rhetorical treatise *De Oratore*[9], and then, after the death of Hortensius (50 BC), as already mentioned, through the dialogue *Hortensius* and the comparison at the end of *Brutus*.

It was in 80 BC that Cicero presented his first plea in a *causa publica*, a public criminal prosecution before the court that dealt with homicide. He spoke, as he almost always did, on behalf of the defence. The punishment of capital offences was originally a matter for the popular assembly. In the second century BC, however, a more practical arrangement had been arrived at: jury courts, appointed at first for individual cases, and then established permanently. A peculiarity of the system was that each of these courts specialized in a particular category of crime, high treason, extortion, murder and so on. They were generally presided over by a praetor; the members of the court, usually thirty to sixty in number, were chosen by lot from a list of judges for each particular case. The compilation of this list was the subject of violent political dispute during the revolutionary period. Gaius Gracchus deprived the senators of the rights as jurors which they had enjoyed hitherto and conferred them on the equites (122 BC); in the context of his constitutional reform Sulla restored the situation. The jury courts operated according to the principle of popular indictment, that is they acted only when a Roman citizen in good standing had lodged a complaint. If the indictment was approved, this laid on the accuser the duty of acting as prosecutor. The procedure was actually thoroughly 'modern' and befitting a free state. Statutory criminal offences and punishments were based on sufficiently precise legal specifications; the judges conducted the hearing, while the prosecution and the defence dealt with the relevant issue; the process leading to a verdict was conducted by word of mouth and in public. The snag was in the criteria for the selection of the jurors in any given case. Since the interests of senators and knights not infrequently clashed, the outcome, particularly in political trials, was occasionally blatant class justice.

The circumstances of the time, in fact, had little, if any, effect on the Quinctius case. The murder trial, on the other hand, in which Cicero then figured, involved an underhand piece of villainy on the political stage which called for little in the way of judicial argument, but – for Cicero as counsel for the defence – all the more in the way of the courage to resist corruption backed by political authority. Young Sextus Roscius from Ameria was accused of murdering his father. There were no grounds whatever for this accusation, it was simply designed to silence Roscius junior. Roscius senior had possessed a considerable fortune. When he was killed in 81 BC, his name was belatedly added to the list of proscribed persons: he was reckoned to be an enemy of the state and his property was confiscated by the treasury. The instigator of this vicious plot was a certain Chrysogonus, a freed man and influential favourite of the dictator Sulla. Chrysogonus purchased the property of Roscius senior for a ludicrously small sum.

None of the established advocates had undertaken to defend Roscius junior – they were afraid of Sulla. And so the case found its way to Cicero. He, however, did not mince his words; he not only refuted the accusation, he also exposed the true motives of the men behind it. Cicero declared that the great Sulla could not concern himself with every trifle, any more than Jupiter could; he had no knowledge of the dastardly doings of his underlings. The triumph of a good cause should not be abused to enable rogues to enrich themselves with the property of others: the judges must take steps to prevent this. Cicero's boldness was successful, the accused was acquitted. And Sulla showed, by allowing justice to take its course in this first murder trial since his victory, that he seriously meant to restore the rule of law. The style of the long speech for the defence has the marks of a certain youthful ebullience: Cicero himself subsequently disowned a particularly mannered passage.[10] However, he was now numbered among Rome's leading lawyers and promptly embarked on a wide range of activities before the courts – nothing of all this has survived, apart from a few scanty references.

Since Cicero was of a weak constitution (I have already quoted his statement to this effect.), and since he did not husband his strength, his zeal led to a physical breakdown, and it seemed as if he would have to bury all his ambitious hopes. He temporarily suspended his legal activities and embarked on a journey to the Greek Orient, for purposes of convalescence, but also as a kind of educational excursion. He intended to visit various celebrated teachers of rhetoric with the aim of acquiring a mode of delivery which would put less strain on his voice and spare his lungs. He combined this business with what was for him pleasure, devoting himself once more to fundamental philosophical studies, particularly on the first stage of his journey, which took him to Athens. In making all these arrangements, he allowed himself plenty of time: he was away from the early summer of 79 until the summer of 77 BC. He had no doubt calculated that he would still have sufficient time to apply for his first appointment, as quaestor, by 75 BC, the earliest date permitted by the law.

In Athens, where he stayed for six months, he found himself in congenial company – with his brother Quintus and his cousin Lucius, and also with Titus Pomponius Atticus and Marcus Pupius Piso. He had probably made friends with Atticus back in the days when both of them were being initiated into the law by Scaevola the Augur. Atticus was of aristocratic descent, like Cicero, and had also enjoyed a careful upbringing. But that was all they had in common: the two friends had pursued entirely different careers. Atticus was a convinced Epicurean and steered clear of any public commitment. He devoted himself entirely to his estate, which he enlarged to a considerable extent; he collected works of art and built up an impressive library; he sustained a wide range of friendships and sought to mediate in disputes. During the civil war between Marius and Sulla he had not felt safe in Rome – he had been living in Athens since 86 BC, where the generous support he gave to his adopted home earned him the epithet Atticus. Cicero hence found him already in Athens when he came to stay there in the spring of 79 BC.

The setting of the fifth book of *De Finibus* reflects the situation in 79 BC: Cicero's stay in Athens, his friends and relations there.[11] In the morning the participants had attended a class held by Antiochus of Ascalon, a teacher in the Academy, in the afternoon they had resolved to take a stroll to the Academy, so as to enjoy the peace and quiet that prevailed there. Pupius Piso says that he feels deeply moved every time he visits a place that is linked with the recollection of great men – so that he seems to see Plato here before him. The others concur, and each of them mentions a place in Athens which has a special meaning for him. Quintus Cicero, the poetry-lover, nominates the hill of Colonus, renowned on account of the second Oedipus tragedy of Sophocles. Atticus picks the garden of Epicurus, Cicero a bench frequented by Karneades, a teacher of the Academy. Finally, Lucius Cicero declares that he used to go to the harbour of Phalerum, to the spot where Demosthenes had endeavoured to drown out the sound of the waves with his voice, and also to the tomb of Pericles. Pupius Piso then suggests that such visits should not merely serve to satisfy idle curiosity; they only make sense if they inspire us with models for our own behaviour.

Cicero did take lessons from the orator, Demetrius the Syrian, but studied mainly with the philosopher Antiochus, mentioned above. The latter was, like Cicero, a pupil of Philon of Larissa, yet he had discarded the sceptical probability theory which had been taught in the Academy for some time. He reverted to a new dogmatism, to a belief in irrefutable knowledge; he was in fact searching for a synthesis of the doctrines of the old Academy, the Peripatos and the Stoa, which, in his view did not differ from each other to any significant extent. What Cicero principally gained from Antiochus was probably a sound knowledge of philosophical history; as far as his basic convictions were concerned, he remained true to Philon's scepticism. Apart from Antiochus, Cicero occasionally heard the Epicureans, Phaedrus and Zenon, during his stay in Athens.

It was probably at this time, too, that he travelled to Peloponnesus. He mentions that in Sparta he had heard about the harsh training and the cruel floggings to which young men were subjected, and had seen for himself how sporting contests were conducted: with fists, feet, nails and teeth.[12] And in Corinth, which the Romans had destroyed barely seventy years previously, in 146 BC, he was shocked by the sight of the ruins. One other detail is known from this period in Athens: Cicero – like Atticus and possibly also his other fellow-students – had himself initiated into the Eleusinian mysteries. He writes that this admirable doctrine had led men from a barbaric mode of life into civilization: 'There we not only received joyful intimations of a true manner of living, but also a better hope of dying.'[13] It is not likely, however, that the initiation was of great significance for Cicero, that it had, for instance, any influence on his religious ideas. Even in his day the mysteries of Eleusis seem to have served as a tourist attraction for eminent Romans. We know that Sulla had been initiated, and that Antony and Octavian, for example, underwent the same ceremony. Cicero, the sceptic, made a strict distinction between certainty and hope. He did not deny the possibility that the soul was immortal, but he was convinced that there could be no more than conjecture on the subject. The most important source of his ideas on a life after death is the first book of the *Tusculanarum*. There he states that Plato's belief in immortality is for him only one view among several, although it was one that he found particularly attractive: 'This view affords me pleasure, and I would much prefer it to be correct; in the second place, however, even were it not true, I should like to be persuaded of it all the same.'[14]

Cicero left Athens in the autumn of 79 BC and travelled to Asia Minor. In an address during a court case he takes occasion to narrate an incident he had experienced in Miletus.[15] A woman had been condemned to death there for aborting her unborn child after being bribed to do so by the legatee in default. Thus, the testator had died before the child could be born, having nominated the child as his principal heir, and certain other persons in default, in case his first nominee should be unable to claim his inheritance.

In Smyrna the brothers were faced with a blatant example of that arbitrary justice entailed by the politicization of the jury courts. They called on the former consul Publius Rutilius Rufus, who had long been living in exile there. In 94 BC Rutilius Rufus, as adjutant to the governor Scaevola Pontifex in Asia Minor, had attempted to defend the inhabitants of the province against unjustified taxation. As a rule the Roman state did not itself collect the taxes it imposed on its subjects, but farmed out the concession to the highest bidder. The concessionaires were the knights, the capitalist class. They were allowed to retain whatever exceeded the sum they had guaranteed to the state; they thus tried to squeeze as much as they could out of the provincial population, and were not infrequently assisted in their efforts by the governors. The measures taken by Rutilius Rufus were therefore directed against illegal fiscal pressure exerted by members of the capitalist class: his reward was arraignment on a criminal charge. At that time the knights had the jury courts in their hands. They had the sheer insolence to find Rutilius Rufus guilty of the very offence which he had opposed, blackmail of his provincial subjects. Rutilius Rufus, however, calmly went off to live among the very people whom he had allegedly exploited, in Smyrna.

There he devoted himself to his studies. He was in fact an exceptionally cultured man, having belonged to the circle associated with the younger Scipio and having studied with the Stoic, Panaetius. Cicero claims that it was on the occasion of this visit that he learned two things from Rutilius Rufus. He quotes him in *Brutus* as the authority concerning a court case from the year 138 BC, which provided in the pleas put forward an instructive example of the varying effects of different rhetorical temperaments.[16] He also claims that it was from Rutilius Rufus that he learned of the conversation which he subsequently has Scipio conduct with his friends in *De Republica*.[17] Although we may well believe that the anecdote concerning the case in 138 BC derives from Rutilius Rufus, it is equally certain that Cicero, in *De Republica*, is employing a fiction that had been common enough in the dialogue since Plato's time. It was customary, in fact, for the authors of such conversations to claim that the speeches they put into the mouths of celebrated personalities from the past had been communicated to them by named witnesses; this convention was intended to invest the dialogue with a greater degree of authenticity.

While he was in Asia Minor, Cicero visited a series of teachers of rhetoric, who have in the main achieved immortality because he thought them worthy of mention in the autobiographical section of *Brutus*: Menippus of Stratoniceia, Dionysius of Magnesia, Aeschines from Cnidus and Xenocles from Adramyttium.[18] Cicero writes that he had traversed the whole of Asia; if the cities he mentions are arranged from north to south (Adramyttium east of the Troas massif, Magnesia on the River Hermus, Stratoniceia and Cnidus in the extreme southwest of Asia Minor), then it appears he had at any rate travelled along the entire west coast.

Cicero was not satisfied with these local celebrities, however, and hence made his way to Rhodes to consult Apollonius Molon, whom he had twice heard in Rome. In *Brutus* it is stated that Apollonius Molon took pains to restrain his pupil's excessively volatile delivery and to curb his excessive ardour.[19] He returned to Rome transformed. His exuberance had simmered down, and his constitution had become satisfactorily robust. Cicero did not study alone in Rhodes, he had his friend Servius Sulpicius Rufus with him. Sulpicius Rufus had originally meant to become an orator, but preferred in the end, Cicero writes, to be the first in the second art, rather than merely second in the first of the arts.[20]

That is, he became a lawyer, the most famous counsel of his day. Cicero emphasizes his ability to arrange legal issues in a systematic manner. He wrote a famous letter of condolence on the death of Cicero's daughter Tullia which features in *Ad Familiares*.[21] In the 'Ninth Philippic' (February 43) Cicero, for his part, paid a worthy, indeed moving tribute to Sulpicius Rufus, who had died while travelling on an ambassadorial mission. In Rhodes Cicero also visited Poseidonius, the most eminent Stoic of the day, but there is no evidence that the great thinker had any lasting influence on him – although he numbers him among his philosophical mentors.[22]

4

Quaestor: The First Appointment

After his return from the East, Cicero once more took up his legal practice; he conducted *causas nobiles*, celebrated cases, he tells us.[1] No details have come down to us, but a reference in the second Verres address suggests that he was especially assiduous in managing the affairs of his own social class, the knights and tax-gatherers.[2] We may suppose, then, that he did all he could to enhance his reputation and to gain supporters, both among the senatorial aristocracy and among the rural population. He had long since decided to embark on an official career, so that as a newcomer, *homo novus*, who was not in a position to invoke the merits of his ancestors, he had to rely on his own resources for a successful electoral campaign. From the period between Cicero's grand tour and his departure to take up his first post as quaestor in Sicily, only one speech seems to have survived – and that is incomplete. It is a plea in a civil suit on behalf of the actor, Quintus Roscius Gallus, in his day one of the most celebrated masters of his art. Cicero had known him for some time: Roscius had asked him to represent his brother-in-law Quinctius. Cicero frequently mentioned him and greatly admired him, regarding him as a matchless performer. The case which he conducted on behalf of Roscius concerned a claim deriving from circumstances which a modern observer might find repugnant. Roscius and another person had shared the ownership of a slave who was trained as an actor by Roscius, and the partners shared his salary between them. The slave was killed, and the settlement of claims thus arising led to a dispute between the two shareholders.

It was about this time that Cicero married. The date of the ceremony is not known, it might have been either before his excursion to the East or else before he took up the quaestorship. However, the idea that Cicero took a wife only to spend the next two years apart from her is somehow disconcerting. So he probably brought his bride home in 77 BC rather than in 80 BC. He was, after all, intent on starting his career by resuming his legal practice and by applying for his first official post. His marriage, too, was certainly designed to serve the same purpose: it was meant to improve his social status. Later, in his defence of his pupil and friend Caelius, he described the hectic lives of the *jeunesse dorée* of the day: 'Entertainments, love affairs and adulteries, excursions to Baiae, beach parties, dinners and drinking bouts, singing, music and boat trips.'[3] He himself probably knew nothing of all this in his youth. He was impelled by ambition, and such mundane amusements must have seemed shallow to him when compared with his own aims. Having once been invited to the same dinner as Cytheris, an actress of dubious reputation, it seems plausible enough that he should have been prompted to write and assure a friend that 'such things left me cold, even when I was a young man' – 'me ... nihil istorum ne iuvenem quidem movit umquam'.[4] He worked hard, true to the maxim which also crops up in his plea for Caelius: 'You must dismiss all thought of pleasure from your mind, renounce hobbies; games and jocularity, festive boards, and perhaps even the company of friends have to take second place.'[5] His decision to marry, therefore, was based on sober calculation: he married for money and for the sake of the useful connections the marriage would bring him.

His wife was a certain Terentia. It must be put like that because we are not dealing with the name of an individual: Roman women were identified only by the name of their families. No details of Terentia's affiliations to the highly respected Terentius family are known. We know only of a half-sister by the name of Fabia who was a priestess of the goddess Vesta. She was accused of breaking her vow of chastity by entering into relations with Cataline, but the trial to which she was subjected ended in her acquittal. Terentia came from a wealthy home: her dowry amounted to no less than 120,000 denarii, that is 480,000 sesterces, a sum well beyond the personal fortune of 400,000 sesterces required for admittance to the equestrian order. She also owned woodland and pasture, probably in the vicinity of Tusculum, and possibly even had tenements in Rome. According to Plutarch she was a tough and strong-willed character who dominated Cicero and played a larger part in her husband's political concerns than she allowed him in domestic matters.[6] In 63 BC she is said to have insisted that the Catalinarian faction be severely punished, and two years later it was at her instigation that Cicero gave evidence against Clodius, who had been charged with sacrilege.

In the summer of 76 BC Cicero applied successfully for the quaestorship. 'The Roman people elected me – in each case unanimously – among the first as quaestor, in preference to my colleagues as aedile, and ahead of all others as praetor: this distinction was accorded to my person, not my family, to my character, not my pedigree, to proven competence, not to acknowledged nobility.'[7] It was in these words that the newcomer Cicero addressed an opponent, a member of the aristocracy. He was assigned one of the two Sicilian quaestorships. His immediate superior, the provincial governor, was called Sextus Peducaeus, whom Cicero once described as 'vir fortissimus atque innocentissimus', 'a thoroughly competent and unselfish individual'.[8] Cicero's official residence was in Lilybaeum (nowadays Marsala), a wealthy community at the furthermost western tip of Sicily. He speaks in slightly inflated but entirely convincing terms about his devotion to duty and his incorruptibility: 'This is how I discharged the office of quaestor in the province of Sicily: I thought that all eyes were focused on me alone and imagined that my quaestorship and my person were set on a kind of cosmic stage. I consistently denied myself all those things that are reckoned to be pleasurable, not only the exquisite indulgences of our age, but even those due to nature and necessity.'[9] Conscientious officials customarily prepared themselves for every new assignment. As his Verres speeches reveal, Cicero was thoroughly familiar with the history of Sicily and the nature of its legal system. He may have acquired his knowledge from, among other sources, the comprehensive *Sicilian History* of Timaeus of Tauromenium, an author well known to the Romans (died *c.* 250 BC).

Sicily, under Roman rule since the end of the first Punic War and hence Rome's oldest province, had become in the course of time the 'larder', the 'breadbasket of the Roman people'.[10] The Sicilian communities were required to hand over a tenth of their harvests to Rome. If this imposition did not meet the need, then the Roman state could decree compulsory purchases. Their officials were commissioned to deliver a specified quantity of grain at a specified price, and the communities were obliged to provide their quota. This routine task was among those that fell to Cicero in Lilybaeum. In Rome prices were rising, Cicero purchased an adequate quantity of corn on behalf of the state, doing his best to be fair to all parties involved, including the Sicilians. In particular, his two clerks refrained from making a customary, but illegal, deduction when paying the communities their due. At the conclusion of Cicero's term of office the Sicilians rewarded his fair dealing with unusual marks of respect. In a farewell speech delivered in

Lilybaeum, he, for his part, promised that he would continue to be at their service in the future.

Cicero was not totally absorbed in his administrative duties, however: he sought out artistic treasures and other celebrated sights in every part of this prosperous island. This may be deduced from the Verrine Orations, especially from the fourth book of the second speech, which deals with the theft of works of art by the blackmailing governor. On one occasion he mentions that he had himself seen a work subsequently stolen by Verres, a bronze statue of Artemis which had once stood in Segesta, a city which boasted an affinity with Rome, since, according to tradition, it had been founded by Aeneas.[11]

The fifth book of the *Tusculanarum* relates an episode characteristic of Cicero's knowledge and expertise.[12] Syracuse had chosen Hannibal's side in the Second Punic War, so that it was besieged and taken by the Romans. It was a Roman soldier who killed the city's most famous inhabitant, the mathematician Archimedes, who had assisted in the defence of the city by devices of his own design (212 BC). According to tradition he was engrossed in geometrical figures and shouted at an approaching soldier: 'Noli turbare circulos meos' – 'Don't spoil my circles!' At the time of Cicero's quaestorship, he tells us, the Syracusans no longer knew the whereabouts of their eminent fellow-citizen's grave. Cicero rediscovered it, surrounded and overgrown with thorn-bushes and undergrowth. He had in fact stumbled on a couple of lines of poetry which he knew were inscribed on the tombstone: they suggested that the grave was topped by a cylinder and a sphere. Cicero had searched around among the tombs by the Agrigentinian Gate and had noticed a low pillar that was barely visible above the shrubbery and that had a cylinder and a sphere engraved on it. Men armed with sickles had been sent to clear the grave, and, sure enough, the epigram appeared in weathered lettering on the other side of the pedestal. Thus, Syracuse, one of the noblest Greek cities, and once one of the most erudite, had rediscovered the tomb of Archimedes with the help of a man from Arpinum. From Plutarch we know that Archimedes himself had wished to have a tombstone in this form.[13] The two geometrical bodies refer to the surviving treatise 'On the sphere and the cylinder', in which Archimedes had defined the ratio of the volume of a sphere to the cylinder enclosing it as 2 : 3. The verses, which Cicero knew by heart, have not come down to us.

At the beginning of 74 BC Cicero returned to Rome from Sicily, exactly like someone who thinks he is playing a leading role on the world stage. He was soon to learn that he had much overestimated the renown he had gained through his official activities. He speaks about this, not without humorous self-irony, in a plea delivered some twenty years later, the speech in defence of Plancius.[14] He had thought at that time, he says, that people in Rome were talking of nothing but his quaestorship, and he had returned expecting that the Roman people would henceforth invest him with all other offices without any further exertion on his part. His journey had led him through Puteoli on the Campanian coast, a major port and high-class resort. To his dismay someone asked him there, when he had left Rome and whether there was anything new to report from there. 'When I replied', Cicero continues in his Plancius speech, 'that I was on my way back from the provinces, he said: "Ah, yes, from Africa, I believe." I was annoyed and said: "No, from Sicily." Then someone butted in who seemed to know everything: "What", he said, "You don't know he was quaestor in Syracuse?"' After this second blunder (he had administered the second Sicilian quaestorship, that of Lilybaeum), Cicero swallowed his irritation and behaved as if he were merely a holiday-maker who had come for the bathing.

5

The Prosecution of Verres

As a sequel to the passage from the Plancius speech quoted above, Cicero tells us that he drew his own conclusions from this experience. 'For, when I observed', he goes on, 'that the Roman people were pretty hard of hearing, but had keen and penetrating eyesight, I no longer thought about what people might hear of me; I tried to make sure they would have me in front of them from now on, I positively lived before their very eyes, I did not neglect the forum; at home no one was ever refused access to me by my porter, or because I was sleeping.'[1] In the midst of all this hectic activity he was very keen to get to know as many of his fellow-citizens as possible by name, without the aid of a 'nomenclator' – the slave who served as a walking address-book and whispered to his master the names of all those he met. According to Plutarch he once remarked that it was a disgrace that craftsmen were able to identify precisely all the tools and equipment they used, whereas a politician, who was required to conduct public affairs through the agency of men, did not take the greatest care to know his fellow-citizens with equal precision.[2] He even knew where his acquaintances lived and where they had their country homes, who they associated with and who their neighbours were.

The 70s, less turbulent than the preceding decade, nevertheless brought grave public disorders, and at times these events had indirect repercussions on Cicero's unremitting activity as advocate. This was especially true of the Spartacus rising. In the years 73–71 BC hordes of rebellious slaves made their way through the whole of Italy, plundering and murdering and defeating Roman troops on several occasions, until Spartacus was himself defeated in Lucania and killed. The last vestiges of the rebellion were crushed in the north of Italy by Pompey, who had just returned from Spain after overthrowing Sertorius, one of Marius's supporters. The armies of Spartacus, however, were no more than the most obvious symptom of a widespread development. Armed gangs of slaves made the country unsafe everywhere, often in the service of masters who were using them as bodyguards and assault troops. No doubt the turmoil occasioned by the rivalry of Marius and Sulla encouraged this alarming trend towards general violent anarchy. Even in the murder trial in which Cicero appeared for the defence shortly before his departure for the East – the accused being a certain Lucius Varenus – armed gangs of slaves had evidently played some considerable part. His speech in defence of Marcus Tullius deals in fact with crimes in which armed slaves acted as accomplices. This speech, from 72 or 71 BC, is the only one that has survived, at least in part, from the period between Cicero's return from Sicily and the trial of Verres. Two neighbouring landowners from the district of Thurii in Lucania – in the immediate vicinity of a camp occupied by the troops of Spartacus – had fallen out over a strip of land. Property was destroyed and slaves were killed. The case was investigated under regulations promulgated in 77 BC with the express purpose of countering such depredations through more rapid judicial procedures and particularly drastic penalties.

In the years 73–71 BC, that is at the same time as Spartacus was terrorizing Italy, the governor Gaius Verres held sway in Sicily. Verres was the very epitome of a venal, greedy and ruthless Roman provincial ruler. The fact that he was able to rule for so long was one consequence of the Spartacus troubles. His successor, Quintus Arrius, was already standing by in 72, prepared to take over from him, but his services were needed in the campaign against the insurgent slaves, so that he failed to arrive. That Verres's governorship was extended into a third year was probably a further consequence of the threat posed by Spartacus.

At the same time, what was going on in Sicily was common knowledge in Rome. In the autumn of 72 BC Sthenius, an eminent citizen of Thermae (on the northern coast of Sicily), had arrived in Rome seeking support against the high-handed behaviour of Verres. He was an extremely wealthy man who had spent his life collecting works of art and valuable furniture. Verres was frequently a guest in Sthenius's house and had gradually coaxed or coerced him into handing over his treasures. In various public places in Thermae stood a number of ancient bronze statues. They had come originally from Himera, a town adjacent to Thermae which had been destroyed in 409 BC by the Carthaginians and which had never been rebuilt. After the younger Scipio had conquered Carthage he returned the booty to the successors of its original owners, the inhabitants of Thermae. Sthenius had tolerated the theft of his private property, but when Verres went on to demand the finest items belonging to the city, including a statue of the poet Stesichoros (sixth century BC), he then persuaded the council of Thermae to refuse any such demand. Verres was furious: he renounced his friendship with Sthenius, allied himself with the latter's enemies and contrived to have Sthenius arraigned on a charge of forging documents. Sthenius fled to evade trial and was sentenced in his absence to a fine of 500,000 sesterces. Not satisfied with this, Verres then had a capital charge laid against Sthenius, with the trial being scheduled for 1 December.

In the mean time Sthenius had arrived in Rome, where he had any number of friends. The consuls reported to the Senate on the affair and proposed that the Senate should rule that no person from the provinces might be charged with a capital offence in his absence. Verres's father – who was a senator – managed to frustrate this proposal, assuring the supporters of Sthenius that he would persuade his son to back down. Verres nevertheless went ahead and pronounced a verdict of guilty, although neither the accused nor the plaintiff had appeared. Now, the people's tribunes had recently promulgated a decree banishing from Rome any person who had been sentenced on a capital charge. Cicero procured from the college of tribunes a statement to the effect that this did not apply to his friend Sthenius. The case illustrates how matters stood with the rule of the Senate as it had been restored by Sulla. An 'old boy network' and mutual favours between colleagues frustrated any measures aimed at the arbitrary practices, however blatant, of members of their own class.

Gnaeus Pompeius Magnus ('Pompey the Great') and Marcus Licinius Crassus Dives ('Crassus the Wealthy') had distinguished themselves on the side of Sulla during the civil war. Crassus then laid the foundation of his vast fortune by appropriating the property of proscribed individuals. Already in 71 BC it became apparent that the pair of them, as consuls for the succeeding year, proposed to follow a 'popular' course and introduce radical reforms aimed against Sulla's reactionary constitution. They did in fact remove the last remaining restrictions to which Sulla had subjected the office of people's tribune. Towards the end of 70 BC the judicial office, the exclusive preserve of the Senate since Sulla's dictatorship, was divided, with the senators, the knights and the *tribuni aerarii* (we are not sure who they were) each being allocated a third of the places.

In this political climate influential circles in the Senate did all they possibly could to prevent the unmasking of one of the most iniquitous members of their class. As early as 71 BC, while Verres was still in Sicily, emissaries from nearly all the Sicilian communities had appeared in Rome. They wished to avail themselves of the only weapon the Roman state allowed its subjects as a defence against delinquent officials – indictment for extortion. There was a special jury court for this purpose. However, the Sicilians were not permitted to plead their case themselves: they had to be represented by a Roman lawyer. They requested Cicero, whose integrity they had already tested, to come to their assistance, and he agreed. It was pretty well the only time in his life that he was prepared to assume the role of prosecutor; in almost all the other criminal cases in which he was involved he acted for the defence.

When he lodged his complaint with the praetor responsible for extortion cases at the beginning of 70 BC, about the time that Verres left Sicily, Cicero encountered the first of the obstacles that the friends of Verres had raised to delay or thwart him. A follower of Verres, once his quaestor, Quintus Caecilius Niger, also applied to undertake the prosecution – with the aim of conducting it in such a way that it would not constitute a threat to Verres. So now a preliminary hearing had to be held to decide who had priority. Cicero delivered the address known as *In Caecilium Divinatio, A Conjecture in Opposition to Caecilius*, and won the day. He was thus appointed official prosecutor in the case against Verres. He promptly asked the quaestor for a stay of 110 days so that he might conduct an official investigation and collect evidence in the form of documents and witnesses.

He then set out for Sicily, accompanied by his cousin. In the course of an uncommonly severe winter he spent fifty days touring the entire island and assembling the impressive mass of incriminating evidence that fills books 2–5 of the second Verres speech. At the same time the opposing party was doing all it possibly could to obstruct him. The governorship was held at that time by Lucius Caecilius Metellus, successor to Verres. He, however, belonged to the Verres clique, together with his brothers Quintus and Marcus and the defence counsel for Verres, the orator Hortensius. Quintus and Hortensius were candidates for the consulship in 69 BC, while Marcus Caeilius Metellus was seeking a praetorship for the same year. Verres, for his part, had undertaken to use some of the money he had extorted from the Sicilians to provide bribes to ensure the outcome that his friends wished. Cicero therefore had to overcome all sorts of resistance simply in order to do what he was entitled to do by law: procure documents, question witnesses and persuade the communities to nominate delegations to attend the trial.

Cicero returned to Rome in good time before the specified term of 110 days had expired. But the Verres clique had not been inactive there, either, and he found a new surprise awaiting him. Immediately after the proceedings against Verres had been sanctioned, another plaintiff had appeared before the same praetor and had requested a stay of 108 days for the hearing of his case, an alleged case of extortion in Achaia. But the praetor was in the habit of fixing dates for hearings in accordance with the period granted for inquiries to be made. And so it came about that the Achaian case was allocated the earlier date, because the delay sought was two days shorter. Cicero claims that this ruse led to a delay of three months, and the trial did not finally start until 5 August.[3]

The ruse was part of an ingenious plan. Because of the popular agitation against abuses of senatorial power, the year 70 BC, when Pompey and Crassus were consuls, offered by far the least propitious circumstances for Verres's purposes, especially for the possibility of bribing the court. The clique therefore endeavoured to delay the trial until the following year, when they could hope that Hortensius and the two Metelli as consuls and praetor would do everything they could to ensure an acquittal. Two circumstances were in their favour. A feature of the Roman trial was the practice known as *ampliatio*, or adjournment: after all the evidence had been submitted, the court might conclude that the issue had still not been sufficiently clarified, so that a further hearing of the evidence was required. In a trial for extortion the law stipulated that the entire body of evidence had to be presented twice: an *actio prima* was invariably followed by an *actio secunda* before a verdict was pronounced. This slowed down the proceedings considerably. What was more, from the middle of August until the middle of November in the year 70 BC very few days were available for judicial proceedings. Apart from the regularly recurring festivals, there were extra games by which Pompey had promised to celebrate his victory in Spain. The election for 69 BC, which took place at the end of July, turned out to be a triumph for the Verres clique: Hortensius and Quintus Metellus became consuls. But Marcus Metellus was not merely elected praetor – he was chosen by lot to preside over the court for extortion. The failure of an attempt to stop Cicero being elected aedile mattered very little in the circumstances, for Verres was already receiving the congratulations of his friends.

When the first day of the trial began on 5 August, instead of making the usual opening address expounding the whole subject of the case, Cicero declared that he would proceed at once to submit the evidence for the prosecution.[4] From the 6th to the 13th August it was demonstrated point by point, with the aid of witnesses and documents, that Verres had extorted 40 million sesterces from the population during the three years of his governorship. The opposition were not prepared for such a fiercely aggressive prosecution, and when the court reassembled for the second hearing following two vacation periods, Verres had already drawn his own conclusions from the failure of his delaying tactics. He had decamped for exile in Massilia (Marseilles), taking his loot with him, as the law of the time allowed him to do, provided that he had not already been found guilty. The court regarded the accused's guilt as proven. In the final phase of the trial, the assessment of damages, as Plutarch reports, it was decided that Verres should pay back no more than three million sesterces.[5] Possibly this was the value of the items that could be repossessed. Nevertheless, the Sicilians were very pleased: the trial had set a precedent. Cicero, however, left the courtroom as a twofold victor. He had vanquished not only the accused, but also the latter's lawyer, Hortensius, and was now regarded as Rome's leading orator.

He published his speeches against Verres forthwith, not only the two which he had actually delivered – the attack on Caecilius and the address of 5 August – but also the vast amount of material which he had not been able to deploy in a coherent form. From this he constructed an imaginary actio secunda, as if Verres, contrary to expectation, had appeared after all for the second hearing. This actio secunda, a remarkable piece of work in a literary as well as an historical sense, is in fact not a trial speech (it would be much too long for that, anyway), but a documentary record of a politically significant affair, put into the form of a forensic plea.

The first book of the actio secunda deals with the accused's previous career, the offices which Verres had held before assuming the governorship. Strictly speaking, this subject is not at all relevant to the issue. But Cicero was conforming to the prevalent forensic practice in Classical times when he began by entering into the 'vita ante acta', and might expect to find a receptive public.

Books 2–5 contain the actual substance of the prosecution, the misdemeanours of the Sicilian governor, arranged under relevant headings. The second book describes typical incidents from the field of jurisprudence and general administration. It illustrates the ruses and subterfuges Verres had used to enrich himself at the expense of the victims of his arbitrary justice. The Sthenius affair forms a central feature in the exposition.

The third book presents the most important part of the charge, tax extortion. It is here that Cicero goes to work most thoroughly. He deals with the complex legal, administrative and economic provisions of the Sicilian tax system before turning his attention to the individual offences committed by Verres. This book is therefore of great value as a document describing Roman administrative practice in the provinces. For this, posterity has to thank the circumstance that Cicero could not assume, as he could otherwise in dealing with Roman domestic affairs, that the Roman public would be familiar with the general and basic principles involved. Sicilian taxes were evidently just as unfamiliar to the majority of his contemporaries as they are to the modern observer, so that he thought it appropriate, as a first step, to explore the fundamental features of the system. The offences themselves boil down to Verres's practice of making common cause with the individuals who acted as tax collectors, abusing his authority in order to frustrate all the safeguards that had been designed to protect farmers from arbitrary impositions in the levying of taxes.

The much vaunted final two books, which clearly rise above the level of what has gone before, are not only high-grade sources of cultural history, they are also fascinating examples of Cicero's mastery of the art of exposition. The fourth book takes as its subject the blackmailing practices and the violence through which Verres was able to appropriate art objects of every kind. It discusses a pathological side-effect of the adoption of Greek culture by the Romans. The Roman aristocracy of the late Republic was obsessed with works of art from the great age of Greece, and it positively became the fashion to assemble miniature museums. The orator Crassus possessed priceless vases and chased metal vessels which he did not dare use because they were so precious. Sulla and others kept statues and paintings of the finest quality in their villas. Marcus Aemilius Scaurus, Sulla's son-in-law, assembled a collection of cameos and even had all the pictures of the famous painter Pausias of Sikyon (4th century BC) brought to Rome. The example of the aristocracy started a fashion among the newly rich: Chrysogonos, Sulla's favourite, crammed his home with the finest items from the property of those who had been proscribed. Verres's passion went to the point where he did not shrink from using any means whatsoever: it was certainly exceptionally unbridled, but it was not unique.

The last book might bear the title, 'Verres as commander-in-chief', or 'Public safety in Sicily during the governorship of Verres'. It deals with the way in which Verres had employed the nucleus of his imperium, his sovereign rights, that is his military authority and his penal powers over Roman citizens. The first major section includes a highly detailed account of the ruin of the Sicilian navy: it had been destroyed by pirates because it was inadequately equipped. Verres, whose avarice had brought about the catastrophe, subjected the blameless Sicilan naval commanders to cruel punishment. The second main section concerns the illegal punishment and killing of Roman citizens. This passage, which was an addition and not strictly relevant (the charge was extortion), Cicero deliberately saved until the end, since it was bound to appeal strongly to this feelings of his Roman listeners and readers.

6

From Aedile to Praetor

From the period preceding Cicero's consulship eleven letters altogether have been preserved: they are addressed to Atticus, who at that time was still in Athens.[1] These letters, which begin at the end of 68 BC or the beginning of 67 BC, tell us a good deal about Cicero's personal circumstances. For the first time we hear about his wife Terentia, who suffered from severe pains in her arms and legs. His daughter is evidently the apple of Cicero's eye. He calls her 'Tulliola, deliciolae nostrae',[2] which Wieland renders, possibly a shade too sentimentally, with the words 'sweet little Tullia, my darling'.[3] As early as the end of 67 BC (she must have been ten years old at the time), her father promised her to Gaius Calpurnius Piso Frugi. He was the great-grandson of the historian Lucius Calpurnius Piso Frugi, who had been consul in the critical year 133 BC. The connection with a house belonging to the high nobility served political ends and was designed to enhance Cicero's prestige. The marriage was celebrated in 63 BC and ended six years later with the sudden death of Piso. In the summer of 65 BC Terentia gave birth to a second child, a son, Marcus. The proud father writes succinctly: 'L. Iulio Caesare, C. Marcio Figulo consulibus filiolo me auctum scito salva Terentia' – 'Under the consulship of Lucius Julius Caesar and Gaius Marcus Figulus, I must inform you that I was given a little son; Terentia is well.'[4] Cicero's brother Quintus had married Pomponia, the sister of Atticus, Cicero having acted as match-maker. The marriage, from which Cicero's nephew Quintus was born in 66 or 65 BC, does not seem to have been a happy one, even at that time. Cicero hints repeatedly that he had tried to placate his brother.[5]

Each of the two earliest letters to Atticus reports a death in the family.[6] Cicero writes that his brother Lucius had died – in fact, he is referring to the cousin who had studied with him in Athens and who had later assisted him in Sicily with the investigation into Verres. He mourns his loss and praises the kindly disposition and agreeable manners of his late friend. A subsequent letter, on the other hand, contains no more than the bald statement: 'Pater nobis decessit ante diem quartum Kalendas Decembres' – 'We lost our father on 27 November.' This terse announcement has caused some dismay, especially as Asconius, a commentator on Cicero, offers a different version, according to which Cicero's father did not die until 64 BC.[7] It has therefore been plausibly suggested that *pater* should be emended to *frater*. In other words, Cicero was briefly recapitulating what he had reported in his previous letter, a common practice which may easily be explained. Since people had to rely on personal favours or on messengers to deliver their mail, they could never know for certain whether, or how soon, a given letter would reach its recipient.

In the early letters to Atticus no subject is mentioned as frequently as the villa in Tusculum – Cicero's favourite retreat for his leisure hours – and the amenities he had planned for it. This was the place, he writes, where he could get away from his labours and from the daily grind.[8] It was there that he immersed himself in his studies when politics disgusted him. Atticus was a great connoisseur and bibliophile, collecting on his own account and also accepting commissions on Cicero's behalf. It is mentioned on several occasions that he had purchased statues from Megara and *Hermes* of Pentelic marble for Cicero.[9] He is to buy some more – for the *gymnasium* (a garden) and for a terrace. This was the modest – and honest – manner in which Cicero satisfied the hunger for Greek art that was widely prevalent among the Roman aristocracy. The term 'gymnasium' was no doubt intended to suggest that the Greek athletic arenas which were so called had also been favourite meeting-places for philosophers in Athens. Another subject frequently mentioned is books. Atticus was apparently thinking of selling a collection of his books (he had skilled scribes among his slaves) and Cicero asked if he could have them.[10]

Cicero's legal practice was flourishing. Three pleas from this period have been preserved: the speech in defence of Fonteius in fragmentary form, and the complete speeches in defence of Caecina and of Cluentius Habitus. There is no lack of evidence, however, suggesting that Cicero coped with much more than this. Only in the case of Caecina can it be claimed with any certainty that it concerned a civil dispute. Here Cicero operated with the same kind of interpretative skills as in the defence of Tullius. No further pleas in civil lawsuits have come down to us from any later period. Following his appointment as praetor Cicero spoke only in criminal and political trials, and as a politician. This development probably ensued in the nature of things: an advocate so much in demand and so involved in major actions simply had no time for petty cases. As counsel for the defence in criminal cases he was particularly concerned with two offences which had come to be regarded more or less as mere peccadilloes in the corrupt Republic: improper influencing of voters (*ambitus*) and blackmail by those in authority (*crimen repetundarum*).

An unusual case arose from an instance where an official clerk occupying a relatively high rank in Roman society by virtue of his profession had been improperly relegated by the censors – which the latter were entitled to do, without any detailed examination of the case, during the census (the quinquennial revision of the civic lists). Cicero was able to have the clerk reinstated and appears to have achieved his object in other cases as well. In the memorandum composed for Cicero when he was applying for the consulship, his brother lists with some satisfaction, a number of individuals who were obliged to Cicero for assistance in their lawsuits.[11] The Quintus Gallus who is mentioned there along with others was, interestingly enough, a friend of Cataline. Among the fragments of Cicero's speech for the defence (Gallius was charged with ambitus), there is a notable description of a drinking party:

There are shouts and screams, screeching females, there is deafening music. I thought I could make out some people entering and others leaving, some of them staggering from the effects of the wine, some of them still yawning from yesterday's boozing. Among them was Gallius, perfumed and wreathed with flowers; the floor was filthy, soiled with wine and covered with withered garlands and fish-bones.[12]

The speech in defence of Marcus Fonteius, of which, apart from a few fragments, only the conclusion has been preserved, shows Cicero a couple of years after the Verres affair involved with the same type of offence – the blackmail of his subjects by a provincial governor – only this time he was appearing for the defence. Fonteius, once governor of the province of Gallia Narbonensis, may not have come anywhere near the criminal stature of Verres. On the other hand, he certainly was not the thoroughly decent and utterly respectable, upright citizen his advocate made him out to be. The surviving parts of the speech at any rate do not enter into the charges of the indictment. Cicero casts voluble doubt on the credibility of the Gallic witnesses and claims that condemnation of the accused, a competent officer, would inflict considerable damage on the state.

The prosecution of Verres and the defence of Fonteius clearly show that Cicero exercised his function as advocate in entirely different ways, according to the part he had to play. As prosecutor, his function in the Verres trial, he painted as black a picture as he could of the defendant. As counsel for the defence, his customary task, he did everything he possibly could to represent his client as totally innocent. There is no reason to reproach Cicero with this practice: the functions of prosecution and defence are legitimate and part and parcel of the judicial system in any free state. They are designed to show the judges the two extremes which seem to be possible in the investigation and assessment of the relevant issues. It is then up to the judges to deduce as objective a view as possible from these opposing angles and to deliver their verdict accordingly.

Cicero's deliberate partiality as counsel may be even more clearly observed in his plea on behalf of Cluentius Habitus, whom he defended in a case of alleged murder. The setting was a small country town and the events were reminiscent of some lurid popular ballad – killings, abortions and the forging of wills with the aim of illicitly gaining legacies. Originally, the main parties to the dispute were Aulus Cluentius Habitus and his step-father, Statius Albius Oppianicus. However, in 74 BC, eight years before the hearing which gave rise to the surviving speech by Cicero, there had been a whole string of lawsuits. At that time Cicero had been on the opposite side, defending a freedman by the name of Scamander, accomplice in the attempted murder of Cluentius, which had been staged by Oppianicus. Cluentius had contrived to have, first Scamander, then a second accomplice, and finally Oppianicus himself convicted. In the trial in 66 BC it was Cluentius's turn to be in the dock: he was alleged to have got rid of his step-father by having him poisoned. Several years earlier, in his first Verres speech, Cicero had spoken in Oppianicus's favour in a corruption scandal that was linked to the verdict of guilty passed on Oppianicus.[13] Now, in 66 BC, as defending counsel for Cluentius, he was hard put to it to explain to the court how he had come to change sides. In this connection there is a passage which is worthy of note as illustrating his view of himself in his capacity as advocate:

> Anyone who thinks that, in our speeches before the bench, he has our cast-iron convictions, is making a grave mistake, for all these speeches are dictated by the interests of the parties themselves and their lawyers.[14]

If a case could speak for itself, Cicero continues, then nobody would need a lawyer. The latter was not committed, to his own convictions but to the interests of his client, so that he always had to put things in a light that most favoured his case. Cicero was here making a candid, but risky confession. The judges might have taken it as a measure, not only of his former, but also of his present, attitude and the two-edged weapon might have been turned against his current protégé. The judges, however, accepted the statement in the spirit in which it was meant, and Cluentius was acquitted. Cicero is said to have declared later that he had hoodwinked the judges – 'se tenebras offudisse iudicibus'.[15] They ought to have borne in mind that his plea in 66 BC had also been dictated by party interest and circumstances. In *De Officiis* (*On Duties*) Cicero later reduced the problem to the simpler formula: 'It is the judge's business always to go for the truth in trial proceedings; it is the advocate's business sometimes to make a case for the probable as well, even if it doesn't correspond precisely to the truth.'[16]

Cicero's campaign for the office of aedile coincided with the time when he was straining every nerve to force through the Verres trial, so that he was torn between the trial and his campaign. Verres, however, used his money all too blatantly, and Cicero was elected with no trouble at all. Of the office itself – which he held in 69 BC – we do not know for certain whether it was the *curule* or the *plebeian* magistracy. By that time, it seems, the special features of the aedilship no longer bulked large in the public mind. Like the people's tribunes, this authority, which was responsible latterly for the games and the supervision of markets, was instituted as a special office of the *plebs*, i.e. those citizens who did not belong to the circle of illustrious patrician families. From 366 BC onwards, however, the plebeian aediles were matched by two *curule aediles*, so called on account of the privilege they enjoyed of occupying the *sella curulis*, the official chair reserved for senior civil servants. Election to the plebeian aedilship continued to be confined to plebeians, but both plebeians and patricians could be elected curule aediles, officials representing the people as a whole. As far as Cicero is concerned, it is known only that he organized games: there is no evidence that he also administered the markets, a function reserved for the curule aediles. Hence, he would have been a plebeian aedile. He was responsible for the festival of Ceres with its circus games, held about 19 April; the boisterous Flora festival, dedicated to the goddess of flowers, at which popular plays were put on and dancers performed striptease acts, round about 28 April; and also for the grand *ludi Romani*, which occupied the entire period from 4 to 19 September, with theatrical performances and chariot races. Cicero later boasted that he had achieved his aim of recommending himself for further official posts without undue exertion.[17]

At first Cicero was not in the least concerned about the next hurdle, the praetorship: he wrote to Atticus saying that he need not come to Rome for the election campaign.[18] But there was in the end a degree of uncertainty, since the elections in the summer of 67 BC had to be interrupted twice – probably on account of unfavourable omens, the flight or the call of birds, say, which the Romans interpreted as a divine warning against the conduct of any state ceremony. It was for this reason that Cicero had the honour of being three times proclaimed first among the candidates elected. Thus, in 66 BC, he was one of the eight praetors provided for in the Sullan constitution. He was entrusted with the chairmanship of a *quaestio*, a jury court, and was responsible for sentencing blackmailers, the offence he had attacked four years previously as prosecutor in the Verres trial. There do not seem to have been any major scandals during his period of office. Nevertheless, it was under his jurisdiction that Gaius Licinius Macer was convicted, a man who had gained distinction, not only as a politician, but also as a historian. His annals probably covered the whole of Roman history from the beginning down to his own day. His son was Gaius Licinius Calvus, orator and poet, and a friend of Catullus. Macer belonged to the popular faction; in his *Historiae* Sallust quotes him as delivering an impassioned address when he was tribune for the year 73 BC. He is hardly likely to have been a vicious extortioner. We do not even know which province he is alleged to have plundered, but his conviction affected him so grievously that he died immediately afterwards.

It was as praetor that Cicero delivered his first political speech – in support of a bill proposed by the people's tribune Gaius Manilius. The bill appointed Pompey commander-in-chief in the war against Mithridates VI of Pontos, that same Mithridates whom Sulla had managed to defeat twenty years previously. The speech, essentially a eulogy of Pompey, reveals that Cicero, a beginner in the area of high politics, was thoroughly imbued with a sense of his important assignment. It is constructed with pedantic precision and indulges in a series of sustained solemn periods.

One would like to know what Cicero, in these years of his laborious rise to eminence, really thought of Pompey, his exact contemporary and the most brilliant star in the Roman firmament before he was eclipsed by Caesar. The careers of the two men were as different as they could be. In Cicero's case everything went by the rules: he assumed one

regular Republican office after another, in each instance at the pre-
scribed age. Pompey's brilliant career consisted entirely of constitutional
irregularities. As a young man he had fought on Sulla's side against the
Marius faction without having any official function. He was entrusted
with further military commissions and exercised his first regular public
function in 70 BC, as consul – in a sense, beginning at the point where
others were wont to finish. In fact, he excelled himself shortly afterwards: in 67 BC an enabling law conferred on him special wide-ranging
powers of command covering all coastal regions for the purpose of
suppressing the depredations of the pirates who were rife in the
Mediterranean.

Now that the Empire had been delivered from the scourge of piracy,
Pompey was once more to be given sweeping powers for the campaign
against Mithridates. The war had already been going on for eight years
under the command of Lucius Licinius Lucullus, the famous gourmet
who had introduced from Kerasus in the realm of Mithridates the
cherry which took its name from that place. Lucullus had first of all
conquered Pontos and had also defeated Tigranes, the Armenian ally of
Mithridates, on several occasions. Reverses had then forced him into
inactivity and he was recalled. This was the situation when Manilius
put forward his bill.

When Cicero began to speak it was already a foregone conclusion
that the popular assembly he was addressing would endorse the proposal – only stubborn defenders of senatorial rule, like Hortensius, for
example, dared to resist it by that time. Cicero did not miss the chance
to bring himself to the notice of the influential Pompey, but he tried at
the same time not to offend the senatorial aristocracy unnecessarily. No
doubt he was prompted to follow this course in large measure by the
fact that he would soon be a candidate for the consulate and needed as
wide a range of contacts as possible. Much later, when his judgement
was no longer clouded by electoral considerations, he severely criticized
Manilius's law, the exceptional character of which entailed a grave
infringement of the Republican constitution.[19]

Cicero's attempt to maintain good relations with Pompey, as well as
with the senatorial aristocracy, ran into grave difficulties during the last
days of his praetorship. According to ancient custom, the people's
tribunes used to assume and demit office on 10 December: hence, from
that date in 66 BC Manilius was no longer tribune. At the end of
December he was instantly accused of extortion – obviously an act of
revenge on the part of radical circles in the Senate. In his speech
supporting Pompey, Cicero had fully committed himself to defending

Manilius in such an eventuality. Now he feared that this would place him too much on the side of the popular faction, and he tried to avoid honouring his pledge by scheduling Manilius's trial for the last day of his praetorship, and, hence, of his chairmanship of the court dealing with extortion. He was not allowed to get away with this, however, and had to assure an agitated crowd of citizens that he would undertake the defence of Manilius the following year, when he had relinquished office. However, the charge was not proceeded with, and Cicero escaped scot-free.

7

The Battle for the Consulship

In his *Jugurthan War* Sallust describes how Marius, the homo novus, decided for the first time to apply for the office of consul, and remarks in this connection: 'Even at that time the other offices were conferred by the people, but the office of consul was passed from hand to hand within the aristocracy. A man without ancestors might be ever so famous and might have rendered outstanding services, it was still thought he was not worthy of the honour and that the office would be profaned thereby.'[1] It is true, the consuls, like all other magistrates, were formally elected by the people, but the influence the senatorial aristocracy exerted on the electorate was so powerful that it could exclude undesirable candidates and make the consular elections appear no more than a transfer 'from hand to hand' within the ranks of the aristocracy.

Once his praetorship was over, Cicero was exclusively concerned with the preparations for his election to the office of consul, for which he would be eligible at the earliest in the third year following his praetorship, i.e. in 63 BC. He was, of course, thoroughly acquainted with the state of affairs so succinctly stated by Sallust in the sentences quoted above. Thus, in a letter to Atticus from the early summer of 65 BC, dealing with his chances a year before the elections for 63 BC, he writes: 'As soon as I have spied out what the *nobiles* [the leading figures in the senatorial aristocracy] intend to do, I shall write to you again' – 'Cum perspexero voluntates nobilium, scribam ad te.'[2] In a somewhat later letter he declares to his friend: 'I very much need you to come soon; this is because people are convinced that there are aristocrats, friends of yours, who mean to oppose my election. You would be extremely useful in getting these people to adopt a more favourable opinion of me.'[3] So Cicero by no means underestimated the barrier he faced: the unwritten law of the senatorial regime that the office of consul should, if at all possible, be withheld from newcomers.

Cicero admired the traditions of Rome and could not imagine Rome otherwise than under the rule of the aristocracy. He fervently desired to be admitted to the circle of the aristocracy, to be included among the authoritative figures there, so that he found himself in an awkward position when obstacles were placed in his way. He had to seek friends and helpers wherever he could find them, even among the opponents of the senatorial party, the *Optimates* (the best people), as they called themselves, and yet he could not afford to discredit himself in the eyes of these Optimates. It was a question, therefore, of manoeuvering on a number of different fronts. Cicero was obliged to create the impression among the aristocracy, among the knights, and with the populace in general, that he was just the right man for this or that group, that it was precisely their interests he would care for most.

Cicero's special difficulties and prospects are graphically revealed in a a document which Quintus drafted for his brother when the latter was preparing to run for the consulship – the *Commentariolum Petitionis* or *Memorandum on Standing for the Consulship*. It was to serve as a guideline for the campaign and show how Cicero might gain the support of as wide and influential a circle of citizens as possible. The first section of the work starts from the fact that Cicero was a homo novus. Quintus refers to his brother's talent as an orator. It was mainly to this talent that he owed his following – among the knights, among the towns of Italy, among numerous individuals – and now the time had come, Cicero must point out, for all these people to repay what he had done for them. Quintus goes on to give advice on how best to foster relations with the aristocracy. After all, it was they who mattered most, and he would have to take special pains to show them that he was worthy of the high office to which he aspired. He should make it clear that he had always been on the side of the Optimates. His occasional 'populariter loqui', 'popular speeches', and his support for Manlius' proposal, say, had merely been intended to secure the favour of Pompey.

Under the heading, 'Magnitudo Petitionis', 'The Significance of the Candidature', the second, considerably longer section of the *Commentariolum* contains the actual instructions, which cover every conceivable detail. If Cicero means to conduct his election campaign prudently, then he must employ two methods: he must gain 'studia amicorum', 'the interest of his friends', as well as 'popularis voluntas', 'popularity with the people'. Friends in all walks of life can be useful in many different ways in the campaign, and a candidate might be more liberal than usual in his use of the term. A special chapter is devoted to the candidate's entourage and to the kind of people he should associate with: a large number of permanent – or occasional – associates enhanced a man's prestige. Among suggestions for gaining the 'popularis ratio' there is a hint that a candidate might once in a while promise more than he was able to perform. But Quintus interjects that this suggestion was hardly likely to be accepted by his brother – a *homo Platonicus*, a man of lofty ideals.[4] The little treatise, drawn from practical experience and designed for practical use, reflects the unvarnished truth about the Roman situation. Anyone inclined to question its occasionally dubious moral standards should bear in mind that it was not such relatively innocuous lapses that corrupted the electoral practice of the time, but much more massive abuses, especially the buying of votes.

In 65 BC Cicero defended the former people's tribune, Gaius Cornelius. He published the speeches he delivered during the four days of the trial (two addresses to the jury). They have not come down to us, but they are known in their probable outline from the commentary on them written by the learned scholar, Quintus Asconius Pedianus. The affair is important because it illustrates Cicero's situation at the time he was standing for election as consul. He could not very well turn down requests for help from members of the popular faction who were hostile to the Senate, but, on the other hand, he had to do everything possible to court or to retain the favour of the aristocratic class. Asconius assures us, in fact, that, in his speech for the defence Cicero achieved the remarkable feat of not offending the pride of the noble gentry he was pitted against, and yet not allowing their influence to prejudice his client's case.[5]

The case itself was by way of being a topical political issue. Cornelius had contrived to have legislation passed that ran counter to the Senate's interest – or had attempted to do so. In one case a fellow-tribune had raised an objection, having been persuaded by the Senate to do so. Cornelius was alleged to have ignored this objection, which would have been a grave offence and an infringement of a fundamental rule of the constitution. At the end of his year of office (65 BC), when the initial trial had been concluded, Cornelius was once more charged with high treason (*maiestas*). It was at this point that Cicero undertook to defend him, because Cornelius was a moderate rather than a radical member of the Populares. It was no doubt predictable that the case would not go against him. And so it turned out, in fact. For, not only the knights and the tribuni aerarii, but also a number of senators acquitted Cornelius, an outcome to which Cicero's astute defence no doubt contributed a good deal.

In the above-mentioned letter from the early summer of 65 BC in which Cicero discusses his chances of election, all the rivals he can think of are mentioned, among them Lucius Sergius Catalina (Cataline). Of him it is said, in drastic terms, that he will certainly be a rival – 'provided the judges ordain that it shall not be broad daylight at high noon' – 'si iudicatum erit meridie non lucere':[6] Thus, in Cicero's view, he does not count as a rival. Cataline was two years older than Cicero and had also achieved the praetorship two years before him – in 68 BC. Immediately afterwards he had gone as governor to the Roman province of Africa (now Tunisia) and, undeterred by the fate of Verres, had set about ruthlessly exploiting the local population so as to improve his ruinous financial situation. When he returned after governing the province for two years, he was charged with extortion. The trial prevented him from running for the consulship in 64 BC (anyone involved in pending criminal proceedings was disqualified from candidacy). Cicero was in fact banking on a conviction which would prevent Cataline standing as a candidate in 63 BC as well.

In a second, rather later letter, also mentioned above, Cicero refers once more to his rival Cataline, but here, surprisingly, he makes the following statement: 'At the moment I am thinking of assuming the defence of my rival, Cataline. We have the judges we want to have, to the entire satisfaction of the prosecution, in fact. If he is acquitted, then he will ally himself all the more closely with me in the election campaign; if things turn out otherwise, then we shall just have to put up with it as best we can.'[7] The passage shows just how far Cicero was prepared to go for purely tactical reasons. Nothing can have changed in the case itself, or in the charges against Cataline, since the time Cicero had reckoned with such aplomb that he would be convicted. But obviously circumstances now suggested that an acquittal was on the cards, probably because of the court, on the constitution of which the parties involved – defence and prosecution – could exert a certain influence via their right to object to undesirable judges.

Cicero would have known Cataline for a long time. Like Cicero, he had served in the Social War and, coming as he did from a patrician family, he belonged even more obviously than the plebeian Cicero to the cohors praetoria of the commander-in-chief, Pompeius Strabo. Later, from 82 BC onward, he was employed as Sulla's hired assassin and was reputed to have murdered a number of knights, including his own brother-in-law, Quintus Caecilius. That he also killed his brother and then – according to the formula used by Chrysogonis in the case of Sextus Roscius senior – placed him on the proscribed list, is vouched for only by Plutarch, so that the report is unreliable.[8] At any rate, he was involved in the brutal slaying of Marius Gratidianus, a follower of Marius and a cousin of Cicero's father. Quintus Cicero describes this incident in his *Commentariolum* as follows:

> Need I add that the man who is standing for election as consul along with yourself is the same man who scourged a highly popular figure, Marcus Marius, through the entire city in full sight of the Romans, hounded him to his place of burial, flayed him with all manner of tortures, and then, as he stood there, struck off his victim's head with the sword he held in his right hand, clutching the hair of Marcus's head with his left, and carried it away with blood dripping between his fingers?[9]

Details of this account may be exaggerated (Quintus Cicero fancied himself as a poet; while he was Caesar's legate in Gaul, for instance, he was said to have written four tragedies in sixteen days!). Nevertheless, it is strange that Cicero, the homo Platonicus, should have thought of making common cause with such a depraved individual. True, Cataline was not unique; men of his type could go pretty far in Rome in those days. Besides, he enjoyed the support of Crassus, and also of Caesar, who, as aedile at the time, was gaining great renown on account of his extravagant games. All the same, we cannot be entirely satisfied with what Cicero later said in his speech in defence of Caelius, when he was concerned to put his client's allegiance to Cataline in as good a light as possible: 'To begin with, Cataline would almost have fooled me, even me: I thought he was a good citizen, well-disposed to all honest men, and a loyal and trusty friend.'[10] However that may be, Cicero did not defend Cataline – who in fact was acquitted in his trial for extortion – either because Cataline declined the offer or because he himself changed his mind.

Quintus's *Commentariolum* names four rival candidates in all: a certain Publius Sulpicius Galba, otherwise little known; Lucius Cassius Longinus, who later joined forces with Cataline; Gaius Antonius, who became Cicero's colleague; and Cataline.[11] Quintus thinks the first two are of no importance whatever, and says that only the other two could pose a threat to his brother. Apparently his judgement was correct. Antonius and Cataline formed an electoral alliance and campaigned together. Since, in the case of Cataline, an evil character, and, in the case of Antonius, a feeble, vacillating character, were candidates for the highest office, authoritative circles in the Senate decided to overlook Cicero's lack of a pedigree and to promote his candidature. As the elections approached, with Cataline and Antonius resorting to extremely dubious and unscrupulous ways of chasing votes, the Senate resolved to pass a more stringent law against improper electoral influence. However, to the indignation of the Senate, one of the tribunes objected. Cicero, for his part, launched a massive attack against his two rivals, the *Oratio in Toga Candida*, or *The Address in a Candidate's Toga*.

Unfortunately, the speech has not come down to us. All the same, what was said of the speeches in which Cicero defended the former tribune Cornelius, applies here also. The commentary by Asconius, which has survived in this case, too, makes it possible for us to reconstruct the essential features of the speech. The two rival candidates, in the speaker's view the worst sort of Sullan partisans, have their previous careers exposed in a wealth of detail. And, in Cataline's case, Cicero outdoes his brother's *Commentariolum* when he describes the murder of Marius Gratidianus: he asserts that Cataline had carried the latter's head, still instinct with the breath of life, to Sulla – from the Janiculum on the far bank of the Tiber, as far as the Temple of Apollo, west of the Capitol. Of himself, Cicero declares, sure of victory, that the Roman people will appoint him to defend their interests. Cataline, on the other hand, could rely on nobody's support, neither the men who really counted, nor the Senate, nor the knights, nor the people. In response to such pyrotechnics, which in many ways anticipate the surviving diatribes against Lucius Calpurnius Pison and Antonius, the victims could do no more than reiterate that Cicero was an upstart.

Cicero was elected unanimously. Antonius fared rather better than Cataline and thus became Cicero's colleague. Cicero liked to look back on that day in July 64 BC as one of the finest in his life. He emphasized that he, a newcomer, had been elected at his first attempt and at the earliest point in time the law allowed. Moreover, that he was elected unanimously by the whole body of citizens.[12]

Just before his period in office began he made another extremely astute move. A law introduced by Gaius Gracchus in 123 BC required the Senate to stipulate in advance of the elections which provinces should be allocated to the consuls for the succeeding year (the remaining provinces were then left to the praetors). In this way an important issue of competence was to be divorced from the consideration of particular persons. Sulla's constitution also allowed the consuls two· years in office, the first in Rome, the second in one of the provinces. From that time on the Senate had to deal with the question of which were to be the consular provinces in each case. And this was what happened in 64 BC preceding the consular elections for 63 BC: the Senate had declared Cisalpine Gaul (Upper Italy, which did not cease to be a province until 41 BC) and Macedonia to be the consular provinces for 62 BC, and, when lots were drawn, Cicero was assigned Macedonia for his second year of office. He offered to exchange with his colleague, who was heavily in debt. The latter eagerly assented, although, in return, he had to undertake to withdraw his support from Cataline. This did not mean that Cicero could rely on him, but it made open opposition impossible. The rest was taken care of by Publius Sestius, Antonius's quaestor, who was on Cicero's side and kept him reliably informed.

8

The Consulship

In a diatribe aimed at Lucius Calpurnius Piso (55 BC) Cicero sums up his consulship as follows:

> On 1 January I relieved the Senate and all right-thinking men of their apprehension concerning a Settlement Act and massive gratuities.... In the trial of Gaius Rabirius, who was charged with high treason, I successfully defended a resolution passed by the Senate forty years before my consulship, relating to malicious attacks. I declared ineligible for election certain respectable and capable young men who had nevertheless been so buffeted by fortune that they would have set aside our constitution, had they achieved office.... By dint of patience and resilience I contrived to keep in check my colleague Antonius, who was dying to get hold of a province and who took part in numerous political intrigues.... I declined the province of Gaul at a public meeting in spite of protests by the Roman people, because political circumstances suggested it was expedient to decline. I ordered Lucius Cataline to leave the city, because he was planning to exterminate the Senate and ruin the city, not secretly, but in the sight of all.... At the last moment of my consulship I snatched from the vile hands of the conspirators the weapons which were poised at our citizens' throats.[1]

Here Cicero lists all the important issues of his consulship, all matters which he considered detrimental to the state because they were directed against the Sullan constitution and the rule of the Senate: the Agricultural, or, rather, Settlement Law proposed by the people's tribune, Servilius Rullus; the treason trial of Gaius Rabirius; the proposal by another tribune that the sons of those proscribed by Sulla should again be permitted to run for office; the unreliability of his colleague Antonius; his renunciation of the province he had obtained through the exchange with Antonius; the Catalinarian conspiracy. He leaves out whatever he regards as ephemeral, the daily routine of politics – for instance his support for Lucius Roscius Otho, who some years previously had won for the knights the privilege of separate seating in the theatre, or the trial of Lucius Licinius Morena, who had been accused of exerting improper influence in the elections.

Cicero's choice is appropriate. The issues he refers to do in fact belong together in that they all implied a threat to the existing regime. Cicero does not state, however, who the instigators of nearly all these subversive activities really were: Crassus and, to an even greater extent, Caesar. His consulship coincided with a critical phase in the political rise of Caesar and consisted essentially in warding off attacks launched by Caesar against the rule of the Optimates. The final and most spectacular assault was an exception: the putsch attempted by Cataline on his own initiative and not merely as the tool of Crassus and Caesar.

Gaius Iulius Caesar, six years younger than Cicero and Pompey, was descended from the patrician class, the original aristocracy of Rome, a breed which traced its ancestry back to Aeneas and Venus. His father had never advanced beyond the office of praetor, while his grandfather was totally undistinguished. A distant relative, Lucius Iulius Caesar had been consul in 64 BC. Caesar's youth was shaped by the civil war between Marius and Sulla: his aunt, Iulia, was married to Marius, and he himself, at the age of sixteen, had married a daughter of Cinna, who held dictatorial powers at that time. Thus, family ties predisposed him to side with the opponents of senatorial rule. He remained loyal to this party in spite of the harrassment he was subjected to under Sulla, and in spite of the apparent futility of the struggle in the early stages.

He began without any significant resources of his own and for many years must have seen that he was no nearer his ultimate and publicly declared aim of overthrowing the Senate's rule. He consequently did everything he could to advance under the protection of more influential contemporaries. Thus, like Cicero, he sought the patronage of Pompey, especially regarding the granting of special powers in the wars against the pirates and against Mithridates. Otherwise, he often joined forces with Marcus Licinius Crassus, who was fifteen years his senior; they jointly supported the electoral campaign of Antonius and Cataline. It was their intention to use Cataline as a tool, a fact which was not unknown to Cicero, as an allusion in his speech *In Toga Candida* indicates.[2]

It was in Cicero's consular year that the attacks launched by Caesar against senatorial rule, generally in collusion with Crassus, became more violent and more frequent. The fact that they all failed was due in no small measure to Cicero – although his success did little to change the course of history, since Caesar, rising inexorably from one office to the next and gaining the supreme ecclesiastical appointment of Pontifex Maximus in 63 BC, never flagged and was never discouraged. Caesar's tactics always remained the same, which explains why Cicero never mentions him by name in the survey he embodies in his attack on Piso: Caesar stayed in the background and let others act on his behalf. This procedure was designed to safeguard his reputation in case of failure. Without taking undue risks he could judge how far it was safe to go; on the other hand, he was in a position to disown individuals like Cataline who dared to go too far. With Caesar Roman politics became devious and enigmatic; henceforth there was a public aspect and an aspect that was concealed from contemporary observers. The public scene featured a variety of projects with a variety of personalities, but in the background there was one single will, Caesar's will, intent on the overthrow of the senatorial hegemony.

During his consulship Cicero achieved great rhetorical triumphs, and the amount of material that survives is exceeded only by the *Philippics* against Mark Antony from the closing years of his life. The consular speeches are concerned, apart from a few obscure allusions, with the public aspect of a whole series of turbulent events. They are part and parcel of that aspect and must therefore be read as documents giving a summary view of those events. This applies at any rate to the speeches opposing the Settlement Act and the speech in defence of Rabirius. Cataline and his followers on the other hand, fought their own battles without being shielded by more eminent figures, and in this case Caesar quite openly did what he felt able to do.

Cicero conceived and published his *Orationes Consulares*, as he himself calls them, in 60 BC,[3] when it was a matter of defending consular policy, especially the summary execution of the Catalinarian conspirators, against increasingly vehement attacks by the Populares. This circumstance impairs the documentary validity of the consular speeches. They do not necessarily show us what Cicero the consul was thinking and saying in public – certain things may have been adjusted to match the less promising prospects of 60 BC.

In the letter to Atticus reporting on the final draft of his consular speeches Cicero enumerates the various items belonging to this body (he uses the expression σῶμα):

Two deal with the Settlement Act, one addressed to the Senate on 1 January, the other to the people; the third concerns Roscius Otho; the fourth is on behalf of Rabirius; the fifth deals with the sons of proscribed persons; the sixth was delivered when I renounced my province before an assembly of the people; the seventh is that by which I expelled Cataline; the eighth I delivered before the people the day after Cataline's flight; the ninth is also addressed to the people ...; the tenth I addressed to the Senate on 5 December. Then there are also two brief speeches, append-ages to the Settlement Act.[4]

The selection is the same as in the speech attacking Piso, except that Cicero here includes his success in the Roscius Otho incident.

Of these twelve speeches, four have not been preserved: one of the brief speeches on the Settlement Act; the address on behalf of Roscius Otho; the statement directed against the sons of proscribed families; and the renunciation of the governorship of Cisalpine Gaul. On the other hand, a speech which does not belong to this group of consular addresses has survived intact over the ages: the speech in defence of Morena, one of Cicero's most brilliant performances. The reason for what appears at first sight to be a rather odd omission is not hard to find. The charge of improper electoral influence which the lawyer Sul-picius Rufus, the unsuccessful candidate for the consulate in 62 BC, brought against his successful rival Murena, was a piece of in-fighting between Optimates. This was a somewhat embarrassing episode from which the conclusion might be drawn that the united front presented by all right-thinking men, as invoked by Cicero, was not holding together too well.

A few days after 10 December 64, the date when the board of tribunes assumed office, the tribune Publius Servilius Rullus proposed a *lex agraria*, a settlement law. The era of civil wars had begun with the settlement legislation of the Gracchi: agrarian reform, the provision of homesteads for the city's proletariate, had henceforth been numbered among the basic issues of popular politics. Rullus had been preceded by Marcus Livius Drusus, who had last attempted to introduce a lex agraria in 91 BC.

The proposal made by Rullus was uncommonly bold. He promised an abundance of land for settlement that would be purchased from existing owners. He envisaged a ten-man commission with well-nigh dictatorial powers which had five years to implement the law. The idea was to facilitate the purchase of votes by permitting only half – seven-teen out of thirty-five – of the constituencies (*tribus*) to participate in the vote. The draft proposal had defects: Cicero was able to exploit the dubious financial implications of the scheme and, in particular, to claim that its social purpose was no more than a pretext. In fact, the proposal was meant to make the *decemviri* undisputed rulers of the state. In the Senate he had no difficulty in obtaining a majority against the proposal. It was only in his second speech, which was meant to discredit the draft proposal in the eyes of its beneficiaries and of the nation as a whole, that he descended into the arena and used all the resources of his persuasive power to represent the law as both irresponsible and pernicious. He did not hesitate to imply that certain individuals behind the scenes were pulling the strings, and even claimed that he, the consul, and not his adversaries, was the true friend of the people, the true Popularis. He succeeded in stirring up so much feeling against the bill that Rullus did not even call for a vote on it. Cicero's triumph delayed a decision for no less than four years, and it was not until Caesar's consulship that the essential aims of Rullus's proposal were implemented.

There then followed two intervals of popular commotion in which Cicero's eloquence celebrated further triumphs. Plutarch tells us that Roscius Otho was hissed by the populace in the theatre because some years earlier he had promoted a law assigning separate seating to the knights.[5] Cicero achieved the feat of making this aristocratic privilege acceptable to the common people, so that they subsequently greeted Otho with applause. Of another episode, the successful defence of Gaius Calpurnius Piso, consul for 67 BC, who was charged with extortion, it is reported that Caesar was for once openly involved: he gave evidence for the prosecution.[6]

It was not long before the next scandal blew up, and it had certain bizarre features. In this case Caesar's accomplice was the tribune Titus Labienus, subsequently a renowned military commander in the Gallic War. During the unrest of 100 BC the Senate had declared a state of emergency and the people's tribune Lucius Appuleis Saturninus had subsequently been murdered by a gang of young Optimates. This deed led, thirty-seven years later, to the trial of the senator Gaius Rabirius. The charge was not murder but – since the victim was an inviolable tribune – high treason. The case was meant to stress, as regards Rabirius, that the Senate was not empowered to declare a state of emergency and hence to give the consuls authority to impose the death penalty on Roman citizens without a regular court having tried the case and pronounced sentence.

Caesar was not content merely to hark back to an event that had happened more than a lifetime earlier; he went on to resurrect from ancient chronicles a long since defunct and gruesome procedure that was designed to heighten the deterrent effect. A commission specially convened to try Rabirius, the *duoviri* for high treason, was supposed to find the accused guilty. If the popular assembly confirmed the verdict, then a savage mode of execution, otherwise inflicted only on slaves, awaited him: scourging followed by crucifixion. The praetor Quintus Caecilius Celer frustrated the implementation of this hoary ritual with the aid of a custom that was nearly as antiquated. He lowered the flag which used to fly whenever the people had gathered on the Campus Martius, their customary place of assembly in the bend of the River Tiber. The voting procedure then had to be abandoned and Rabirius was not convicted.

Labienus then seems to have given up the idea of the more rigorous legal process: Cicero's speech for the defence, dignified but emotional in tone, was obviously part of the normal process of law. Hortensius first of all repudiated the charge, then Cicero dealt with the political implications of the case. Rabirius was acquitted – and Caesar suffered a second woeful setback. The third soon followed. Sulla had barred from public office the sons of those followers of Marius whom he had proscribed. But a people's tribune, no doubt backed by Caesar, proposed that this restriction be lifted. Cicero made a speech which was presumably highly effective. As in the case of the legislation put forward by Rullus, he probably argued that the seemingly popular nature of the proposal was not in fact in the public interest.

Little is known about the sixth item in the collection of consular speeches. By an exchange of provinces Cicero had put his unreliable partner Antonius under an obligation. Now he gave up his claim altogether; he declared that, following his term as consul, he would not go to Cisalpine Gaul as governor – acting, he claimed, in the interest of the state. He was no doubt already firmly convinced that Cataline, who had stood for consul unsuccessfully for the second time in the summer of 63 BC, would risk open rebellion.

The last quarter of Cicero's consular year was occupied by his most spectacular feat: the discovery and suppression of Cataline's *coup d'état*. The sources that report this incident are uncommonly copious. (Apart from Cicero's four speeches and Sallust's account, there are relevant passages in the biographer Plutarch, as well as in the historians Appian and Cassius Dio.) There is thus scarcely an event in the decline of the Roman Republic that is as well documented as this episode. What is more, Cicero considerably exaggerated the significance of the event and the part he himself played in it. Both these factors, the

fortuitous survival of records and Cicero's egocentric view, have secured for Cataline's putsch a notoriety in succeeding ages which it does
not really deserve.

By the summer Cicero had successfully warded off a far more dangerous opponent of senatorial rule, namely Caesar. What he accomplished
in the last three months of the year amounted to little more than a
police operation conducted with uncommon skill and a modicum of
luck. Cataline and his kindred were pursuing the policy of desperadoes.
Led astray by the Sullan disorders, they were aiming at rebellion for its
own sake, hoping to improve their own material situation at the expense of their fellow-citizens. They overestimated their own strength,
while their adversary, Cicero, overestimated the threat they posed. This
was all the more the case as Cataline, following his second electoral
defeat in the summer of 63 BC, had ceased to count as a serious politician in the eyes of his erstwhile patrons, Crassus and Caesar. The battle
against Cataline's faction was fought on a different level from the battle
against a Rullus or a Labienus. In the latter cases it was a matter of
countering opposition to the Senate which, however unscrupulous it
might be, still acknowledged certain rules and, above all, was careful
not to expose itself needlessly. In the former case it was simply a question
of eliminating a gang of gamblers who had stooped to the level of
common criminality.

It is not necessary to retrace the outward course of events here. What
matters is that on the night of 20–1 October Crassus and two other
noble gentlemen presented themselves at Cicero's home and handed him
anonymous letters warning him of Cataline's murderous plans. In this
way Crassus dissociated himself from the rebels in the most emphatic
fashion, and Cicero might assume that Caesar's attitude was no different. The Senate thereupon pronounced the 'senatus consultum ultimum', that is, it declared a state of emergency and thus initiated the
train of events that led to the summary execution of those followers of
Cataline who had been unmasked in Rome – and ultimately to Cicero's
exile, since the Populares turned the affair into a major political issue.
On 7 November, after Cataline had tried unsuccessfully to dispose of
him by assassination, Cicero addressed the Senate in the famous speech
by which he drove Cataline from Rome. On the following day, in his
second Catalinarian speech, he addressed the people, speaking mainly
of Cataline's supporters.

It was on 3 December that Cicero contrived to expose the leaders
of the conspiracy in Rome. He was highly praised in the Senate, and
Quintus Lutatius Catulus, a much respected Optimate, conferred on

him the title of 'Father of the Fatherland' (*parens patriae*). The arrested ringleaders were held in custody by various senators, among whom were Crassus and Caesar – a shrewd move on the part of Cicero, who meant to suggest in this way that he did not suspect the two politicians of being involved in the insurrection. The third Catalinarian speech reported the success of these measures to the people.

A debate in the Senate on the punishment of the arrested Catalinarians took place on 5 December. It has become famous because of Sallust and on account of Cicero's fourth Catalinarian speech. Caesar advocated relatively mild treatment: lifelong preventive detention. Cicero responded with studied courtesy that this was exactly the policy of the Populares. That uncompromising partisan of the Optimates, Cato, argued vehemently for the death penalty and ultimately had his way. When Caesar then dared to suggest that, at least the Catalinarians' property should not be confiscated, he aroused such fury that Cicero had to guard him as they left the meeting in the Temple of Concordia. Cicero had once more got the better of Caesar and the latter stayed away from the Senate for the rest of the year.

It was in the second half of November, amid all the excitement aroused by the trial of the Catalinarians, that Cicero produced his masterly defence of Murena. As mentioned above, this concerned a dispute between Optimates: Murena, consul designate for 62 BC, had, according to his defeated rival, Sulpicius Rufus, employed illicit means to gain his high office. Also involved in the prosecution was the aforementioned Marcus Porcius Cato, the great-grandson of Cato Censorius, later dubbed Uticensis after the place of his suicide. Marcus Porcius enjoyed a high reputation as a moralist and was no doubt co-opted on account of his strict Stoic principles (he was thirty-two years old at the time and had occupied the office of quaestor the previous year). On the defence side Cicero was preceded by Hortensius and also by Crassus, who thus demonstrated his affinity with the senatorial aristocracy. Cicero managed to defend his client without seriously offending his adversaries, whom he regarded as his friends. In two celebrated passages he gave free rein to his wit, so that even Cato is said to have exclaimed, 'What a witty consul we have!'[7] In one of these passages he presents a caricature of the typical lawyer in order to deride Sulpicius Rufus's profession: dedicated to a pettifogging terminology, he spends his time agonizing over issues that any ordinary person could grasp without the slightest difficulty.[8] The other passage surveys the strait-laced moral code of the Stoics, not without a hint of irony. In both cases Cicero exploits the entire range of his educational background to good effect, and his plea was doubtless an intellectual delight such as had rarely been experienced hitherto in a Roman court. The judges were probably mainly impressed by the argument that a verdict of guilty would disqualify Murena, and anyone who wanted only one consul to take office on 1 January was playing into the hands of Cataline and all other enemies of the constitution. The judges were not deaf to this patriotic appeal and they acquitted Murena.

Cicero's consular year did not end without menacing intimations of storms to come – the initial signs of those attacks on Cicero's policy against Cataline that were to lead, first to his isolation and then to his exile. Pompey was still detained in the East, and Cicero tried to enlist his support by writing him a long letter about what he had achieved during his consulship. The attempt was a lamentable failure. In one of the earliest letters from *Ad Familiares* (April 62 BC) Cicero tells Pompey how disappointed he was with the latter's frosty response.[9] Evidently Pompey was put off by Cicero's boasting, for he makes no reference in his reply to the consul's achievements.

Even more wounding were the attacks of Quintus Caecilius Metellus Nepos, a man who inclined towards the Optimates, but who was probably trying to make his mark as an adherent of Pompey. His brother, Quintus Caecilius Metellus Celer, praetor in 63 BC, had backed Cicero in the military suppression of the Catalinarian insurgents. The conflict between Cicero and Nepos led to a bitter quarrel between Cicero and Celer, as is all too evident from a couple of letters written at the beginning of 62 BC.[10] Nepos had assumed the office of tribune on 10 December and at once attacked Cicero, who, he claimed, had unscrupulously seized power and set himself up as leader of the Senate: the help of Pompey should be enlisted in order to thwart him. To a popular assembly he stated that someone who condemned others without allowing them to defend themselves in a regular trial should not be entitled to speak in public. Thus, Nepos adopted the view of the Populares, as did Caesar, namely that Cicero had had the convicted Catalinarians executed without due legal process. Accordingly, he prohibited Cicero from speaking about his actions again on the last day of his term in office. He was only permitted to swear the customary oath that he had observed the law conscientiously. Thereupon Cicero swore an entirely different oath, to the effect that he had saved Rome – and the assembly then concurred that he had sworn truly.

9

The Turning-point

It is rare for the life of a famous personality to be divided into two such clearly defined phases as is the case with the rhetorician, politician and philosopher Cicero. The first phase covers the period down to his consulate (63 BC), the second covers the time from his consulate down to his cruel death in 43 BC. The first phase has been appreciatively recorded by virtually every moderately benign biographer. It was during this period that Cicero acquired the comprehensive knowledge and the competence that made him the prime intellectual force in late Republican Rome, and it was with the aid of these accomplishments that he made his way from next to nothing to the highest office of state. The second phase, however, has always worried or annoyed his biographers and moved them to express regret or irritation. These two decades are marked by a series of blunders and failures on the part of the politician Cicero, who tried in vain to steer his own conservative course amidst the revolutionary forces that were increasingly governing the tide of events. They are also characterized, however, by the literary substitutes for action that made Cicero the most important philosophical writer in Rome.

The consulate is, as it were, the axis linking the two phases. It was with his appointment as consul that Cicero achieved, on the one hand, the primary aim of his ambition, the crowning success of his official career. On the other hand, it was on the consulate that the political illusions and the political failure of the two succeeding decades were based. The pivotal function of the consulship was in part desired by Cicero himself and was to that extent something subjective. The ambitious newcomer had worked his way up from one office to another by dint of shrewd manoeuvering without ever committing himself to a clearly defined political programme. The consul, on the other hand, whose term of office teemed with popular and revolutionary aspirations, firmly backed the interests of the senatorial aristocracy with an ideology which he tried in vain, as a consular, i.e. a former consul, to promote in the forties and fifties.

This pivotal function of the consulship was, however, dictated to a much greater extent by external factors. Cicero's rise was achieved entirely within the context of the traditional constitution: forces backed by arbitrary military power outside the constitution were indeed present (in the person of Pompey), yet they did not intervene in the daily routine of politics. But from the time of his consulate onwards Cicero continually came up against forces outside the constitution. First it was Caesar alone, then it was the quasi-revolutionary triumvirate of Caesar, Pompey and Crassus, and finally it was once again Caesar – by this time a dictator.

From the outset Cicero, as a trial lawyer, especially in political trials, expressed his view on the political background to criminal offences and on the current political situation in general. The first unambiguous statement of this kind crops up in his speech on behalf of Sextus Roscius. There he states that the aristocratic regime reinstated by Sulla could only survive if it dissociated itself from the criminal machinations of the war profiteers.[1] The basis and thrust of his argument are plain enough: Cicero takes for granted the traditional order as restored by Sulla, but in pursuit of his forensic goal he exposes the system's excesses and tries to single out those responsible. Cicero proceeds on similar lines in his speeches attacking Verres: the traditional order had to be protected against pernicious individuals like Verres.[2] The courts, however, which at that time were presided over exclusively by senators, he accuses of having brought themselves into disrepute by their scandalous administration of justice. They must try to remove this stigma by punishing Verres severely in order to prove that law enforcement was in the right hands. He himself, as aedile, would take ruthless measures against any attempt at corruption. Towards the end of his speech in support of Pompey, Cicero also refers to the shortcomings of the aristocratic regime: only a Pompey was proof against the brutal mentality of the profiteers under whom the provinces suffered.[3]

This, then, is the general tenor of the political statements which Cicero propounded during his rise to prominence. The aristocratic system needs to be reformed and purged; it must be preserved from the damage which an unscrupulous minority – in Cicero *pauci* ('the few') – are liable to inflict on it.[4] Cicero's attacks are thus aimed at radical representatives of the senatorial party, and he adopts, more tacitly than openly, the standpoint of the moderate Optimates. In keeping with this view he vigorously repudiates, in his speech in defence of Cluentius Habitus, the rabble-rousing campaigns of the popular faction.[5] It is not altogether paradoxical that his speech in support of Pompey advocated a 'popular' measure, although he was accused of duplicity on that account. A large section of the senatorial aristocracy had also bowed to the needs of the moment and voted for the proposed legislation. In any case, a minor deviation of this kind was dictated by tactical considerations. For the sake of his career Cicero had to seek the support of Pompey and of popular circles generally.

Cicero's attitude at the time is clearly revealed in his brother's *Commentariolum*: the knights and the majority of the senators did not stand in his way when he applied for the consulship, while he had gained the sympathy of the people through his support for Pompey and his defence of Cornelius. Only the nobiles, the gentry of the superior aristocracy, posed a threat, since Cicero had aroused their suspicions. It was to them that he would have to explain that he had always sided politically with the Optimates and had never been in any sense an adherent of the Populares ('nos semper cum optimatibus de re publica sensisse, minime popularis fuisse'). He had merely sought the support of Pompey with the aid of certain phrases that had a populist ring about them.

From all this it emerges that the speeches Cicero delivered during his rise to high office do in fact reveal a certain political attitude – a moderate Optimate position which repudiates the corruption in administration and judiciary allegedly caused by a minority. But these speeches still tell us nothing about overall political conceptions or a political programme defined with anything like adequate clarity. This does not mean that, prior to 63 BC, Cicero had no ideas that went beyond current issues. He simply relegated such ideas to the background with the aim of first achieving as influential a position as possible, in keeping with the principle to which he subscribed in the introduction to *De Republica*: a man who wished to help the state must first achieve power.[7]

Cicero's situation changed with the consulship, and so did his conduct. Whereas hitherto he had acted mainly against the excesses of the oligarchic system, now he is concerned above all to repel attacks by the Populares and to frustrate an attempted putsch by extremists. From 1 January Cicero proceeded to define his political goals, as well as the power base from which he proposed to achieve those goals, abandoning his previous reticence and openly stating his political programme. The following statement occurs already in Cicero's first speech opposing Rullus's Settlement Act.[8] Rullus was mistaken if he thought that he and his colleagues could set themselves up as popular politicians in opposition to him, Cicero, the truly popular consul. There was nothing the people cared for more than *pax, concordia, otium*, peace, harmony and tranquillity; Rullus's proposal had achieved precisely the opposite effect. The senators, to whom these remarks were addressed, could hardly miss the point: pax, concordia and otium were watchwords of the policy of the Optimates which aimed to maintain the status quo. Cicero was hence adopting this policy, but using, the bold expedient of declaring it to be truly 'popular', truly in the interests of the people.

Cicero used a similar approach with slight changes of emphasis when he addressed the people in his second speech opposing the Settlement Act.[9] His supreme aim, he claims, was to pursue a popular policy, but this term had to be understood in the correct sense. There were those who undermined the people's welfare on the pretext of 'popularity'. Thus, the proposal by Rullus had brought about a situation which filled the *boni*, all reasonable folk, with dread, whereas it aroused hopes in the *improbi*, the unscrupulous. He, Cicero, would commit himself to the true aims of a popular policy – *pax, libertas, otium*. The substitution of the new category 'freedom' was obviously derived from the Populares' own propaganda. At the end of his speech Cicero reverts to this programme and appeals to the citizens to join him.[10] They were the people whose political influence depended on the elections, whose rights depended on the courts and on the propriety of the officials, and whose prosperity depended on the preservation of peace.

It is in his speeches on the Settlement Act that Cicero for the first time views the state and its citizens as a single entity. He proclaims goals that are binding on all, an amalgam of phrases from the popular faction *and* the Optimates. He suggests, too, which groups are, on the one hand, committed to maintaining the state and which, on the other, are potentially subversive. The 'boni', the Optimates and their supporters, as Cicero believes, the entire nation, are opposed by improbi, that is, radical, subversive forces. With these propositions Cicero gained a good deal. He claimed the party title Popularis, which sounded well, being derived from *populus*, and appropriated it for himself and the cause of the Optimates. He then came up with a reformulation of the traditional political vocabulary. Cicero tried to isolate those who inclined towards the Populares by representing them as a small group of improbi. If he had been able to influence the actual facts of the situation by this move, then he would no doubt have been vouchsafed real and lasting success. Unfortunately, the facts could not be altered by a simple change of vocabulary.

The speeches opposing the Settlement Act tell us more about political aims than about the groups to which Cicero looked for support. A passage in the fourth speech against Cataline, however, deals with this question as clearly as anyone could wish.[11] Cicero announced to the Senate, which was to give its view on the treatment of the arrested Catalinarians, that a suggestion had come to his ears that the resources of the state might not be adequate to enforce a verdict condemning the Catalinarians. He retorted that his prudent care and the keen vigilance of the Roman people had seen to all the necessary precautions. 'Omnes adsunt omnium ordinum homines, omnium generum, omnium denique aetatum.' – 'Everyone is at his post, men of every class, of every condition and of every age.' There had never been such perfect unanimity since the city was founded; only a handful of improbi or, rather, enemies would sooner die along with everyone else than perish on their own.

Cicero then proceeds to enumerate the various groups in this common front, beginning, since he takes the disposition of the Senate for granted, with the knights, who had been reconciled with the Senate after a long period of dissension. He goes on to name the tribuni aerarii and the scribes, one of the more elevated lower orders, and then continues his list with the *ingenui*, the common people (freedom and fatherland were the slogans to which they rallied), and finally even includes freedmen and slaves in his catalogue of forces sustaining the state. Cicero repeatedly assures his hearers that all these *ordines* were prepared to come to the rescue of the state. With the aid of all good men and true, 'omnium bonorum auxilio', he would easily prevail in the war he was waging against dastardly individuals, *perditi cives*, and no power on earth could ever shake the alliance between the Senate and the knights, or the collaboration of all right-thinking men.

This was Cicero's programme of consensus, the 'consensus omnium bonorum', as he often said:[12] the common cause of all those who were ready, together with the Senate and the knights, to defend the traditional order, by which Cicero meant, on the one hand, the preservation of class distinctions and private property, and, on the other, Republican liberty. *Ordo* and – albeit less strongly emphasized – libertas were the slogans by which Cicero hoped to win over the overwhelming majority of Roman citizens. The attempt to conceal the true distribution of power by embracing a large section of the population scarcely altered the course of events. Cicero's 'consensus omnium bonorum' turned out to be just as much an illusion as his audacious usurpation of the party label 'popular'. The subjective aspect of the turning-point which took place during the consular year consists in the fact that Cicero henceforth put forward a conservative programme. It was a programme which gained him no more than a few fleeting initial successes (if in fact these successes were due to the programme), and which soon turned out to be totally ineffective (and this was among the objective factors associated with the turning-point).

It was no mere accident that the objective aspect of the major turning-point in Cicero's life, which was brought about by external factors, coincided with the consulship. It was probably also occasioned, at least in part, by the consulship itself, that is, by the outstanding triumph of the consulship – the exposure and suppression of Cataline's insurrection. A curious concatenation of events seems to have brought this about. The reform of the army by Marius – with dispossessed citizens serving as mercenaries – had imparted a military character to the basic scheme of Roman society, the system of personal allegiance. The unrest of the 80s showed for the first time that the generals of the day and their troops could take over the established state. This disintegration of society – the military confronting the civilian population, the revolutionary leaders opposing the senatorial aristocracy – did not bring about any immediate restructuring of the legitimate political order. On the contrary, in spite of various upheavals, both systems continued to exist side by side for a considerable period. The military held the real power, and the Republican constitution represented the authority which served, apart from dealing with routine political matters, to invest the military leaders and their actions with a semblance of legality.

During this process, in fact, the constitution progressively disintegrated. This did not happen consistently and at a uniform pace, but by fits and starts or, rather, by leaps and bounds. The most drastic leap hitherto had occurred during the early stages of Cicero's career, but the atrocities of those years were so appalling that they retarded the process of radical change. All those involved were reluctant to take up arms for fear of a repetition, so that for an entire lifetime almost unbroken peace prevailed – although it was an illusory peace. At that time, in the 70s and 80s, the Republican constitution, with its public meetings, the Senate and the officers of state, continued to operate as though nothing had happened. The military, especially under Pompey's leadership, and the senatorial rulers did their best to get along with one another, and Pompey got his way by political means. It was during this period that Cicero achieved his spectacular rise to the consulship, a perfectly legal rise, an ascent, as we noted, within the context of the Republican constitution.

Cicero achieved this, the first of his ambitious goals, in a conventional manner. He did not manage, however, to attain his second goal, which was to govern the destiny of the Roman state after his consulship, as princeps senatus, the leading politician of the day. Far from it: there ensued almost instantly nearly two decades of disappointment and humiliation, an agonizing impotence which he himself only partly acknowledged. This setback, reminiscent of a drama, was clearly occasioned by the fact that Cicero was now facing a quite different set of opposing forces.

Until the time of his consulship he had been able to rely on the smooth functioning of the Republican order. Following his consulship he was confronted by forces outside that order – the revolutionary leaders backed by their troops and their henchmen in Rome, i.e. an alliance that used obstruction and violence to steer the popular assembly and the Senate in the direction desired by those in power. Cicero, no soldier and a legitimist with a profound belief in the immutable validity of traditional standards, was no match for these forces.

During and after his consulship Cicero's sphere of influence collided with that of his most powerful contemporary, Pompey, and it was this collision that sealed his political fate. By tactics that were shrewd as well as bold, and essentially by political means, he had frustrated Cataline's attempt to demolish the rotten structure of the Republic. But it was precisely his success which, by a tragic combination of circumstances, hastened the downfall of the Republic and dragged him into a maelstrom of revolutionary feuds. While Cicero was totally absorbed in crowning his career through the brilliant discharge of his consular duties, Pompey was busy earning supreme military honours in the East, in Asia Minor and in Syria – by dint of the plenary powers so urgently recommended by Cicero. In 62 BC Pompey returned to Italy, seeking the customary form of pension for his troops – land and farmsteads. By his successful resistance to Cataline, however, Cicero had inspired the Senate with so much confidence (too much, as it soon transpired), that it began to make difficulties for Pompey, to offer stubborn resistance to his demands.

Now the collision between the two hitherto separate spheres of influence, the civil and the military, was an established fact. Pompey himself could see no way out, but he was offered a helping hand, the hand of Caesar, who promised to back him – if necessary, by force –

during his impending consulate. And so Caesar and Pompey, together with a third partner, Crassus, the wealthiest Roman of his day, formed the coalition which has gone down in history as the First Triumvirate. They entered into a mutual agreement to pursue a common policy and to come to an understanding on all major political issues. This was in 60 BC, the year before Caesar's consulship.

From this point onwards the ambiguity of Roman politics was total. The triumvirate had sufficient power to allow the Republic ostensibly to continue in existence, with their accomplices manipulating the apparatus of the state as they pleased. But Cicero did not understand what had come about in such a short time and with so little commotion. He believed he was still in a position to steer an independent course in keeping with the traditional order. He sought an association with Pompey so as to get him on his side, and thus made himself suspect in the eyes of the senatorial aristocracy. On the other hand, he was not prepared to entertain Caesar's advances and enter into a full alliance with the triumvirate. And so, veering this way and that, and full of illusions about the courses open to him, he worked himself into a position between the parties without being credible to either. He thus contrived his own exile and, after his return, earned himself the evil reputation of a 'turncoat', the derogatory term which the Optimates attached to his erstwhile servility to the triumvirate.

Cicero evidently found that the premises on which his eminence was based – his rhetorical gifts and his faith in the mission of the Roman Republic – imposed insurmountable limits on that eminence. He was a middle-class politician: in order to exercise his influence he needed the solid framework of the traditional constitution and the institutions it guaranteed. He was no 'man of action', in that his most hallowed beliefs deterred him from converting the established order into a position of personal power, conforming to it during his rise, only to overturn it once he had gained the supreme authority. His tragedy consisted in the fact that he hopelessly overestimated the moral potential and the regenerative resources of the senatorial aristocracy. Cicero, at heart a reformer, had the misfortune to be born in an age of revolutionaries, men who were not seeking to preserve the status quo in an improved form, but who were intent on shattering it to make way for something else.

It is true, Cicero was too richly endowed by nature simply to give up in the face of the overwhelming forces which were harrassing and oppressing him. His political failure forced him into a field for which he was suited as none of his contemporaries were – the field of political theory and philosophical writing in general. He thus turned failure into triumph, and we wonder whether we ought not actually to be grateful for the adverse circumstances which forced him to alter course. In normal circumstances he would have been totally engrossed in playing the part of a capable politician, but in the chaos of the foundering Republic he became Rome's most influential philosopher and prose writer.

10

On the Defensive

'Your good wishes heartened me', Cicero wrote to a friend towards the end of 62 BC, and goes on to state:

> You wrote to me some time ago, hoping that the purchase of Crassus's house would turn out to be a good move: this is actually the house I have now bought for three and a half million sesterces, a little while after your good wishes. You must know, I'm so deeply in debt that I wouldn't mind joining in a conspiracy, if anyone would have me. But they want nothing to do with me, partly from sheer hatred and because they detest me as an adversary of conspiracies, partly because they don't trust me and are afraid that I would trap them – they cannot believe that a man who liberated the money-lenders from their state of siege could be short of money.[1]

This passage refers to the purchase of a substantial property and its financial consequences, alluding, in a curious mixture of gravity and facetiousness, to the awkward situation between the camps of the Populares and the Optimates in which Cicero found himself at the time.

Through the purchase of the house Cicero undoubtedly wanted to make it known that, as Rome's leading advocate and now also a consular, he belonged to the cream of society. The property which he acquired was situated in the exclusive residential area on the Palatine where eminent politicians lived and where later the Imperial palaces were erected, on a spur of the hill running north-east, between the Via Nova and the Clivus Victoriae. From that point there was a magnificent view of the forum and the city, while a visitor who wished to pay the owner his morning respects did not have too far to walk. The house had been built by Marcus Livius Drusus, the far-sighted tribune for the year 91 BC, and it was there he had died by the hand of an assassin. The historic mansion had then passed into the possession of Crassus, and thence to Cicero in 62 BC. At the time there were all sorts of rumours in Rome regarding the way in which the finance to buy this expensive property was raised; the affair was linked to the suppression of Cataline's rising.

What happened was that, after the fall of Cataline, a campaign of prosecutions aimed at his surviving followers was started by the Optimates. On the other hand, politicians of the Populares, led by the people's tribune, Quintus Caecilius Metellus Nepos, had protested vigorously against the execution of the Catalinarians. There had been rioting, and the Senate was barely able to restore order. In view of this tense situation, Cicero thought it expedient to follow a middle course. In the legislative battle mentioned above he promoted the condemnation of the most heavily compromised conspirators, so as to make the measures he had taken as consul seem justified. Nevertheless, he tried to prevent people being ruined, from political or personal motives, who had been involved in Cataline's undertaking only marginally or not at all – apparently because he hoped in this way to ease the pressure to which he was exposed from the popular side. This explains why he defended Publius Cornelius Sulla, a relative of the dictator, a pretty shady character, who was alleged to have conspired repeatedly with Cataline. He succeeded, too, in getting his client acquitted.

A rumour current at the time claimed that Cicero had received a loan of two million sesterces before the conclusion of Sulla's trial – a privilege which, even if it was not actually subject to the legal prohibition on the acceptance of gifts, could hardly be reconciled with the lawyers' ethics of the day. When Cicero was taxed with this, he denied outright that he had any intention whatsoever of buying a house: 'It will be true that I received money from Sulla', he is reported to have said, 'if I buy the house.'[2] When the transaction had been completed, Cicero justified himself on the grounds that, as a prudent houseowner, he was obliged to deny his intentions, because otherwise he would have forced the price up. His enemies did not fail to pounce on this weak point. Clodius reproached him with the purchase of the house in the Senate; Sallust's invective claims that Cicero had acquired his house by blackmail[3] – the Catalinarians had to pay up, if they were able, and if not, they were found guilty. It may be assumed that this high-handed behaviour on the part of Cicero, a homo novus, did not escape critical comment, even from those who otherwise thought favourably of him.

For the sake of his mansion, Cicero had embarked on a second somewhat dubious transaction. Antonius, his former colleague, had departed for Macedonia in the spring of 62 BC. In the same year unfavourable reports were received in Rome regarding his governorship, and there were voices demanding his recall. He, for his part, justified his impositions with the argument that he had to collect a share for Cicero, and that the latter had even despatched a freedman to keep an eye on him. It is Cicero himself who states this in a letter to Atticus.[4] The information suggests that he had indeed come to some kind of an arrangement with his shady former colleague. This fits in with repeated references to a go-between known by the code-name Teucris, 'the Trojan woman'.[5] Ultimately 'the Trojan woman has fulfilled her promise' – Cicero's money had evidently arrived. Only a few weeks earlier Cicero had defended Antonius against the critical voices, so that he was not recalled.

Towards the end of 62 BC Pompey arrived with his victorious troops in Brundisium (the modern Brindisi) and the soldiers were disbanded. The great general was able to celebrate a magnificent triumph in September 61, but he could not force through his two demands in the face of stubborn opposition by the Optimates – i.e. the confirmation of all the arrangements he had made in the East, and, above all, provision for his veterans. Pompey and Cicero did in fact come closer together in these years, and the letters to Atticus contain a good many details concerning their relationship.[6] Cicero's friend even repeatedly expressed his concern that Cicero might be drawn into the wake of his more powerful associate and alienated from the Optimates. Cicero, for his part, claimed that his understanding with Pompey would not draw him on to the side of the Populares, but would draw Pompey over to the Optimates. However, the alliance with Pompey did not in the least change the fateful course of events, with obstruction by the Optimates forcing Pompey to ally himself with Caesar. Cicero did nothing definite for his friend and apparently made no serious attempt to do anything. This was a grave political mistake, one of the gravest of which Cicero was guilty.

The main cause of Cicero's failure is perfectly obvious: it lay in his exaggerated self-confidence, in the overestimation of his own personality. The successes of his consular year had led him into the mistaken belief that he was a political force in his own right and that he could steer events in the direction he wanted by manoeuvring adroitly between the Optimates and the Populares. It was certainly in order for Cicero to seek to be on good terms with Pompey, but he should have proceeded from a clearly defined position and with a clear aim in view. If he wished to retain his credibility, his position could only be that of the Optimates. It was from this position that he had to try to convince the Optimates, if not of the justice, then at least of the ineluctable nature of Pompey's demands. Instead, he attempted to tack to and fro between the parties or, to be more precise, he was under the illusion that he could commit both sides to his idea of how things should go.

In this connection his precarious relationship with the Optimates and with leading personalities in the party, like Lucullus or Hortensius, has to be borne in mind. There is no lack of evidence that he strongly resented them – possibly the more so following his successes. Evidently he was still being made to feel that he was not considered their equal. Lucius Manlius Torquatus, Sulla's accuser and member of a patrician family, called him not only a 'tyrant' but also a 'foreigner', because he came from a country town. Abuse of this kind may well have rankled, although Cicero might dismiss it lightly in public ('We can't all be patricians', he said in his defence of Sulla,[7] assuming a superior air.) but the insult may have rankled nevertheless. The wretched state of affairs following his consulship, and especially the resentment of the gentry, the 'fish-pond owners', as he calls them on occasion, had prompted him, he writes to Atticus, to seek more effective powers and the more effective protection of Pompey.[8]

The fish-pond owners, he repeats shortly afterwards, looked askance at him; they were either incompetent or else they did nothing. Since the death of Quintus Lutatius Catulus he had been following the path of the Optimates; but nothing would induce him to abandon the cause of the Senate. As this passage shows, he felt himself isolated and thrown back on his own resources. Cicero's insistent self-awareness erupts with positively shattering force in another letter to Atticus:

> Please realize that at the moment I lack nothing so much as someone with whom I might discuss all my troubles, someone who is fond of me, with whom I could talk without pretending or concealing or suppressing something.

His brother was absent, Cicero goes on, and he had no idea where Atticus was. Then we read:

> I have been so totally forsaken by everyone that my wife and my little daughter and my darling little Cicero are my only relief. My ambitious and resplendent friendships do indeed make a brilliant show in public, but they are of no use to me within my own four walls. So that, when the house is thronged with visitors of a morning, when we make our way to the forum surrounded by a host of friends, I still cannot find anyone in the whole crowd with whom I might crack a cheerful joke or share a heartfelt sigh.[9]

Cicero, who was aware of his own unique character, did not possess the ability of the average aristocrat to adapt and to conform to the *esprit de corps* that governed his caste. He repelled others and was himself repelled, and was unable to ignore the arrogance of the 'fish-pond owners' for the sake of their common cause.

He tried to compensate for his discontent with the present by immersing himself in his past triumphs, writing accounts of his consulship. Autobiographical notes of this kind written by eminent politicians were not entirely a novelty: *hypomnemata* or *commentarii*, as they were called, had been a recognized genre in Greece since the Hellenistic period, and in Rome since the beginning of the first century BC. Sulla, in particular, had commemorated his deeds in elaborate literary form. A novel feature in Cicero's case, however, was that he confined himself to a specific phase in his life and that he attempted to compose a number of versions in various forms and to circulate them. He made a start with the long letter to Pompey which I have already mentioned and which was so ill-received. He then reported to his friend Atticus in March 62 that he had sent him a memorandum in Greek.[10] At the same time he announced a Latin memorandum as well as an epic on his consulate: 'ne quod genus a me ipso laudis meae praetermittatur' – 'so as not to omit any manner of self-praise', as he rather naively adds. Atticus had also committed to paper an account of Cicero's consulship, but Cicero felt that it was not written in a sufficiently polished style.[11] He himself had not been sparing in the use of ornament after the manner of the Greek orator, Isocrates. He had passed his work over to the philosopher Poseidonius so that the latter could turn it into something even more lustrous. Poseidonius extricated himself from the affair astutely by replying that he had been dismayed by the sheer quality of Cicero's draft.

Cicero's Greek memorandum has not survived, but it has been conjectured that Plutarch used it when describing the consulship in his biography of Cicero. It is not known whether Cicero actually wrote the prose work in Latin that he refers to, but traces of the panegyric epic on his consulate are clearly evident. It consisted of three books, and in his essay *On Prophecy* Cicero himself preserved a fairly lengthy passage from the second book, a prophecy by the Muse Urania.[12] Two lines gave rise to much hilarity and derision among Cicero's contemporaries and succeeding generations:

> O fortunatam natam me consule Romam!
> Cedant arma togae, concedat laurea linguae!

Oh fortunate Rome, born anew under my consulate!
May the sword give way to the toga, and the laurel yield to
the word![13]

In the first line Cicero praises his rescue act, the suppression of Cataline, as a second founding of Rome. The second line, as Cicero himself later maintained, was not intended to stress the superiority of himself, the civilian, over the general, Pompey, but was merely meant to suggest in vague terms that peace was preferable to war.[14] In this way Cicero attempted to enhance his influence by means of topical and laudatory literary works – with his own person in the leading role. What he achieved was certainly the exact opposite. The collection of consular speeches he was preparing at the same time was a distinctly more rewarding exercise.

In the summer of 60 BC Caesar was elected consul for the succeeding year. At about the same time he contrived to clinch his alliance with Pompey and Crassus, an alliance which determined the direction and aims of Rome's fortunes for a whole decade – until the outbreak of the civil war. Cicero learned more details of these agreements in December. 'Cornelius was here', he wrote to Atticus, 'I mean Balbus, Caesar's henchman. He assured me that Caesar meant to rely on the advice of Pompey and myself in all matters, and to try and ensure that Crassus would also ally himself with Pompey.'[15] Thus Cicero, a friend of Pompey, was to be recruited for the common cause represented by the trio. Joining the alliance, as he immediately realized, would bring Cicero peace and quiet and secure him against attacks by hot-headed adherents of the Populares. But he recalled the maxim he had stated in the poem he had written about his consulship: he was under an obligation to hold to the course he had followed so far and to commit himself to the cause of the boni, the good men and true.

From April until June 59 Cicero was in the country, staying on his estates in Antium and Formiae, while Atticus was in Rome. The letters they exchanged during this period have been preserved. From these it seems that Caesar and Pompey were trying to get Cicero on to their side by a series of tempting offers – prestigious appointments and the like. Cicero hesitated and was unable to make up his mind. On the one hand he had obligations to Pompey, on the other he had an obligation to himself and to his former actions – and so he remained a disgruntled and despondent onlooker. (He meant to watch the shipwreck of the politicians from the shore, he writes on one occasion.)[16] In his self-imposed isolation he could neither support the cause of the Senate, which was increasingly under threat during Caesar's consulship, nor commit himself to the measures introduced by the triumvirate, for example, Caesar's settlement legislation. His hesitancy and readiness to accept the *tyrannis* of the powerful trio and to retreat into a life of learning and scholarship were also motivated, now as previously, by resentment against 'his' party, the Optimates. 'I would rather have a rough passage with someone else steering than take over the helm for such thankless passengers.'[17] The triumvirate, he remarked on another occasion, could not cripple him as effectively with their troops as the ingratitude of those who called themselves 'the good men': not only had they failed to reward him, they had not even thanked him.[18]

This period of political lethargy was increasingly overshadowed by a chain of events which had begun in December 62. The *bona dea*, the good goddess, was a female deity, of Italic or Greek origin, and a nocturnal ceremony which took place at the beginning of December in the total absence of male participants was dedicated to her. The rites were celebrated in the home of some high official or other, but he was not permitted to be present himself. It formed part of the official state worship, and the participants were women of the aristocracy, together with Vestal Virgins. In 63 BC Cicero had made his house available, and in the following year the feast was celebrated in the house of Caesar, who was praetor at the time. In defiance of the law, Publius Clodius Pulcher, alleged lover of Caesar's wife, took part in the ceremony. In January 61 Cicero wrote to his friend Atticus as follows: 'No doubt you have already heard that Publius Clodius, the son of Appius, was discovered disguised as a woman in Gaius Caesar's house while the sacrifice for the people was being performed there. He was able to make good his escape with the aid of a slave-girl, but it's a dreadful scandal.'[19] Clodius had proved to be an awkward customer already in his youth while serving in the army of his brother-in-law Lucullus and in other respects as well. In 65 BC he brought an unsuccessful prosecution against Cataline; two years later he is said to have distinguished himself as assistant to Cicero.

In the first months of 61 the bona dea scandal spread in ever-widening circles. The *pontifices* had declared the incident to be sacrilegious; the Senate set about appointing a special tribunal, which Clodius strenuously resisted. Cicero was restrained at first, but after he had himself been attacked, he, too, joined in a campaign of vilification. In May a trial was finally held before a court that had been constituted in

Clodius's favour. Clodius denied the sacrilege. At the time in question he had been in Interamna, that is, probably in a town of that name on the River Liris, some 75 miles south-east of Rome. Then Cicero entered the witness-box and declared that Clodius had paid him a visit on the day of the crime. It was reckoned that Clodius would be found guilty; nevertheless, he was acquitted three days later by 31 votes to 25, no doubt thanks to massive bribery. But Cicero had made a deadly enemy of Clodius, who was now intent on revenge.

In the summer of 60 Clodius let it be known that he would stand for the office of people's tribune. There was, however, an obstacle, since this office was not open to him as a patrician. In March 59 the obstacle was set aside by none other than Caesar himself. Antonius was being prosecuted at the time, and Cicero was trying to help his former colleague, however low his opinion of him might be. In his speech for the defence Cicero expatiated on the violent methods Caesar was using to force through his first Settlement Act – although he would have avoided mentioning Caesar by name. Caesar reacted with lightning speed: that very same day Clodius was made a plebeian by adoption and could thus stand for the office of tribune. He was duly elected and assumed office on 10 December 59. The triumvirate now had a willing tool at their disposal, should they wish to thwart any attempt on Cicero's part to work against them.

In spite of his dejection and political passivity, Cicero did not neglect his legal practice. There was a dearth of major cases, but he appeared successfully for Quintus Caecilius Pius Scipio Nasica, who was accused of gaining office by illegal means. His defence of Antonius, on the other hand, failed: his former colleague was forced into exile. For a certain Aulus Minicius Thermus, of whom no further details are known, he even gained a double victory. Apart from the plea on behalf of Sulla, two speeches have survived from this period: one for Archias and the other for Lucius Valerius Flaccus. The poet Archias, Greek by birth and once Cicero's teacher, faced the charge of having improperly acquired Roman citizenship. Cicero's brief plea is not just a rebuttal of the prosecution's case, but also a document of great historical and cultural value, since it affords graphic glimpses of the literary life of the time. Flaccus, as praetor, had been of considerable assistance to Cicero in exposing Cataline's conspiracy. In 54 BC he was charged with having abused his powers as governor in Asia for purposes of extortion. The trial was a run-of-the-mill affair, remote from high politics, and Cicero's defence resembles in many respects his plea on behalf of Fonteius some ten years earlier. In the central section Cicero gives free rein to his wit, so that the judges were moved to laughter and acquitted the defendant, although there is little doubt that he was guilty.

Flaccus's successor was Quintus Cicero. He had been praetor in 62 BC and had then governed the province of Asia from 61 to 58 BC. The fact is worth mentioning, because, when his brother's term of office was extended for a year against his will, Cicero sent him an elaborate letter explaining the principles on which a model provincial administration should be run. This letter, which opens the collection *Ad Quintem Fratrem*, is a kind of counterpart to *Commentariolum Petitionis*, although it is less of a practical manual than an ideal scheme replete with high moral principles. Cicero states here plainly what he owes to the Greeks: it was to them, the cultural harbingers of all mankind, that we owe the civilized ideals to which all mankind, even savage barbarians, may lay claim.

11

Exile and Return

Caesar used his consulship to secure a permanent position of power, not only because otherwise he would have laid himself and his policies open to attacks by his enemies, the Optimates, if he were subsequently out of office and hence liable to prosecution, but also because he had before him the example of Pompey. The wars against the pirates and Mithridates had been waged under plenary powers not subject to the customary annual term of office. Consequently, the people's tribune, Publius Vatinius, a loyal, capable, but none too scrupulous, henchman of Caesar introduced a bill which gave Caesar extraordinary powers of command in the provinces of Cisalpine Gaul (Upper Italy) and Illyricum (Dalmatia). To these territories the Senate further added Narbonensian Gaul (Southern Gaul). Caesar had also taken steps in agreement with Pompey and Crassus to ensure that he need fear no difficulties with the consuls for 58 BC: Lucius Calpurnius Piso Caesoninus was the father of Calpurnia, his fourth and last wife. Aulus Gabinius had, as people's tribune, secured for Pompey the command of operations against the pirates and had since then been reckoned as one of his adherents. Finally, Clodius, the most unscrupulous of the gang leaders, occupied the office of people's tribune; he was prepared to do anything, especially to attack his mortal enemy, Cicero.

This constellation promoted a development which made Cicero's exile inevitable, although probably neither Caesar nor Pompey sought to bring it about initially. Clodius at once announced proposals, among them two which were designed to clear the way for his further plans. He restored the freedom of association, which the Senate had subjected to certain restrictions, so that he could organize his gangs of thugs with impunity. He also deprived the magistrates of a simple means of obstruction – the right to prohibit or disperse public meetings on religious grounds. After achieving this he made ready at the end of January 58 to strike a grievous blow at Cicero. He published the draft of a law under which anyone who was guilty of killing a Roman citizen without the consent of the people, i.e. without due trial, should be liable to proscription. The wording in itself merely stressed a long-standing principle of the Roman constitution, but by implication it declared unconstitutional the state of emergency which the Senate was wont to declare in the event of a common danger. It was thus aimed mainly at Cicero, although he is not mentioned by name.

Cicero could have risked waiting for the people's decision, which would have given Clodius's proposal the force of law, and the subsequent trial with himself as the accused. Instead, he reacted instantly with a haste which he later bitterly regretted. He discarded his senatorial dress and appeared as a simple knight. Demonstrations and counter-demonstrations followed. Clodius's gangs hounded Cicero whenever he appeared in public, pelting him with stones and ordure. A crowd consisting mainly of knights assembled on the Capitol and resolved to put on mourning as a sign of solidarity with Cicero, and the Senate followed suit. Clodius was then provoked into staging further riots, and the consuls forbade the Senate to wear mourning. Cicero almost automatically found himself at the centre of growing opposition to the triumvirate. In the Senate two praetors attempted to contest the validity of the official actions taken by Caesar during his consulship. Caesar himself, stationed outside the city ready to depart, watched the course of events with mounting irritation. News that the Helvetians were planning to migrate called him away, however, to the northern frontier of the province he governed.

Cicero became the focal point of events, an object of negotiation and dispute between the parties. Things had now come to a pass where those in power evidently intended to make an example of him. There was another individual whom they also regarded as so much of a threat that they wished get rid of him – Cato. They silenced him in a rather more genteel fashion by persuading him to accept various tasks in the eastern dominions. In the case of Cicero, who had declined a post as adjutant in Caesar's forces as well as a seat on the commission that was to implement the settlement act, there could be no question of any such polite fiction: he was left to the mercy of Clodius and his strong-arm methods.

Cicero himself now placed his hopes on Pompey, who had repeatedly said that he would defend him – but his hopes were vain. A delegation of highly respected Optimates, which went to Pompey's estate on Lake Albano, was dismissed and told to apply to the ruling consuls. The delegation then waited on Piso, with whom they thought they might make more headway than with Gabinius. Piso replied that he wasn't as brave as Lucius Manlius Torquatus (a member of the delegation) or as Cicero had been when they were consuls. He wanted no bloodshed, Cicero could save the state once again – by his departure. Cicero tells of another attempt at intercession which he undertook with his son-in-law Piso, a distant relative of the consul.[1] The consul is reported to have said he knew of no way to thwart Clodius, it was a case of every man for himself.

Two days later Clodius convened a meeting in the Circus Flaminius. The consuls, when asked for their view of Cicero's consulate, expressed severe disapproval, while Caesar advised against the retrospective application of the law to Cicero. Cicero consulted his friends, and almost without exception they advised him to leave the city. He was all the more inclined to follow this advice, since he never imagined that he would have to wait a year and a half for his return. He possessed a statue of Minerva, Rome's protectress, and brought it as a votive offering to the temple of Jupiter on the Capitol. Then, accompanied by a number of friends, he left the city in the dead of night.

About the same time – shortly before the middle of March – Caesar had departed for Gaul, and the day after Cicero's flight Clodius had his banishment law ratified by a popular assembly. The mob did not wait for any further formalities before wrecking Cicero's property. His house on the Palatine Hill was plundered and set on fire, and the country houses at Tusculum and Formiae were also ransacked and wrecked. There is no report of anything similar happening to the other villas – near Arpinum and in Antium – so we may suppose they were spared, at least to begin with. Since Cicero's flight had made a prosecution under the banishment law impossible, Clodius proceeded to promulgate the text of a resolution by the people, according to which Cicero was to be banished because he had caused Roman citizens to be executed without legal warrant. His entire property was to be forfeit to the state, and a supplementary clause decreed that he must remain at a distance of at least 500 miles from Italy. Contravention of the ban was punishable by death, and anyone who offered aid within the banned area was liable to incur the same penalty. This second proposal of Clodius aimed at Cicero was probably ratified and became law at the end of April.

Cicero did not travel alone. He was certainly accompanied by freedmen and servants, and a friend by the name of Gnaeus Sallustius saw to his security and well-being. He intended at first to make his escape to Sicily. In a villa near the Lucanian town of Atina where he spent the night he had a dream.² As he wandered alone, it seemed, through a desolate landscape, Marius appeared to him and asked him why he was so downcast. He replied that he had been expelled from his fatherland, and Marius comforted him, saying that salvation would come from the Temple of Honour and Virtue – which was indeed where the Senate resolved a year later to begin proceedings for his recall. This story actually occurs in a much later work, *De Divinatione*, not in any of the letters from that period which are couched in a uniformly hopeless and despondent tone.

Round about 5 April Cicero arrived in Vibo, not far from the Straits of Messina, where he learned that the Sicilian governor would stop him landing on the island, and that Clodius had stipulated a prohibited zone of 500 miles. Sicily was now out of the question; Cicero turned away from Vibo in a north-easterly direction and made for Brundisium in order to embark for Greece. There he spent a few days with a friend by the name of Marcus Laenius Flaccus. On the last day of April he sailed across to Dyrrhachium (now Durazzo) on the west coast of Macedonia. Since Epirus, where Atticus had an estate, and Athens were too close, he thought of travelling on to Cyzicus on the Propontis (the Sea of Marmora) and consequently took the road to Thessalonica, where he arrived on 25 May. Here he was safe from enemies, especially exiled Catalinarians, since he was permitted to stay in the official residence of the Macedonian quaestor, Gnaeus Plancius. The governor, Plancius's superior, raised no serious objection, although he had his misgivings. Cicero stayed in Thessalonica until November before returning to Dyrrhachium, which he reached on 25 November. At that time he thought that his spell of exile would soon come to an end, but in fact he had to kick his heels in Dyrrhachium until August 57 BC.

Cicero's behaviour during his exile has attracted a good deal of criticism, even from his contemporaries, especially from his friend Atticus – and in full measure from succeeding generations. His letters – twenty-seven to Atticus, besides four to Terentia and a couple to his brother Quintus – do indeed tell a sorry tale. Apart from a few details about his journey and the places where he had stayed, together with sundry remarks about efforts being made for his recall, there is nothing but a monotonous account of Cicero's despondent state of mind. Nowhere do they show any sign of an attempt at self-control or any inclination to cope with the dismal present by means of a despairing sort of humour. He later reacted quite differently under Caesar's dictatorship, which elicited not merely grumbles but also witticisms and self-irony. In these letters from exile he never stops bewailing his grievous plight. He is overcome by tears and so distraught that he cannot bring himself to go on writing.[3] His weeping well-nigh obliterates the letters he receives, and he is so distracted that he cannot write coherently. Never was such misfortune visited on any mortal. The dejection criticized by Atticus is fully justified by the fact that no man so well situated, with such intellectual gifts and experience, so respected and with such patronage in high places, had ever been cast down from such eminence.

In Rome rumours began to circulate that Cicero had been driven out of his mind by grief, and a visitor reported that he was drawn and haggard.[4] Cicero's sufferings in exile seemed to assume tragic dimensions. Worse even than his self-pity was the ceaseless brooding search for 'blame'.[5] He had made the mistake of trusting false counsellors and friends who were really jealous of him; even Atticus was in part to blame, because he had left Cicero in the lurch at the crucial moment and allowed him to leave Rome. Atticus tried to convince his friend of the absurdity of these reproaches, which were totally unwarranted, but Cicero continue to think that he had been betrayed and ruined by false friends and envious schemers.[6]

There is no way to gloss over all this, but certain things are explicable. Cicero had not reckoned with such a lengthy period of exile, and the strenuous, often abortive efforts to have him recalled were bound to put a heavy strain on his nerves. These were, however, no more than superficial factors; the real reason for his state of utter demoralization was inherent in his character as a brilliantly talented self-made man. Pretty well all that he was he had achieved by his own efforts, so that he felt it had all been obliterated and destroyed when his standing as a citizen, a senator and a former consul was called in question. Gentlemen of the old aristocracy were wont to inherit their *amour-propre* along with the traditions of their families. The individual counted for something as a member of his house, he formed part of a structure and a system that transcended the individual, so that a failure on his part, provided it was not altogether his fault, would not demoralize him so totally. Cicero's dejection in exile is obviously just as much a part of him as his elation at his successes. Both suggest an individual who was lonely in a very basic sense, who knew that he must rely on himself, and work entirely from his own inner resources.

If any Roman of his day should have found support and solace in philosophy, then it was Cicero, but this resource totally failed him. The moral theory of the Stoics and Cynics, according to which there was but a single good, with everything else regarded as merely illusory good or evil, had long since been converted into the common currency of a voluminous literature of spiritual comfort. The subjects treated in such works included, not only death, poverty, slavery and the like, but also exile as a very common feature of political life in the city-states of Classical times. An excerpt on 'Banishment' from an itinerant preacher called Teles (third century BC) has come down to us. During his own exile Seneca devoted a whole treatise to the subject, *Ad Helviam Matrem*. It was dedicated to his mother, who, as it happened, was descended from the same family as Cicero's mother. Cicero touched on the subject in the fifth book of his *Conversations in Tusculum*.[7] Banishment, he argues there, scarcely differed from a lengthy journey, and one's fellow-travellers, poverty and ignominy, were no real evil for the wise man. It is here that we come across the celebrated quotation, 'Patria est, ubicumque est bene'. By the time Cicero came to write *Tusculanarum Quaestionum*, his own exile, the actual occasion for such reflections, already lay some ten to thirteen years back in the past – and at that time the consolations of philosophy had availed him very little.

While Cicero was thus entirely wrapped up in himself and brooding on who was 'to blame' for his misfortune, his friends, led by the influential Atticus, were doing their best to bring about his recall. By April 58 the situation had already changed in Cicero's favour: Clodius had assisted in the escape of an Armenian prince, a prisoner of Pompey, and he and Pompey had fallen out on this account. On 1 June the Senate made a first attempt to pass a motion reprieving Cicero, but it failed because one of the tribunes who was friendly with Clodius raised an objection. It was not until the end of October that the attempt was renewed: eight tribunes who were well disposed towards Cicero put forward proposed legislation for his recall, but this attempt also failed when the opposition intervened. All hopes were now focused on the new consuls who would take up office on 1 January 57.

Publius Cornelius Lentulus Spinther had given assurances that he would definitely use his influence in Cicero's favour, while Quintus Caecilius Metellus, the man with whom Cicero had quarrelled at the end of his consulship, promised to conform to the Senate's wishes. In view of this situation, Cicero travelled back from Thessalonica to Dyrrhachium at the end of November. But in January 57 the same ploy was repeated as in the preceding year. A Senate motion was not passed because a tribune objected, while a popular meeting convened to approve a law permitting Cicero's return was dispersed by Clodius's thugs. During the following months the bludgeon ruled in Rome, and it was only after bitter battles that the bodyguards of two tribunes of the

Optimates, Titus Annius Milo and Publius Sestius, were able to get the
better of Clodius's bully-boys. In May Cicero's cause began to make
progress at last, with Pompey playing a leading part. It was then that
the Senate resolved that the voters of all Italy should be summoned to
attend the public meeting that was to debate the law for Cicero's return.
At the beginning of July the Senate approved the wording of the law
and all the other formalities connected with his return. On 4 August a
packed public meeting passed the law.

Cicero gave an account of his homecoming to Atticus. He wrote:

> I left Dyrrhachium on 4 August, on the very day that the law concerning
> me was introduced. The day after I arrived in Brundisium. There my
> Tullia was waiting for me, and it happened to be her birthday ... On 11
> August I learned from a letter that Quintus sent me, that the law had been
> endorsed by the popular meeting, with amazing acclaim on the part of all
> ages and conditions of men, and amazingly large participation from the
> whole of Italy. I left Brundisium with every mark of respect, and all along
> the way delegations from here, there and everywhere had turned up to
> offer their good wishes. As I approached the city there was not a single
> citizen whose name was known to a nomenclator who did not come to
> meet me ... When I reached the Capenian gate crowds of people were
> thronging the temple steps; they showed their sympathy by loud applause.
> A similar crowd and the same kind of ovation accompanied me to the
> Capitol; there was an incredible crowd of people in the forum and on the
> Capitol.[8]

The day following his arrival in Rome Cicero delivered an effusive
speech in the Senate expressing his gratitude. Apart from this speech,
a similar address to the people has also been preserved – although it
is possible that Cicero did not deliver it in person, but merely had it
published as a kind of pamphlet.

It was in these two addresses that Cicero first propounded his own
account of his banishment, a kind of myth, if we compare it with the
bare facts. He, who had saved Rome from Cataline in 63, had now
averted the city's ruin a second time. For Clodius and, in collusion with
him, the two wickedest consuls in Roman history, Gabinius and Piso,
had vowed to destroy him and the state – so that he had gone into exile
of his own free will, in order to prevent a dreadful civil war. True,
freedom, together with the dignity and the good name of the Senate had
accompanied him into exile. Nevertheless, the actual existence of the
Roman people had been preserved intact, so that the Republican constitution and all the glory of the traditional state could now return to
Rome along with Cicero.

The law of 4 August 57 which rescinded the ban on Cicero, also decreed the restoration of all his property, besides compensation for damage. Cicero encountered a problem with his city residence on the Palatine Hill. The house adjoined a colonnade erected by Quintus Lutatius Catulus, general (together with Marius) in the Cimbrian war. When Cicero went into exile, Clodius contrived by means of a proxy to acquire the house at auction, intending to take up residence there. He also modified Catulus's colonnade, linking it to part of Cicero's property and erecting a marble statue of a female figure. He dedicated the colonnade and the statue, together with the plot of land on which it stood, to Liberty, the symbol of Roman civic freedom.

When Cicero's property was restored to him, Clodius raised an objection relating to the plot of land he had added to the sanctuary of Liberty. Anything which had once been dedicated to a deity was reckoned to be divine property and might never again revert to human ownership. The Senate then resolved to seek an opinion on the validity of Clodius's dedication from the pontifices. Both Clodius and Cicero appeared before the priests in order to make their case. In a long speech which has survived, *De Domo sua* (*On his own Home*), Cicero stated that in his view the dedication undertaken by Clodius was null and void. The pontifices accepted Cicero's argument that an official could dedicate a sanctuary in the name of the state only if he were empowered to do so by a specific law. Since Clodius had not observed this principle, his consecration was invalid. The Senate then dismissed Clodius's objection. Now Cicero was able to rebuild his town residence. An attack on his workmen staged by Clodius at the beginning of November seems to have been no more than a passing episode.

12

Under the Sway of the Triumvirate

During the months from autumn 57 until the spring of 56 the political scene was in a state of uncommon disarray. Caesar, probably the only man with clear ideas and aims at the time, scarcely made his presence felt. The alliance of the triumvirate was showing signs of collapse, and the Optimates, instead of agreeing on a common policy, dissipated their forces in futile petty scheming, so that Rome presented a prospect dominated by obstruction and intrigue. The cliques of Optimates, Pompey, Crassus, Cicero, the mob and their leaders who battened on the state were all intent on minding their own business. They had not the faintest notion that Rome's future would depend on decisions taken by Caesar, who was in Gaul at the time.

A perfect example of the contemporary standard of politics was the argument about the restoration of King Ptolemy XII, known as Auletes, 'the flautist'. Egypt had long been a subject state and about the middle of the second century BC it had become a Roman dependency. Insurrections and assassinations rocked the kingdom, and Ptolemy, who had occupied the throne since 80 BC, was not given the status of 'friend and ally' of the Roman people until 59 BC – having paid Caesar and Pompey considerable sums of money for the privilege. Only a year later he no longer felt safe in his own country and fled to Rome, where he took refuge with Pompey. Now an unedifying tug of war began over the issue of his reinstatement, which offered the prospect of large profits to those involved. In the autumn of 57 the Senate assigned the job to the current consul, Lentulus Spinther, the future governor of Cilicia. The supporters of Pompey thereupon tried to frustrate this decision. Certain circles of Optimates promoted an oracle which warned against supporting the king 'with a host' – the intention being to prevent the formation of a task force to the advantage of Pompey. This kind of sanctimonious mumbo-jumbo played no small part, even in those times, although one wonders who did not see through it and realize it was nothing but a put-up job staged by interested parties. The Senate did in fact conclude that the state would be jeopardized by any attempt to reinstate the king 'with a host', leaving open the question of who would reinstate him without the benefit of an armed force.

Cicero and others tried to retain the commission for Lentulus. One tribune wanted it assigned to Pompey, and another tribune even tried to have Lentulus's authority in Cilicia revoked by law. Gnaeus Cornelius Lentulus Marcellinus, one of the consuls for the year 56, contrived by means of a trick to prevent a final vote on the proposed bill. He cancelled all the 'comitial' days, i.e. those days on which public meetings might be held, until the spring, when Pompey had lost interest in the whole business. Ptolemy had to wait for another year until Gabinius, governor of Syria, marched his troops into Egypt in the spring of 55. Ptolemy then got his throne back in return for a promise to pay 10,000 talents.

The first book of the *Ad Familiares* collection consists of letters that Cicero sent to Lentulus Spinther in 56–4, and the first items deal in minute detail with the Egyptian affair. In the whole web of intrigue Cicero was perhaps the only individual who was not motivated by blatant self-interest. He was profoundly grateful to Lentulus Spinther, who had agitated vigorously for his return from exile, and he found it extremely embarrassing not to be able to do something in return for his friend and supporter.

As far as domestic affairs were concerned, the situation was not much improved in the months following Cicero's return. The vicious gang warfare of the preceding winter had left many outstanding accounts to be settled. The issue was initially Clodius's – ultimately successful – attempt, following his year out of office, to secure a legal basis for his subversive activities by acquiring the status of aedile. Milo, however, intended to bring charges against Clodius, so that the elections for aedile were postponed until January 56. Then certain circles of Optimates prevailed who – incredible as it may seem – had chosen Clodius as their ally. This was because these individuals had noted with satisfaction the insolent manner in which Clodius had treated Pompey, and even Caesar, during the latter's consulship. They thought that this unruly lout might serve them as an instrument against Pompey. They thus contrived to frustrate Milo's plan to prosecute Clodius, who was duly elected aedile.

He proceeded at once to turn the tables, starting a prosecution for *vis* (the use of force) against Milo and setting one of his henchmen on

Sestius, the second tribune of the preceding year, who had thwarted him. During the trial of Milo disturbances aimed against Pompey were engineered by Clodius. Gangs armed with clubs were formed and it looked as if the situation would revert to what it had been a year previously. But the case against Milo was never completed and other subsequent trials passed off in an orderly fashion. In February Cicero defended the former aedile, Lucius Calpurnia Bestia, who had been charged with improperly influencing elections. He took this trial, un-important in itself, as an opportunity to show the accusations against Sestius in their true light. In one of the brawls in 57 BC Bestia had saved Sestius's life, and Cicero praised his deed in heartfelt terms (as he writes to his brother Quintus; the speech itself has not been preserved).[1]

Cicero's high-minded speech in defence of Sestius seems to share the narrow-minded and short-sighted view common to all the political in-itiatives of the day. It reveals no more insight into the true balance of political forces than was common on the contemporary Roman scene. However, it goes far beyond the dismal tactics and practices of that scene by reason of its vitality and its endeavour to mobilize the finest traditions of the Roman state in order to cope with the problems of the day.

In a wide-ranging historical introduction Cicero once more describes the events surrounding his exile, as he had done in his two votes of thanks and in the speech *On his own Home*. In a second, systematic, section he proceeds to outline an idealized picture of the traditional order and the rule of the Optimates. It is here, in his opening remarks, which contain his political programme and credo, that he launches the fascinating phrase, 'cum dignitate otium'.[2] By this he means that in-ternal peace (otium) should be sustained on the basis of the undisputed validity of a hierarchical social structure (dignitas). Cicero suggests that there is no way in which one of these aims may be pursued to the exclusion of the other. Stability may not be sought without regard to social order, or social order without regard to stability. The inner equilibrium of this social order, Cicero argues, is threatened by two dangers. The primary danger of the opposition represented by revolu-tionary elements and political adventurers, and a secondary danger arising from laxity on the part of those who would be called upon to defend the social order, were it imperilled. It is true, Cicero boldly claims, the bitter conflict between the Optimates and the Populares had long since been settled, and all that was left were factitious brawls between gangs of hired hooligans.

The scheme of this speech in defence of Sestius is evidently linked to the catch-phrase of the consular speeches, the 'consensus omnium bonorum'. Here, again, it is a question of the good men, the boni, i.e. the majority of the citizenry adopting the political aims of the Optimates. In 56 BC there were individuals, particularly in the upper classes from which juries were selected, who would respond to such an appeal. The court acquitted Sestius unanimously, that is, it accepted unreservedly Cicero's argument that Sestius had responded in self-defence to provocation by Clodius.

The soaring rhetoric of the Sestius speech had a distinctly banal epilogue, both before the bench, and subsequently in Cicero's speeches. Publius Vatinius, people's tribune in 59 BC and a supporter of Caesar, had introduced the law which gave Caesar extraordinary powers of command in Gaul. He appeared as a witness for the prosecution in the trial of Sestius, and in his statement tried to represent Cicero's plea for the defence as the meaningless claptrap of a trivial time-server. Cicero struck back with extraordinary violence and allowed himself to be drawn into one of those unbridled attacks which he used to launch in the fifties – not on the true instigators of political events, but on their accomplices, or on the people he imagined were to blame. He thought his retort was important enough to publish, albeit in a modified form. It has come down to us as a savage piece of abuse. We ought to bear in mind, however, that it is not just an indictment of its author but also of the age in which he lived. At that time it was customary to go to extremes of coarseness and vulgarity in abusing a political opponent.

The attacks represented by the so-called cross-examination of the witness Vatinius – in spite of all Cicero's protestations to the contrary – did not merely hit Vatinius. They also hit the triumvirate on whose behalf he had acted, and Caesar in particular. It is hard to imagine that Cicero was prompted to pick on Vatinius by sheer fury. His attack, like the trial of Sestius itself, took place at a time when the balance of forces was unclear: the influence of Caesar seemed to be waning, and the consensus between him and Pompey appeared to be somewhat shaky. At the beginning of the year Vatinius had applied in vain for the office of aedile, and Cicero may have been encouraged in the assumption that this was his chance to strike a blow at Caesar's man.

Cicero's productive capacity was at times well-nigh inexhaustible. It was at this time, in the spring of 56, that he produced a masterpiece of the advocate's art, virtually as an interlude of light relief – his plea on behalf of Marcus Caelius Rufus. Caelius, the highly talented but feck-less son of an eques, had been trained in oratory by Cicero. There then followed years in which they were estranged. Caelius had allied himself for a time with Cataline, and in two trials where Cicero appeared for the defence, the trials of Antonius and Bestia, Caelius had acted for the prosecution. Cicero was nevertheless broad-minded enough to come to the aid of this youthful hothead, whose litigiousness had involved him in a somewhat perilous affair. He was alleged to have taken part in various acts of violence and homicide by which King Ptolemy had tried to silence a delegation from Alexandria that had come to protest against his reinstatement. The prosecution were able to introduce a notorious woman from Roman high society as their star witness – Clodia. She was, one of the three sisters of Cicero's mortal enemy and probably the same woman who was immortalized by Catullus as Lesbia.

Cicero's speech for the defence, a first-rate source of evidence concerning the morals of the time, offers us intriguing glimpses of the dissolute behaviour of a certain circle in late Republican society. It does so in a cheerfully frivolous manner, without moralizing or condescension. There was no call, said Cicero, to be strait-laced about youthful high spirits, even our respected ancestors had gone in for this kind of jollification now and then, when they were young. If Cicero was merely acting the part of the ageing liberal when he adopted the common moral standards of the day for his young protégé's sake, then he did so very convincingly: Caelius was acquitted.

At the same time, the beginning of April 56, the *ager Campanus*, the Capuan marches, came up for discussion. Caesar's second Settlement Act had designated this belt of land for the establishment of small-holdings, thus depriving the treasury of valuable estates that yielded substantial revenue. This measure, which Caesar had taken during his consulship, had been a particular thorn in the flesh of the Optimates. They were now thinking of contesting it, hoping for the support of Pompey, whose alliance with Caesar seemed to have entered a critical phase. Cicero did not hesitate to join in the assault on the 'bulwark' of Caesar's policy, as he termed it.[3] It was at his suggestion that the Senate resolved to hold a debate on the Capuan marches on 15 May.

The debate was never held, for Caeser did not take lying down either the resolution sponsored by Cicero or various other threats on the part of the Optimates. In the middle of April he met Crassus in Ravenna and Pompey in Luca and contrived not only to eliminate their smouldering antagonism, but also to formulate a policy for the coming years. Crassus and Pompey were to claim the consulships for 55, together with five-year appointments as military commanders, with a similar extension to Caesar's tenure in Gaul. These agreements were in fact kept strictly secret. Cicero and the other leading senators learned no more

than that the debate on the Capuan marches would not be allowed and
that they must eschew any policy hostile to Caesar. Shortly before 15
May one of Pompey's agents called on Cicero and instructed him to
take no action regarding the Capuan marches before Pompey's return –
he was then in Sardinia and later on in Africa. Accordingly, Cicero took
no part in the Senate meetings on 15 and 16 May, and the whole
business came to nothing.

A change had thus taken place almost imperceptibly. A couple of
discussions had been held in northern Italy, a number of messengers
had travelled post-haste to Rome, and what had seemed to be the
prevailing balance of forces had been upset, very much to the disadvantage of the Senate. A sudden stop had been put to the independent
policy of the Optimates, and to their scheming and plotting. It was
Cicero who most obviously misjudged the situation. His grandiloquent
speech in defence of Sestius had not been meant merely to serve its
immediate purpose. Above and beyond that purpose it was intended to
suggest a fundamental revaluation of the maxims underlying the traditional structure of the state and society – an aim which it inevitably
failed to achieve. Rome was now nothing but the place where political
action was ratified, not the seat of political action itself, as the confer-
ences in Ravenna and Luca had shown. The revival of the triumvirate
left only the 'otium' of Cicero's slogan; the 'dignitas', the dignity of a
sovereign Senate guiding the destiny of Rome, no longer existed. The
opponents of the traditional order did not merely comprise, as Cicero
thought, a handful of urban gangs, but also many members of the
poorer citizen class, who flocked to Caesar's banner, as well as Caesar
himself and his staff. Cicero differed from the Optimates around him in
that he had ideals which he propagated because he believed they could
be realized, whereas the gentlemen of the old aristocracy were totally
absorbed in their petty cliquish affairs.

Cicero adapted very rapidly to the new situation. The overall change
was instantly followed by his own about-turn – total commitment to
the interests of the triumvirate. Already by the end of May Caesar had
obtained the Senate's approval for demands which Cicero had called
'monstrous' only two months earlier.[4] The treasury was to pay the
wages of four legions that Caesar had recruited on his own initiative,
and Caesar was to be allotted ten subordinate commanders. It was none
other than Cicero himself who put forward these proposals, because, as
he said some months later, he did not think it right to retain his original
negative attitude. He thought it better to adapt to the new political
circumstances and aim at concordia, mutual understanding.[5]

Not long afterwards Cicero had occasion to take Caesar's part even more decisively. It was a matter of which provinces should be administered by the consuls for 55 in the succeeding year. As already mentioned, a law introduced by Gaius Gracchus required the Senate to take a decision. There were proposals concerning Gaul, hitherto Caesar's territory. If they had been adopted, they would, to say the least, have made it more difficult to prolong Caesar's command there, as planned by the triumvirate. Cicero backed a counter-proposal involving Syria and Macedonia. Thus, Caesar was spared, and, at the same time, governorships were denied to two men who – along with Clodius – were mainly to blame for Cicero's exile. He was successful on the whole, in that there was no majority for the bold, not to say crazy, attempt to challenge Caesar's political potential. The speech which Cicero delivered on this occasion, and which he proceeded to publish, proclaimed to the world at large that he had gone over to the triumvirate, and this was how things remained for the next four years – until his courageous defence of his friend Milo in 52 BC.

In the late summer there was a heated exchange between Cicero and Clodius during a Senate meeting. Cicero seized this chance for a showdown with his arch-enemy in the speech *De Haruspicum Responso, On the Soothsayers' Expert Opinion*. In keeping with Roman tradition, certain groups of Optimates had engaged Etruscan soothsayers and sages to assess the possible consequences of recent events, especially certain religious or cultic transgressions. At a public meeting Clodius had the audacity to stigmatize Cicero as one of the offenders. Cicero, in return, used the clash in the Senate as a pretext to apply the report, sentence by sentence, to Clodius. His speech culminates in an appeal. In a bold generalization, both the Senate and the triumvirate are subsumed under the notion of Optimates, and Cicero claims that the political crisis can be resolved only if the Senate disowns Clodius and shows it is prepared to negotiate with the triumvirate. Cicero failed to realize that any accommodation with the triumvirate would amount to the total surrender of the Republican constitution. He tried to represent his way of coming to terms with the situation as the only possible solution, which says very little for his sense of what was politically feasible.

The series of defences which Cicero undertook in the service and at the behest of the triumvirate began with the speech on behalf of Lucius Cornelius Balbus, which probably dates from the autumn of 56. Of these speeches, only the pleas for Balbus and Rabitus Postumus have come down to us. At that time Balbus was Caesar's principal agent and more or less the *éminence grise* of the triumvirate. He came from

Gades, in Spain, and certain Optimates tried to bring about his downfall by challenging his Roman citizenship in the courts. Cicero quite correctly made the point that the attack was really aimed at the triumvirate, and advised the prosecution to abandon a lost cause. Balbus was acquitted. Cicero had never come into conflict with him, and the case involved issues of constitutional and international law where a competent lawyer had nothing to lose.

Cicero was all the more disconcerted when Pompey suggested that he should conduct the defence of Lucius Caninius Gallus, an opponent of his efforts to have the task of reinstating King Ptolemy allocated to Lentulus Spinther. He wrote in relation to this case: 'I expect nothing more for all my trouble, indeed, I sometimes find myself obliged to defend men who have done me no service – at the request, if you please, of those who have done me favours.'[6]

But the most unreasonable demands made on Cicero were those requiring him to appear for the defence of former adversaries: Vatinius, a supporter of Caesar, and Gabinius, a follower of Pompey. It was in connection with these cases that he had to endure the most severe reproaches on the part of the Optimates. While the defence of Gabinius ended with the additional humiliation of a defeat, Cicero fared rather better in the subsequent trial of Gabinius's accomplice, Gaius Rabirius Postumus. Here he was representing the adopted son of a man whom he had defended barely a decade earlier in a political trial staged by Caesar. In return he had been actively supported by the son during his exile.

In the late summer of 55 Piso Caesoninus returned from his governorship of Macedonia. Together with Gabinius, the other consul of the year 58 BC, and Cicero's arch-enemy Clodius, he was the main target of the outbursts of hatred to which Cicero was repeatedly prone following his return from exile. After being forced to relinquish any sort of independent policy, and since his activities in the Senate and the courts as an accomplice of the triumvirate, Cicero had been in a very unbalanced state of mind. This is no doubt the reason for a verbal assault on Piso which far outdoes in length and lurid detail the attacks on Vatinius and Clodius (in his speech *On the Soothsayers' Expert Opinion*).

Piso had done no more than attack the interpretation which Cicero never wearied of placing on his exile, namely that he had been forced to withdraw in the face of a conspiracy led by Clodius and the consuls for 58 BC. In response to this view Piso simply stated that Cicero was venting his rage on individuals who he thought were of less account than himself, since he did not dare to attack the true instigators of his exile, Caesar and Pompey. However accurate this analysis of events might have been, Cicero could not bring himself to accept it. His *amour-propre* forced him to stick to his own version, against his better judgement as it were. Attacks like that by Piso hurt him deeply, so that he tried to deny their justification by drowning them out in unparallelled bombardments of abuse.

The result which he thought fit to put before the public and which has not been preserved in its entirety contains a whole arsenal of conventional topoi of invective. It was possible to quote parallels for almost everything that Cicero wished to urge against the antecedents, the appearance, the character and the deeds of his enemy. All the same, the massive accumulation of insults and abuse which the pamphlet attacking Piso serves up has a certain scarcity value. With this piece of writing Cicero secured himself a place among the satirists of Latin literature which might just possibly be rivalled by Catullus and is not matched again until we get to the Church Father, Hieronymus.

Cicero's energies and his zeal were by no means totally absorbed by the tiresome, quasi-voluntary services he rendered the triumvirate, or by senseless verbal skirmishes with his foes, some of them real, some of them merely imaginary. There was still room, not only for the first of the great dialogues – *De Oratore* and perhaps for *De Legibus* too – but also for a number of forensic works. The triumvirate intervened in the affairs of the city only when their authority was at issue. There were many other topical issues, however, which were unaffected by the arguments between them and the senatorial aristocracy.

There is evidence of this in two of Cicero's speeches from 54 BC: a speech, of which only about a third has survived, defending Marcus Aemilius Scaurus, a typical Optimatis, who had shamelessly filled his pockets as governor of Sardinia and Corsica, and the plea on behalf of Gnaeus Plancius. Here, Cicero shows himself once again from a favourable angle, if we discount one infelicitous passage concerning his relationship with the triumvirate.[7] In 58, when he was quaestor in Macedonia, Plancius had looked after the exiled Cicero courageously and unselfishly. Now, when his benefactor was in court facing a charge of having won an election by improper means, the time had come to express his thanks, and Cicero, who was glad to bear his duty in mind, embarked on a brilliant eulogy of gratitude. This speech, a kind of annexe to the plea for Murena, once again conveys an uncommonly vivid impression of the manifold social complexities of late Republican Rome, and moreover of the principles and practices by which the life of the community was guided with the aid of this system of personal allegiances.

Cicero, who acted for the defence in a series of trials, apart from those mentioned here, took far fewer risks in the Senate under the rule of the triumvirate than he did in court. In effect he never ventured beyond the speech *On the Consular Provinces*, which he delivered following the political changes in the spring of 56. Obviously, the ruling clique availed themselves mainly of his abilities as a lawyer. They allowed him to miss Senate meetings or to be present merely as a silent listener, while Cicero himself followed Atticus's advice and was very careful to restrain himself.[8] He took no part in the squabble about the consulships of Pompey and Crassus, either for or against. He also held his peace concerning the next step taken by the triumvirate – the securing of appointments as commanders for Pompey and Crassus and the prolongation of Caesar's command in Gaul.

Only routine matters occasionally tempted him to abandon his reserve. Thus, complaints about the Syrian governor Gabinius once led to a violent clash with Crassus. Pompey and Caesar urged the pair of them to make up and be friends again, so that Grassus and Cicero dined together in the garden of the latter's son-in-law. Shortly afterwards, Crassus departed for Syria, from where he waged war on the Parthians. The operation ended in the humiliating defeat of Carrhae which cost Crassus his life. There was one consequence which affected Cicero: Crassus had been a member of the college of augurs, and Cicero was appointed to the vacancy which thus arose.

The change in Cicero's political allegiance in the spring of 56 had not merely attracted a good deal of criticism from his contemporaries, it had also plunged him into a distressing inner conflict. A relatively rapid sequence of letters – to Atticus, to his brother Quintus and to Lentulus Spinther, who was then governor of Cilicia – offers eloquent testimony to this personal crisis. There is an uncommonly moving statement in a letter to Atticus of May 56:

> What can be more distasteful than the life we lead, especially mine? Although you are by nature a political animal, you do not personally have to perform servile tasks, you are merely affected by the generally wretched state of affairs; but if I speak about our body politic in a manner befitting the subject, then I'm reckoned to be crazy, if I speak as circumstances dictate, I'm looked upon as an abject creature, and if I hold my peace, then I'm regarded as a spent force – am I not bound to feel that this is all highly embarrassing? The embarrassment is rendered all the

more acute by the fact that I dare not show any sign of it, for fear of seeming ungrateful. But what if I were to give in and retreat into the haven of idleness? Out of the question: I have to join up and go to war. So am I to be a mere retainer, having turned down any more elevated appointment? So it shall be; you, too, agree, I see – if only I had always listened to you![9]

Cicero knew that the discretionary powers of the Senate no longer existed, that he was in the service of dictators – but still he could not simply withdraw. Why not? Did he think he would then once more be at the mercy of Clodius, if he did not do the triumvirate's bidding, or did politics, and especially his legal practice, still exert such a fascination for him? At any rate, he was bound to be grateful to the triumvirate: he had been allowed to return from exile. We should beware of misinterpreting Cicero's emphasis on his obligation to be grateful as nothing more than opportunism. Cicero was bound to consider Pompey in particular as his benefactor, for the latter had worked tirelessly for his recall, so that Cicero developed a kind of inner dependence on him. Here, as everywhere in the life of Rome, personal loyalties and objective problems were inextricably bound up together, which could give rise to serious dilemmas, especially in times of crisis.

Among the letters to Lentulus Spinther (*Ad Familiares* 1), the penultimate item, dated December 54, stands out particularly. It is here that Cicero gives a detailed account of his political conduct. It is here, if anywhere, in correspondence with a man whom he esteemed and whom he took seriously, that he stated his honest opinion and, after mature reflection, summed up all the arguments which he believed he could advance to justify himself. Lentulus had written to him saying he could understand the reconciliation with Caesar, but he would like an explanation as to why Cicero had been prepared to defend Vatinius.

Cicero offers a wide-ranging survey of his policy since his return from exile. At that time, he claims, he had clung firmly to his Republican principles – although he had clearly seen that certain people had malicious reservations about his reinstatement and the compensation he had received for his losses. In particular, it had been he who promoted the decision to debate the Capuan marches. But then there had been the conference in Luca and Cicero had received instructions to drop the Capuan marches issue. He had, however, more or less made it a condition *vis-à-vis* the *res publica* that he should be permitted to discharge his obligation to his benefactors and not give the lie to his brother, who had vouched for him. Certain Optimates had noted the stresses and strains in his relations with Pompey and Caesar with malicious satisfaction; indeed, they had been on the best of terms with his mortal enemy, Clodius. The state had not fallen into the clutches of scoundrels, as in Cinna's time; on the contrary, at its head stood Pompey, a man of outstanding merit. Cicero had no fear of acquiring a reputation for disloyalty, if, in some respects, he changed his tune for the sake of his benefactor: 'non putavi famam inconstantiae mihi pertimescendam, si quibusdam in sententiis paulum me immutassem.'[10] His pact with Pompey had necessarily entailed a good relationship with Caesar, with whom he was also linked through his brother Quintus (who was stationed in Gaul at the time as one of Caesar's regimental officers). After a lengthy disquisition on the ill-treatment he had suffered during his flight and following his return, he claims, with some justice, that even the so-called Optimates had not adhered consistently to their former attitude. His conciliation with Vatinius and Crassus, on the other hand, Cicero goes on, had been the inevitable consequence of requests by Pompey and Caesar. Cicero sums up:

> You have now learned, for which reasons I espoused which cause, and which position I propose to adopt in politics. Please believe me, I would have thought along exactly the same lines, if I had a free hand in every respect; I would not think that I was obliged to resist such massive resources, nor that I ought to put an end to the rule of our most capable citizens – even supposing that were possible; nor would I think that I had to stand inflexibly by the same opinion, although circumstances and the attitude of right-thinking people had changed; I would rather adapt to the times – temporibus adsentiendum.[11]

Even in stormy seas one sometimes had to run before the wind. The policy of 'cum dignitate otium' did not necessarily entail always saying the same thing, only keeping the same end in view.

The reasons which Cicero gives here – what he says about the abilities and achievements of Caesar and Pompey, and about the tepidity and the tendency to compromise on the part of wide circles of the Optimates – we may agree with in essence. A reasonable view reveals, however, that the position which would have suited Cicero simply did not exist. He was measuring both the Optimates and the triumvirate by traditional political and moral standards which had almost everywhere lost their binding force – with a majority of the Optimates, and even more so with the triumvirate. His illusion of the res publica, the venerable Republic, inhibited uncompromising collaboration, either with the

Optimates, or on the side of the dictators. He was prevented from opposing the regime on principle, as Cato and his followers did – not least by his realization that such resistance would be futile. But all such soothing consideratiosn, however well-founded, whether on the part of Cicero himself or of others, could not alleviate the disquiet that Cicero felt: both his impotence and his services to the triumvirate were a constant source of frustration. As early as 59, during Caesar's consulate, he had written to Atticus that he had done enough in the service of Dicaerchus, a pupil of Aristotle, who recommended a practical, active mode of life.[12] He now meant to join the disciples of Theophrastus, which would permit him to lead a contemplative life of studious leisure. 'So we shall devote ourselves totally to our delightful studies and return to the place which we never ought to have left.' But in the interim this withdrawal into literary and philosophical pursuits remained in the realm of wishful thinking. It was only after his exile and the Luca conference that he began to occupy himself seriously with literary enterprises. At first he continued his ill-starred attempts to expatiate on his own life and deeds: following *De Consulato Meo* (*On my Consulship*) he proceeded to compose an epic, *De Temporibus Meis* (*On my Misfortune*), dealing with his banishment and return, and also consisting of three books. He did, however, refrain from publishing the work: certain people who had supported him but who were not mentioned might be offended.[13] Possibly the epic came into the hands of Lucius Lucceius, as a 'source'. Cicero had asked this friend, who was a historian, to compose a work dealing with the period from the start of Cataline's conspiracy down to Cicero's return from exile.[14] The aim was to glorify Cicero, and to this end it might deviate slightly from the truth. Lucceius consented, but it seems that he never wrote the work.

'But truly, having lost my taste for everything else on account of our political situation, it is only literature which sustains and refreshes me now.'[15] When Cicero wrote thus to Atticus in the spring of 55, he was already hard at work on the greatest of his rhetorical writings, the three books comprising the dialogue *De Oratore*. Admittedly, we know very little about the genesis of the work. In the middle of November 55 Cicero tersely informs his friend, 'I have been working carefully on the rhetorical essay; I have had it in my hands frequently and for long periods. You may have it copied.'[16] A year later we read in the long letter of justification he wrote to Lentulus Spinther that the dialogue *De Oratore* goes beyond the customary rhetorical precepts; he was seeking to represent the doctrine of the ancients as a whole, the teachings of Aristotle as well as those of Isocrates.[17] Cicero is claiming, then, that he has more matters of principle to impart than may be found in the ordinary manuals.

He is perfectly correct: his work offers an unusual approach to the subject, and is perhaps the most important account of the rhetorical art that has come down to us from antiquity, precisely because it attempts to combine Aristotle and Isocrates, that is, it tries to convey a philosophical and reflective as well as a technical and practical approach to rhetoric. *De Oratore* sums up a tradition extending over four hundred years and, for its part, exercised an influence on the rhetorical practice of the Middle Ages and modern times down to the eighteenth century. This tradition of a spoken culture subject to specific rules has long since expired, so that it is not easy for the contemporary reader to gain anything like a vivid impression of Cicero's work. In former times, anyone trained in academic rhetoric who picked up the book would find it delightful reading, because they would instantly observe the masterly and intelligent manner in which Cicero handles his material, without the least trace of pedantry. The present-day reader lacks the necessary qualifications.

Cicero wished *De Oratore* to be numbered among his philosophical works, along with all his other writings on rhetoric, apart from the youthful piece, *De Inventione*.[18] He had all the more justification for including *De Oratore*, in so far as he had chosen the form which had been established in philosophical discourse ever since Plato's time, a form which required not only sovereign command of the subject, but also great literary skill: the dialogue. For his setting the author moves back to the period of his youth. In keeping with the conventions of the genre, the dialogue is represented as an actual event, taking place in 91 BC and involving a number of Roman aristocrats. The chief figures are Lucius Licinius Crassus and Marcus Antonius, two politicians whom Cicero reckoned to be the leading speakers of their generation. In each of the prefaces to the three books it is the author himself who speaks. He addresses his brother Quintus and informs him about his personal relationship with the subject of the dialogue and with the two main participants.

The preface to the first book anticipates the basic problem of the work in a nutshell. It says that Cicero had frequently discussed the subject of eloquence with his brother, and that differences of opinion had emerged. Cicero was convinced that a broad cultural background was the indispensable basis of true rhetoric. Quintus, on the other hand, believed that a modicum of talent and a certain amount of practice would suffice. The two opposing conceptions of rhetoric quoted here

– the universal, as opposed to a specialized, technical view – appear again in the dialogue and are developed there as the basic positions adopted in the conversations. Towards the end of the preface Cicero draws the reader's attention for the first time to the wide variety of knowledge which he believes must be a prerequisite for a great speaker, the 'perfect speaker' (*orator perfectus*), as he is termed later. Immediately afterwards he is prepared to make concessions to Roman practice with its predominant type of forensic speaker who was limited to his own special field. This antithesis, too, has programmatic significance for the entire dialogue, for the constantly recurring division between the ideal and the real, for the indefatigable dialectical process by which Cicero rises again and again from this reality towards his ideal.

To support his notion of a culture aiming at totality he is not only able to advance abstract arguments: he is also able to specify a historical model. The exposition here, which seems to be based on the contrast of two modes of existence, erstwhile totality and current fragmentation, seems to anticipate certain features of the cultural criticism of the German Classical movement – Schiller, for instance. Once, so we are told in the third book, there prevailed in Greece a kind of wholeness which encompassed thought, speech and action: it was succeeded by a state of disintegration and fragmentation. This *discidium linguae atque cordis* (discord between tongue and heart) was manifested, for one thing, in the fact that the intelligentsia withdrew from the political leadership, so that theory and practice, learning and politics were divorced from one other.[19] It was also manifested in a corresponding change in the educational system. A broadly based education directed towards philosophy and rhetoric, aiming at correct moral action as well as a precise and striking mode of expression, was replaced by a disintegration into a series of specialized subjects – and the man who had brought about this change was Socrates. Anyone who seeks to restore the unity that once existed – a rhetorical unity, Cicero emphasizes – can no longer be content with the exclusive study of a rhetoric which has degenerated into a purely formal technique. He must seek to acquire from the philosophers the additional knowledge and capabilities he will need in order to become a true master of the speaker's art.

The grandiose programme of *De Oratore* seems to have inherent in it an excessively speculative element, and we may detect at every point that Cicero was being guided more by consideration for his Roman environment than by his own wishes and needs. Our misgivings are justified if we judge the work purely by the value it may have had in its own day. They cease to be valid, however, if we look more closely at the evolution of rhetoric in Imperial Rome. This evolution proved that Cicero was correct – although in a sense which he himself did not desire, because it was a non-political sense. The instruments of rhetoric were incorporated into a larger whole, a general education on Graeco-Roman lines which bore a philosophical and literary stamp.

De Republica (*On the State, On the Community*) is first mentioned in a letter to Cicero's brother Quintus in May 54: 'I'm engaged in writing the work I spoke to you about, dealing with political theory; it is a difficult and laborious task. If it goes according to plan, then my trouble will be well repaid; if not, then I'll throw it into the sea, in sight of which I'm writing. I'll find something else to do; after all, I simply can't sit idle!'[20] Inspired by the same creative restlessness, and yet still not sure of success, Cicero writes not long afterwards to Atticus in a similar vein: 'If only I can manage to finish what I have started. For, as you realize, I have taken on a large and ambitious enterprise that needs a great deal of time, which is precisely what I most lack.'[21]

A letter of November 54 gives a more detailed account of the work.[22] Two of the nine books planned were already finished, Cicero writes to his brother, comprising a conversation held shortly before the death of the younger Scipio, with Laelius and others participating. Then his friend Sallust (not the later historian, but someone otherwise unknown of the same name) had advised him to include himself in the dialogue, in order to give the subject more weight, as Aristotle had done. This suggestion had appealed to Cicero, since he would then be able to refer to contemporary upheavals. He would therefore adopt a different approach and introduce himself and his brother as figures in the dialogue. Apparently Cicero soon changed his mind again: the setting remained that associated with the younger Scipio, but the number of books was reduced to six.

What became of the work during the next two and a half years is not known. On one occasion Cicero assures his brother Quintus that he had totally withdrawn into private life: 'litterae me et studia nostra et otium villaeque delectant' – 'my academic studies and a leisurely life on my estates give me a great deal of pleasure.'[23] It is at any rate certain that Cicero laboured for three years over the dialogue *De Republica*, a longer period than he had spent on any other of his works. Whereas he had been familiar from his youth with the substance of *De Oratore*, here he had to prepare himself for the subject through wide reading and thorough research. Evidently he was barely able to complete the work before leaving Rome to take up his post as governor of Cilicia. His friend Caelius reported to him at the end of May 51: 'Everybody is talking about your book on political theory.'[24]

As Cicero once succinctly put it, the work is a 'sermo ... de optimo statu civitatis et de optimo cive' – 'a discourse on the best possible condition of the state and on the best citizen.'[25] By his ideal of the *optimus civis* Cicero means the leading statesman; he is repeating from a different angle what he had already tried to express with his notion of the orator perfectus. In both works the main figure is linked to the ideal as its embodiment: Crassus stands in the same relation to the orator perfectus as Scipio to the optimus civis. We would not be far wrong in assuming that Cicero intended, through these cyphers – the ideals and the figures incorporating them – to hint at his own person. He, the 'perfect speaker', would also have had the temerity to stand at the head of the Roman state as its 'finest citizen'. Since reality wore a different aspect, since it withheld from him all that he had expected and aspired to, he tried to make clear to his contemporaries in literary fictions what he might have meant to them. At the same time, these works conveyed an implicit appeal. The dialogues of the 50s, with their mood of mingled hope and despair, were designed not only as a kind of surrogate action to help the author overcome grave disappointments; they also appealed to the sense of responsibility of his contemporaries and were a final attempt to point the way to better things.

De Republica, which would have been worthy to have been bequeathed to posterity as one of the great legacies of the political thought of the ancient world, like Plato's *Politeia* and St Augustine's *City of God*, has come down to us in fragmentary form only, and the greater part of these remnants did not come to light until the beginning of the nineteenth century. In late antiquity the work was still being eagerly studied, particularly by the Church Fathers, Lactantius, Ambrosius and Augustine – and then it perished. The early Middle Ages had no idea of what to make of a subject so remote from the medieval world. Only the conclusion was preserved. There, whatever went beyond the range of rational argument was embodied in the metaphor of a myth devised for the purpose, on the Platonic model. Its speculative and eschatalogical content prompted the Neoplatonic writer Macrobius (fifth century) to compile a detailed commentary on Cicero's myth, so that both the text of the *Somnium Scipionis* (*Scipio's Dream*) and the commentary have been preserved. In 1820 a palimpsest consisting of two overwritten parchment sheets was discovered in the Vatican library. The original text was still fairly legible, and it transpired that these pages contained about a quarter of Cicero's work, mainly disjointed passages from books I–III.

The dialogue takes place in Scipio's garden in the year 129 BC, shortly before Scipio's death, and during a festival lasting three days. Scipio is the central figure; facing grave signs of crisis (it is only four years since the revolution instigated by Tiberius Gracchus), he is discussing in a circle of friends the question of how a state should be constituted so as to be the best possible. Whereas Cicero had reverted to his youth for the background to *De Oratore*, this time he chose a setting that antedated his youth by a whole generation and that, nevertheless, belonged to him – in two senses, in fact. For one thing, it was the advent of Tiberius Gracchus that had made manifest the distresses of the Roman Republic. The dialogue took place against the same horizon of the great crisis that beset Cicero, so that his readers could relate to their own time the fears and hopes which he put into the mouths of his characters. For another thing, with his choice of setting he had returned to the origins of the tradition which had essentially set the seal on his intellectual constitution and his political ideas. For both Crassus, the orator, and Cicero's tutor, the lawyer Scaevola the Augur, had links with Scipio's circle. Scaevola was the son-in-law of Scipio's lifelong friend Laelius, while Crassus was married to Mucia, one of Scaevola's daughters. Cicero may have considerably exaggerated the actual facts and endowed his Scipio with a number of fictitious features, but two essential characteristics of his existence seem to have their roots here – his love of Greek culture and his conception of a moderately conservative policy. In the case of Scipio, as a friend of the historian Polybius and the philosopher Panaetius, and a man who emphatically dissociated himself from the deeds of his brother-in-law Tiberius Gracchus, one of these characteristics is just as significant as the other.

The first couple of books, which are the best preserved sections, place abstract argument and historical model side by side, as was the case in *De Oratore*. The first book is devoted to the general proposition that the so-called mixed constitution – a system combining elements of monarchy, aristocracy and democracy – is best calculated to guarantee ideal circumstances. In the second book the correctness of this proposition is demonstrated through the example of Rome. The first book deploys a conceptual apparatus that was derived from Greek constitutional philosophy and that had already been applied to Rome by Polybius. It is mainly in the second book that Cicero's own contribution makes its appearance. The constitutional history of Rome is here interpreted as a deliberate process leading step by step from the domination of the monarchy at the beginning of the age of kings to an increasingly balanced relationship between monarchical, aristocratic and democratic elements, as represented by the interaction of officials, the Senate and the popular assembly. Through his mode of thought, which adroitly subordinates phenomena to a teleological principle, Cicero shows himself to be a Hegelian before the term existed. In this he was outdone a generation later by Virgil, whose *Aeneid* spans the entire era from Aeneas, the mythical ancestor of the Romans, down to the Emperor Augustus – an enterprise that was more audacious but a good deal less inhibited by historical facts.

In the depressing years of the 50s Cicero was probably working on a third dialogue, *De Legibus* (*On Laws*) – on the model of Plato, who had also followed his *Republic* with *Laws*. The work was perhaps never completed, which explains why Cicero thought it not worth mentioning. And *De Legibus* appeared only after his death. Its passage through the ages effectively reduced this torso still further to the two and half books that still exist. The dialogue is set in the present and involves Cicero himself, his brother Quintus and Atticus. Cicero's native Arpinum provides the background. The work opens with some general observations on natural law, which are probably based on a Stoic source, and then proceeds to deal with Roman religious and constitutional law. The Roman criteria, although considerably modified by Cicero, are compared with the standards set by natural law and declared to be identical with the latter. Cicero thus tries once more to combine Greek theory and Roman practice. He does not succeed in this case without begging the question: after all, has not the Roman component been trimmed to fit the purpose of the demonstration?

'Privata modo et domestica nos delectant' – 'Only my private life affords me any sort of pleasure', Cicero writes to Atticus, with the dismal political circumstances in the autumn of 54 in mind.[26] As the context suggests, he is thinking of his studies, his estates, his family and his closest friends. There is no lack of evidence in the letters from these years that Cicero applied himself diligently to his private affairs. Thus, it is with some satisfaction that he writes to Atticus from Antium, where he had kept an impressive library of books even before his exile, that his home had acquired a soul since his amanuensis had put the library in order.[27] Nothing could be more handsome than the shelves recommended by Atticus, with the scrolls of his books and their title-pages.

A friend by the name of Marcus Fadius Gallus, an Epicurean, often helped in acquiring the statues that Cicero needed to adorn the reception rooms of his country houses. In a fairly lengthy letter, however, he expresses himself as highly dissatisfied with transactions conducted by his agent.[28] Fadius had acquired works on his behalf which did not appeal to him – as regards either price or subject. His objections reveal the criteria which guided his choice: works of art must harmonize with his character and his environment. Fadius had compared some Bacchic women he had bought with certain statues of the Muses: 'In the first place I would never have thought that those Muses were all that valuable – and the Muses would have agreed – but, at any rate they would have been suitable for my library and for my literary labours, but where would I find room in my home for Bacchic revellers?' Cicero expressed a similar view about a statue of Mars: 'What am I to do with it, man of peace that I am?'

Piso, Tullia's husband, had done his utmost to have his father-in-law recalled from exile, but he had died shortly before Cicero came home. In the spring Cicero arranged for the widow, who was about twenty years old, to be engaged to a young man, Furius Crassipes, a member of an old patrician family which, however, no longer had much standing. The marriage probably took place shortly afterwards, but it was dissolved by divorce several years later – we do not know exactly why.

Cicero's brother Quintus had spent the winter of 57–6 in Sardinia, where he had acted as adjutant to Pompey, who had been made responsible for the supply of grain through a law enacted by the popular assembly. Subsequently Quintus seems to have lived in Rome and on his estates. It was at this time that Cicero dedicated *De Oratore* to him. Idleness does not seem to have been to Quintus's liking; in any case, he was burdened with debt. He sought relief from both these problems by moving to Gaul in 54 and enlisting in Caesar's service. During his first winter there his competence was severely tested. Ambiorix, the prince of the Eburones, a tribe dwelling between the Meuse and the Rhine, had instigated a rising in which a Roman force numbering a legion and a half had instantly perished. This success encouraged the Nervi, the neighbouring tribe to the west, likewise to take up arms. This was the area where Quintus Cicero was stationed with his legion. In the fifth book of his *Gallic War* Caesar recounts how Quintus in his winter camp defied the enemy's superior forces until he – Caesar – learned of his subordinate's plight and marched out to relieve him.[29] His account suggests that Quintus acquitted himself with distinction. He fared less well during the following summer, when Caesar was leading a punitive expedition against the Eburones. Quintus, who had been entrusted with the defence of headquarters, was attacked and managed to hold the camp only with great difficulty, losing the troops whom, without any real justification, he had sent out to forage for grain.

Among the letters which Cicero sent to his brother, first in Sardinia, and then in Gaul (books 2 and 3 of the surviving collection) the first letter of the third book stands out particularly. It begins with a detailed report of an inspection Cicero had made of Quintus's estates, describing the progress of various building projects. The passage clearly illustrates the pains which the *grands seigneurs* of the time took to maintain, embellish and improve their country residences. Cicero starts with a villa called Arcanum (Hideout); there, a water main under construction was almost finished and giving satisfactory service. On a plot of land recently purchased and called Manilianum after the previous owner, the architect's slowness was giving grounds for complaint. Cicero notes that the bathroom, the colonnade and the aviary are still not finished (aviaries were very much the fashion with the wealthy at the time), and he comments in detail on the porticoes, the pillars, the floors and so on. Then it is the turn of another newly acquired estate called Fufidianum, a shady place suitable for summer residence, but Quintus should consider adding a fish-pond, a fountain and an exercise ground. The plot of land in Bovillae (on the Appian Way, a few miles from Rome) is discussed only as the possible subject of a sale. Finally there is the Laterium, an estate not far from the Appian Way, but situated rather more to the south. Here it is a question of the access road, which leaves something to be desired at one point. The house definitely needs the extensions planned by Quintus. At the moment, Cicero says, it seems like a philosopher accusing the other villas of being unduly lavish.

The letters to Gaius Trebatius Testa demonstrate for the first time with exemplary clarity the scintillating intellectual brilliance and wit of which Cicero was capable in the company of friends, when he was in a cheerful mood. These letters occupy almost half of the seventh book of the collection *Ad Familiares* and mostly come from the years 54 and 53. Trebatius, probably descended from a family of knights, was a lawyer. Cicero had made the acquaintance of this knowledgeable young man as a congenial companion, and proposed to take him with him and to promote his interests if ever he himself were to achieve an office of state. In the spring of 54 he sent him to Caesar to seek his fortune, giving him a flattering testimonial. Trebatius, having been accepted as one of Caesar's advisers, did not find it easy to settle down and no doubt thought he was not being promoted quickly enough, for which Cicero rebuked him in a humorously paternal tone. His letters to

Trebatius tend to be couched in a relaxed and teasing style, but they also reveal how high an opinion he has of Trebatius, and how it is only for the sake of his advancement that he has been prepared to dispense with his presence in Rome. Thus, we read on one occasion:

> I have read your letter and gathered from it that our Caesar thinks you are a high-powered lawyer. You have every reason to be pleased that you have found your way into places where people believe that you know a thing or two. If you'd gone as far as Britain [where Caesar had just embarked on a campaign], truly, no one on that huge island would have been smarter than you.[30]

And so it goes on, with parodies of legal prolixity and judicial authorities being quoted in support of banal advice to guard against the cold with the help of a good open fire. Towards the end, however, Cicero writes:

> Please be quite sure: the only reason I find it rather easier to come to terms with your absence is that you are profiting by it; if that's not so, then there are no greater fools than the two of us – I, because I don't call you back to Rome, and you, because you don't hasten back of your own accord.

Trebatius survived the trying times of the civil war unscathed, possibly because of his cheerful, equitable disposition, and died at a ripe old age in 4 AD. As four letters from 44 BC show, his relationship with Cicero remained unbroken, although Trebatius was Caesar's man. Indeed, Cicero dedicated a brief essay on rhetoric, *Topica*, to Trebatius.

The collection of letters under the title *Ad Quintum Fratrem* breaks off at the end of 54, and the *Ad Atticum* collection is interrupted for two and a half years, so that there is very little correspondence from 53 and 52. There are, however, a number of letters to the youthful Gaius Scribonius Curio that are worth noting.[31] Various features remind us of the correspondence with Trebatius. In both cases Cicero is conversing with a highly gifted individual living abroad who is his junior by twenty years – Curio was quaestor in the province of Asia. The comparison also reveals one major difference. Whereas politics plays no part in the letters to the mild-mannered, unpolitical lawyer Trebatius, this is in fact the main theme of the letters to the spirited hothead Curio. In Rome everything is topsy-turvy and there is a general expectation (*exspectatio* is the leitmotif in this sequence of letters) that Curio will be a stalwart supporter of the Optimates. No doubt he really did have a brilliantly promising career before him. On the other hand, as a friend of Clodius and Caelius, and also of Antony, the future triumvir, he belonged to the feckless *jeunesse dorée* of the time. After his return from Asia he pursued strictly the policy of the Optimates, as Cicero had hoped. In 50 BC, however, he was suborned by Caesar, who paid his debts, and he became the spokesman of Caesar's party in the negotiations preceding the outbreak of the civil war. The historian Velleius Paterculus called him a 'homo ingeniosissime nequam', 'a scamp but a genius'.[32]

Above all, Cicero expected that Curio would take the lead among those who were supporting Milo's candidature for the consulship in 52. It was already July 53, and no officials had been appointed, since Pompey, who was aiming at a dictatorship, simply allowed matters to take their course. This pernicious ploy was repeated during the campaign for office in the succeeding year: obstruction, bribery and intimidation dominated the scene on an unprecedented scale. Milo, who was bent on pursuing a constitutional policy as visualized by the Senate, was attacked by Clodius and not acceptable to Pompey; his chances of success were correspondingly slim. In the course of a Senate meeting Clodius accused Milo of being heavily in debt and hence not worthy to hold the office of consul. Cicero responded with his *Enquiry Regarding Milo's Debts* (*Interrogatio de Aere Alieno Milonis*), a violent attack on Clodius, of which only the odd word or two has come down to us. There was no sequel to this episode. On 1 January 52 the Roman state was once again without duly appointed officers, and no one could foresee an end to the anarchy which was being exploited, by Pompey in particular, as a means of coercion.

Then something happened which speeded up the train of events considerably and led ultimately to the climax of Pompey's special powers and the agreement between him and the Senate, the most significant preliminary to civil war. It also proved to be a turning-point for Cicero, in that it roused him from his reluctant apathy and impelled him to bold and independent action. On 18 January a bloody clash occurred on the Appian Way, about twelve miles south of Rome, between the followers of Clodius and those of Milo, and Clodius was killed. The murder instantly provoked violent riots: the followers of Clodius carried his body into the Curia and cremated it there on a pyre constructed from benches and platforms. The Curia itself was destroyed in the flames. Since elections were more than ever out of the question, the Senate resolved to declare a state of emergency, and Pompey was granted plenary powers to recruit troops throughout Italy. Pompey was now negotiating for a special appointment to cope with the situation, with the Senate party led by Cato on the one hand, and with Caesar on the other. The result was a constitutional freak, a 'consul sine collega', i.e. a thinly veiled dictatorship.

Pompey now took vigorous action. The draft legislation he proposed included a special law against violence – designed to ensure the rapid conviction of Milo. In spite of vehement opposition in the Senate it was passed by the popular assembly, and a special tribunal was instituted. Cicero felt a powerful sense of obligation towards Milo – after all, it was Milo's private army which had prepared the way for his return – so that he had to undertake Milo's defence. By this act he placed himself in opposition to the aims of his influential 'friends', Pompey and Caesar, as he had not done since the spring of 56, when he had persuaded the Senate to schedule a debate on the Capuan marches. At the same time, the adherents of Clodius – among them the historian Sallust – tried to make life more difficult for Cicero by their inflammatory speeches.

Milo's trial began on 4 April. Disorders gave Pompey a welcome pretext to cordon off the forum with his troops. On 8 April, the day when proceedings were to be wound up, the shops were closed, the army was in control of all the approaches to the forum, and Pompey was standing by in the immediate neighbourhood. After the prosecution had submitted their case, it was Cicero's turn to speak. Because of the limited time available for speeches he was the only counsel for the defence. But the show of military force and the clamour instantly unleashed by Clodius's party unnerved him: he presented his case nervously and incoherently. Defeat was inevitable: 38 judges out of 54 found Milo guilty, and the convicted man at once went into exile in Massilia.

The speech, together with all its shortcomings, was recorded by a stenographer as delivered and it was still possible to read it a hundred and fifty years later. Subsequent tradition, however, has preserved only what Cicero himself instantly submitted to the public, a rather more polished summary of what he would have said had he not been intimidated at the time by the manifest signs of terrorism and dictatorship. He is said to have sent Milo a copy of his completed masterpiece. Milo is reported to have replied that he thought himself lucky – if Cicero had spoken as well as this before the court, then he, Milo, would not now be in a position to enjoy barbel of a quality to be found only in Massilia.[33]

Cicero was not discouraged by his defeat in the Milo trial. He obviously thought that there was some sense in resisting the will of those in power, since developments were slowly but consistently moving towards a reconciliation between Pompey and the Senate. The incident on the Appian Way and its repercussions unleashed a veritable storm of lawsuits in which Cicero participated to his utmost ability. To begin with, he succeeded in gaining two acquittals for one of Milo's followers named Marcus Saufeius. On the other hand, a man from the opposing party, the former tribune Titus Munatius Plancus Bursa, was convicted in a trial in which Cicero had appeared for the prosecution. This success afforded Cicero a great deal of satisfaction. He and the judges had managed to foil Pompey, who had gone to great lengths to intervene in the trial on behalf of Bursa. Cicero, liberated from the dilemma in which he had found himself for years as an accomplice of the triumvirate, experienced a powerful sense of exhiliration – and rightly so, because, in standing up for Milo, he had shown himself to be not only a loyal friend but also a courageous citizen. In one of the few letters from 52 he hints, in connection with Bursa's conviction and not without some satisfaction, that he once again feels he belongs to the boni, the good men and true: 'And I was particularly glad that they gave me so much support in the face of the incredible influence brought to bear by his high and mighty lordship.'[34]

The Governorship of Cilicia

Sulla had ordained that the consuls and praetors should remain in Rome during their year of office and then govern a province in the following year. This arrangement was changed by Pompey in 52 BC: the consuls and praetors were permitted to depart to their provinces only after an interval of five years at the earliest. In assigning governorships, therefore, the Senate had to have recourse to officials from earlier years. This explains why Cicero, who had been employed in the provincial administration merely as a quaestor, was enlisted. In 51 BC he received instructions to assume the governorship of Cilicia for one year.

Cilicia proper was a region in the south-east of Asia Minor (opposite Cyprus), which was bordered on the west by Pamphylia, on the north by Lycaonia and Cappadocia, and on the east by Syria. Between Cappadocia and Cilicia rise the Taurus mountains, while the Amanos range runs between Syria and Cilicia. The western part was known as the Cilician uplands, and here the mountains ran right down to the sea. High quality timber for shipbuilding was produced here, but it was also the haunt of pirates who caused the Romans a good deal of trouble. The eastern part, the Cilician lowlands, is a coastal plain traversed by rivers; there, agriculture flourished, partly on the basis of artificial irrigation.

Like the whole of Persia, the region fell to Alexander the Great and his successors; for the most part it belonged to the empire of the Seleucides. In the second century BC their authority declined and bands of pirates found a haven there, from which they spread terror throughout large areas of the Mediterranean. This was where the Romans came on the scene: Marcus Antonius fought the pirates, established the province of Cilicia, and celebrated a triumph (in the years 102–1). It was in this campaign that Marcus Gratidius, the brother of Cicero's grandmother on his father's side, was killed. The Romans' success did not last long; the pirates were soon once more sallying out on the high seas, from Cilicia and also from Crete. An eminent victim of their depredations in the year 75 was the youthful Caesar. Following various ineffectual attempts to cope with this pest, it was Pompey who finally restored order – with the aid of the plenary powers secured for him by Gabinius's law. The captured pirates were treated with relative leniency: Pompey made them settle down permanently, partly in the Cilician town of Soli, known for its 'solecisms' – a Greek dialect corrupted by a mixture of other languages.

Cicero's province extended westwards, far beyond the bounds of Cilicia proper. It included Lycaonia and Pamphylia and stretched as far as Laodicea on the River Lycus, which was only 100 miles from Ephesus. Besides, the island of Cyprus also belonged to Cicero's administrative area. The strength and quality of his troops – two depleted legions – left a great deal to be desired. This worried Cicero, especially because Crassus had recently provoked a war with the Parthians, and Syria and Cilicia were now seriously threatened. Cicero had competent officers to assist him, including his brother Quintus, who had already been tested in combat, so that this made up for his own lack of military skills. His personal staff also included his son Marcus and his nephew Quintus, as well as Tiro, his secretary, whose freedom he had purchased some years earlier.

From the outset Cicero regarded the governorship which had been imposed on him as an onerous duty and he was anxiously concerned that it should last no longer than the year which the Senate had ordained. An unusually large number of letters have been preserved from the year and a half of his absence from Rome. Two and a half volumes are addressed to Atticus, then there is the correspondence with his young friend Caelius, the letters to his predecessor in office, Appius Claudius Pulcher, which take up the whole of the third book in the collection *Ad Familiares*, the letters to the Senate, to Cato and to other Optimates, which occupy two thirds of the fifteenth book, and sundry other items. In all these letters no theme recurs as frequently as the wish, the request, the admonition to the recipient that he should do everything in his power to ensure that the governorship was not extended. It was at this time that the devious dispute about Caesar's successor in Gaul broke out. Cicero feared, not without justification, that the wrangling about the allocation of provinces might delay his discharge.

It seems that he looked on his governorship almost as a second spell of exile, so obsessed was he with the date of his return. We are reminded of his exile, too, by the total lack of that philosophical composure which he had once enjoined on his brother, who had been to obliged to endure his post for three long years.[1] Nor was he able, it seems, to apply to himself the point which he had made to his brother, namely that a long spell as governor, provided it was conscientiously carried out, afforded all the more satisfaction and renown. 'It is unbelievable how this job disgusts me', he writes to Atticus on his arrival in Laodicea, 'the field is not wide enough for the broad sweep of my mind and for my zeal, which are not altogether unfamiliar to you.'[2] He believed that he could only really live in Rome: 'The light, the forum, the city, my home, I miss them all', he goes on in the same letter. 'The city, the city, my Rufus', we read in a letter to Caelius, 'that is what I respect, see that you keep your place in *that* light! Ever since my youth I have been convinced that any time spent abroad is dreary and dismal for anyone who is capable of making his fortune in Rome by dint of unremitting hard work!'[3]

This attitude obviously had a considerable influence on the content of his letters. Neither the countries nor the nations he saw, neither geographical nor ethnographical observations found their way into them. He seems to have been blind to distinctive features of the landscape, and he did not think it worth his while to record a single anecdote or a single curiosity in the letters from the period of his governorship, which were otherwise often very detailed. On the other hand, he was keenly interested in events in Rome, not only in politics and court cases, but also in gossip and scandal. On his departure he enjoined his young friend Caelius to inform him in the greatest possible detail about all *res urbanae*. Caelius was not at all remiss in this respect: the eighth book of the collection *Ad Familiares* includes seventeen letters from him to Cicero, most of them from the period of his governorship.

Cicero set off on 1 May 51. The rapid sequence of letters to Atticus leaves us in no doubt about the route he followed. First of all, he went round inspecting most of his estates: Tusculanum and the farms he owned near Arpinum and Cumae and in the neighbourhood of Pompeii. He then continued his journey on the Appian Way via Benevento and Venusia, the birthplace of Horace, to Tarentum, where he arrived on 18 May. There he had lengthy political discussions with Pompey. By this time fear of a civil was widely prevalent, and Cicero sums up his impression of Pompey as follows: 'I left him as an irreproachable citizen resolutely determined to avert what we are afraid of.'[4] Cicero was delayed for a time in Brundisium because of a slight indisposition, and he disembarked in Actium on 14 June. The group was now on provincial territory and at liberty to billet themselves on the local inhabitants, but, even so, Cicero impressed on his people that he insisted they should be as modest as possible in their demands. On 25 June Cicero arrived in Athens. Apart from Rome, this was about the only place on earth where he felt at his ease; he extolled the city, its buildings and its inhabitants.[5] An Epicurean by the name of Patron called on him. It seemed that Gaius Memmius, the erstwhile governor of Bithynia, known to us through Catullus, was living in exile in Athens; he proposed to tear down the house where Epicurus had lived in order to erect a new building on the site. At Patron's request, Cicero wrote Memmius a courteous letter, asking him not to carry out his plan.[6] From 6 until 22 July Cicero was travelling by sea via Delos and Samos to Ephesus. There, the local inhabitants as well as the tax-collectors gave him a cordial welcome. In view of this event, Cicero resolved to satisfy all those concerned. The final stage of the journey followed after a stay of four days. Cicero arrived in Laodicea on the River Lycus, the principal town of his administrative area, exactly three months after his departure from Rome.

His schedule was adapted to the facts as they existed. He intended to join his troops and use the rest of the summer for military operations; he would then devote himself to judicial matters during the winter. To begin with, military operations were overshadowed by the Parthian peril. Caelius is certainly expressing Cicero's view when he writes:

> I cannot tell how much trouble you are having in keeping the peace in your province and in the adjoining regions, but I at least am very worried. For if only we could arrange matters in such a way that a war ensues which can be dealt with by the forces you have, and if we could only achieve enough to secure your reputation and a triumph, without becoming involved in a difficult and dangerous conflict, then nothing could be more desirable. In fact, as I well know, if the Parthian once stirs himself to action, the struggle will be a pretty serious business; your army is barely capable of defending a single pass.[7]

Caelius goes on to add that no one in Rome is worried; they were expecting him to do the job as if they had supplied him with everything he needed. Even four months later, towards the end of 51, Caelius still seems to be concerned: it is said that the Parthians have crossed the Euphrates.[8] Given the weakness of his forces, Cicero will have no choice but to retreat.

Matters took a more favourable course, however. Cicero's troops were mustered near Iconium in Lycaonia, where he arrived in the middle of August. He moved on to Cybistra near the Taurus mountains, from where, according to the situation, he could either advance north-eastwards into Cappadocia (should the Parthians appear there), or south-eastwards across the Taurus range into Cilicia proper. He was at first very worried and wrote to the Senate asking for urgent reinforcements. He then learned, however, that the Parthians' threat was directed more at the south. They were advancing on Antioch, where they were at once defeated by Gaius Cassius Longinus, deputy to the governor of Syria, and hence forced to retreat. The danger from the Parthians had been averted for the time being.

Cicero's administrative and judicial functions were based on an edict which every governor – on the analogy of the praetors in Rome – issued at the beginning of his period of office, usually adopting the major part of his predecessor's edict. In Cicero's edict, two sections sufficed: the first concerned matters of general public law and regulated the financial and fiscal practices of the local authorities; the second dealt with particularly important issues of civil law and civil litigation – the law of inheritance and of bankruptcy. As far as the rest of the civil law was concerned, Cicero referred to the edicts of the urban praetors in Rome. It was on the basis of these guidelines that Cicero proposed to administer his province justly and impartially: *iustitia, abstinentia, clementia* (justice, probity, clemency) were the principles to which he subscribed.[9]

In this respect his governorship differed markedly from that of his predecessor, Appius Claudius Pulcher. This mettlesome Optimatis, a brother of the notorious Clodius, had followed the usual practice of despoliation. Cicero was instantly besieged with complaints. 'I don't propose to tear open the wounds left by Appius', he writes shortly after his arrival in Laodicea, 'but they are too obvious to be concealed.'[10] In the letter to Atticus which follows, Cicero deals in more detail with these wounds:

> You should know that on 31 July I arrived in my unhappy – and doubtless irrevocably ruined – province, where I was ardently awaited, and then spent three days in each of the three municipalities, Laodicea, Apameia and Synnada. There I heard over and over again that they cannot pay the poll tax levied on them, that they have sold everything that could be sold – I have heard the groans and lamentations of the municipal authorities and learned of atrocities that seemed to be the work of some abominable beast rather than a human being.[11]

After the departure of a governor it was customary for his subjects to dispatch a delegation to Rome in his honour, the costs being borne by the municipalities. When Cicero heard that it was proposed to follow this practice in the case of Appius Claudius, he ruled that no delegation paid for by the local community was to depart without his authority. No wonder that Appius Claudius was anything but enthusiastic about his successor's proposed measures: the third book of the *Ad Familiares* collection offers graphic evidence of this. To begin with, and during Cicero's journey to the province, there is talk of Appius Claudius ensuring that everything is kept in proper order for his successor. Besides, Cicero wished to have a meeting with his predecessor in office, and he chose a route conforming to the latter's wishes. In the sixth letter, for the first time, there is a trace of irritation in the correspondence, which had hitherto been conducted in terms of exquisite politeness and larded with affirmations of friendship. Appius had failed to turn up for a meeting in Laodicea, he was said to be away on official business. Moreover, Cicero did not know where three detachments of his troops were stationed. Appius Claudius no doubt behaved in this way because he was annoyed by the measures Cicero had taken, of which he was fully informed. He went on avoiding Cicero, and when he left the province, he passed Cicero's camp during the night.

He also sharply criticized his successor's policy in his letters, and his criticism was repudiated with equal asperity. The main issue in this ill-tempered exchange, which was couched in terms of strained politeness, was the matter of ceremonial delegations. Cicero writes that he had relieved the municipalities of this needless expense because he had been requested to do so by their leaders.[12] 'It was not only a love of justice but also compassion which moved me to ease the distress of these ruined communities – ruined, indeed, by their own officers; I could not afford to be negligent in regard to such pointless expenditure.' Cicero is sufficiently discreet to place the main blame for the municipalities' distress on corrupt indigenous officials, but terms like 'iustitia' and 'clementia' were certainly alien to Appius. The tone of Cicero's letter becomes positively ironic towards the end, when he compares his correspondent's generosity with his own nature, which had always been wary of generosity at the expense of other people's property.[13]

Did Appius Claudius sense that he was Cicero's moral inferior in the dispute? However that may be, Cicero' next letter sounds more conciliatory, apparently because Appius Claudius had given way: 'So I have at last had the chance to read a letter', he writes, 'that is worthy of

Appius Claudius: full of humane feeling, helpfulness and consideration.'[14] That this conciliatory attitude was largely dictated by diploma-
tic considerations, is shown in a long letter to Atticus written at almost
the same time: 'Appius is behaving as if a doctor, whose patient has
been transferred to one of his colleagues, were to be angry because the
latter had altered the previous treatment here and there. After using
withdrawal therapy on the province, after letting its blood and depriving it of everything he could take from it, and handing it over to me at
death's door, he disapproves because I wish it to recover.'[15]

Cicero left Cybistra together with his troops after it had become
known that the Parthians would not advance via Cappadocia. He
crossed the Taurus mountains and pushed on via Tarsus and Mopsuestia in the direction of the Amanos mountains which marked the frontier
between Cilicia and Syria (now called Gâvur Daglari). His target was
the mountain tribes, the Eleuthorocilicians who were settled there, who
had never been subdued by the Romans and who could easily obstruct
communications with the neighbouring province of Syria. Cicero
ordered four columns to be formed which combed through the mountains, burned down a handful of villages and fortifications, and put the
inhabitants to the sword, or else took them prisoner. Only one of
Cicero's officers, Pomptinus, who commanded one of the columns, was
engaged in actions lasting several hours. The troops then re-formed and
set up camp near Issus, where altars erected by Alexander recalled the
battle that had been fought there in 333 BC.

Since the Second Punic War it had been customary for victorious
commanders to be hailed as 'imperator' by their troops, and anyone
who received this honorific title could claim the right to celebrate a
triumph. Following Issus Cicero was entitled to regard himself as imperator in this informal sense, and Asiatic coins have been preserved on
which the abbreviation 'imp.' features alongside Cicero's name. In his
heart of hearts Cicero was certainly aware that such laurels counted for
very little. 'You don't realize', he writes jocularly to a friend, Lucius
Papirius Paetus, 'what sort of a general [imperator] you're dealing with.
From start to finish of the campaign I was able to apply the *Cyropaedia*,
which I had devoured from cover to cover.'[16] This was a work by
Xenophon, a biography of the Persian King Cyrus in the form of a
novel embodying a great deal of military lore.

In the late autumn Cicero delivered a second blow against the
Eleutherocilicians: the mountain fortress of Pindenissus was invested
and forced to capitulate on 13 December after a siege lasting two
months. These were merry saturnalia for the troops, writes Cicero.[17] He

had handed over the entire booty to them, apart from the horses, adding – without any reference to clementia – that the sale of prisoners to slave-traders had so far brought in 120,000 sesterces. After concluding this operation Cicero instructed his brother to lead the troops into winter quarters; he himself proceeded to Tarsus, where the Governor of Cilicia had his official residence.

During the winter and spring Cicero busied himself with the civil administration, especially with judicial matters. A few months previously he had reckoned such activities to be inappropriate to his abilities, but now he began to realize that they did have aspects which appealed to him. 'I have never felt such a sense of satisfaction in my whole life', he writes to Atticus, 'as that which I derive from the correct discharge of my official duties, and it is not the renown, which is after all considerable, but the business itself which I like. Why did you ask? It was well worth while. I didn't know myself, I wasn't aware of what I could achieve in this area. I am justly proud of myself: nothing could be finer.'[18] His administration was keen to economize, even on admissible expenditure. He respected the autonomy of the local courts and did his best to keep the debts of the local authorities within bounds.

One affair is discussed at length in a number of letters.[19] The town of Salamis in Cyprus had taken out a loan with Marcus Iunius Brutus, who was to be Caesar's assassin. The interest was to amount to 4 per cent per month. Brutus asked Cicero to help his agents collect his money by granting them commissions in the army. Cicero declined to allow this abuse of official authority for private purposes. He also drew Brutus's attention to his edict, by which interest of more than 1 per cent per month was prohibited, and tried to arrange a compromise between the parties. The matter remained unsettled, however. Out of consideration for Brutus Cicero was not prepared to enforce a judgement in which only the sum permitted by the stipulated interest rate could be legally claimed. Here, then, there was a limit to Cicero's passion for justice: the interests of a member of his own class could not simply be overlooked.

Besides his problems as governor, Cicero had a number of family matters to think about and to deal with. His brother's marriage to Pomponia, Atticus's sister, was still not a happy one, and he tried to act as mediator between the parties. As he was leaving for his province he had witnessed an ugly quarrel between husband and wife, and he reports this to his friend with singular precision so as to suggest that it was Pomponia who was the cause of the trouble.[20] In Cilicia Quintus was wondering whether to draw the logical conclusion and to send

Pomponia a farewell letter. Quintus junior, who was allowed to read his father's correspondence, learned one day of this smouldering dispute. 'The boy was, as I could see, deeply distressed', Cicero writes, 'and he was in tears as he told me his sorry tale. In short, I realized that he has an uncommonly loving heart, which encourages me in the hope that nothing unseemly will happen.'[21] Indeed, a few weeks later, Cicero was able to inform his friend that young Quintus had reconciled his father and mother.[22] Another family problem crops up in letters to Atticus or, rather, it is hinted at here and there: Tullia and Crassipes had dissolved their marriage and Cicero was looking round for an appropriate suitor for his daughter. What the precise details were, we cannot tell, because Cicero deliberately speaks in very vague terms, but apparently a number of interested parties were being considered. Finally, Terentia took the initiative, and Tullia became the wife of Publius Cornelius Dolabella. This placed Cicero in a somewhat awkward position. He was well on the way to a reconciliation with Appius Claudius Pulcher, and now he saw himself acting the part of father-in-law to the latter's accuser, so that he was obliged to assert on several occasions that he was in no way responsible for this combination of circumstances. The choice of Dolabella, a notorious rake some eight years younger than Tullia, very soon turned out to be a grave mistake. Dolabella treated his wife with the utmost brutality, and during the civil war he behaved like a fanatical supporter of Caesar.

During the spring of 50 Cicero was concerned that the Parthian peril might detain him in the province beyond his single year of office. The Parthians withdrew from Roman territory, however, and Cicero was justified in leaving the province at the end of July. He entrusted the quaestor Gaius Coelius Caldus with the conduct of affairs and left Tarsus by sea, arriving in Rhodes already on 10 August. Then he got no farther than Ephesus, where he had to wait until October for favourable winds to carry him on to Athens. While he was there he became involved in events in Rome, which were now moving ever closer to civil war. Pompey and Caesar, the twin dictators, who had now fallen out with each other, had both written him friendly letters asking for his support. Whom should he join, supposing it came to an open conflict? Cicero was hoping, moreover, that the Cilician operation would secure him a triumph. After all, he had been accorded a festival of thanksgiving, a *supplicatio*, and he believed he would find sufficient support for a triumph.

In Patrae on the Gulf of Corinth his secretary fell so seriously ill that he had to leave him there with people who were in a position to look

after him. No fewer than eight letters written in the next few days
during his passage to Brundisium show the concern and the care which
he had devoted to the patient.[23] In Brundisium, where he arrived on 24
November, he met Terentia, who had travelled down to welcome him –
he had asked her to do so in a cordial letter he had written her from
Athens.[24] In December he spent some time on his estates, mainly in
Cumanum. On 4 January 49 he reached the city limits of Rome, which,
as a candidate for a triumph, he was not permitted to pass.

Like so many other things, this custom was evidence of the formal-
istic mentality of the Romans, who clung with special tenacity to
outward appearances. Rome was encircled by an inviolable border, the
pomerium. This delimited the areas of the civil and the military authorities respectively. It was the outward and visible sign that senior officials, the consuls, praetors and provincial governors, could exercise
unlimited powers only outside Rome. Senior officials departing for their
provinces exchanged their civilian toga for military garb at the pomerium, and their official bailiffs, the lictors, added to their bundles of rods
the axes that were not tolerated in the city. Correspondingly, senior
officials returning from the provinces turned back into civilians at the
pomerium. By virtue of this act, however, their plenary powers were
abrogated, so that they then lacked an essential precondition for the
triumph, the solemn procession to the Capitol. Anyone who believed
that he had earned the right to a triumph was obliged to wait at the
pomerium for the Senate's approval – as Cicero did on this occasion.

14

The Civil War

During the years 54–52 the balance of power had shifted decisively against Caesar. His daughter Julia, Pompey's wife, had died giving birth in 54, so that a close bond between the two dictators was broken. Two years later Pompey married the daughter of a radical supporter of the Optimates, Quintus Caecilius Metellus Pius Scipio Nasica. He was the natural son of Scipio Nasica, but had been adopted by Quintus Caecilius Metellus Pius, hence his uncommonly clumsy name. In 53 Crassus was killed and there was now no third man to hold the balance. In the following years the dangerous insurrection led by the Gallic prince Vercingetorix absorbed all Caesar's energies.

It was not surprising, then, that Caesar's determined adversaries among the Optimates set about contriving his downfall in the Senate, using political methods that were in fact legally sound. The issue had been clear ever since 52: Caesar wished his governorship of Gaul to be followed immediately by a second term as consul. The Optimates did everything they could to have him recalled to Rome without any official status, so that he could be arraigned before a court. The argument had been carried on ever since 51 against a complex legal background.

Caesar had calculated on the following lines: the prolongation of his governorship of Gaul, which had taken place in 55, meant that the Senate could not nominate a successor to him before March 50. But, as has already been pointed out, it had to be settled before the elections which provinces the consuls designate were to govern during their second, proconsular year of office. Thus, a relevant resolution passed by the Senate after 1 March 50 was bound to refer to the consuls of the year 49, and hence to the governorships in 48. Consequently, Caesar could not be removed from office before 1 January 48. It was on this date, however, that he proposed to assume his second consulship. To this end he had, with the consent of Pompey, obtained a popular resolution that permitted him to stand for the consulship *in absentia.*

So far, so good. But new regulations had undermined this ingenious scheme. The above-mentioned law passed by Pompey, which stipulated a five-year interval between urban office and governorship (the basis of Cicero's Cilician posting), offered a chance of saddling Caesar with a successor in 49. Henceforth, proconsulships were not to be allocated to future, but to former consuls. Besides, a law prohibiting candidacy *in absentia* called in question the special ruling in Caesar's case.

In 51 Caesar's supporters had succeeded in blocking a Senate resolution concerning Gaul. In the following year Curio, who had radically changed his position, intervened adroitly and successfully on behalf of his new master and even induced the Senate to pass a resolution on 1 December recalling Pompey *and* Caesar, a move agreed by Caesar. But now a group of implacable senators led by Cato, together with others, gained the upper hand. As events became more and more critical at the beginning of Jannuary 49, Cicero, who had just arrived on the outskirts of the city, took part in negotiations. However, his disarmament proposals, although agreed by Caesar's people, were not approved by the Optimates. On 7 January Caesar was dismissed and a state of emergency declared; the people's tribunes, Mark Antony and Quintus Cassius Longinus, who tried in vain to protest, escaped and joined Caesar. Civil war was now an established fact.

The *senatus consultum ultimum* had empowered not only the consuls, but also the praetors, the people's tribunes and the proconsuls to take steps to protect the state. Cicero was also involved, since he still had his imperium and was escorted by his twelve lictors as an outward and visible sign of his dignity. He was also given a job to do: he was to keep watch on the coast of Campania. This post provided him with the opportunity he sought to stay away from Rome, on his estate near Formiae, and otherwise to remain inactive. He disliked war and at first he did not abandon hope that peace might be restored. In the course of March, as he began to realize that his desire for peace would not be fulfilled, he took the decision, after a severe inner struggle, to leave Italy, which by now was completely occupied by Caesar. He proposed to join the Senate party, which had set up headquarters in Greece. It was June, however, before he acted on this decision. Succeeding generations were uncommonly well informed about his motives during the period between his return from Cilicia and his clandestine departure for Greece. About ninety letters have survived from these six months, about ninety per cent of them addressed to Atticus: 'Ego tecum tamquam mecum loquor' – I talk to you as if I were talking to myself.'[1] This constant ebb and flow of reflection has the marks of a ceaseless soliloquy.

Cicero believed that war could be avoided; he saw it as the monstrous progeny of unbridled aggression – on both sides, in fact. His efforts to keep the peace, he writes at the beginning of January to Tiro, who was still prostrated by illness in Patrae, had been brought to nothing by the passion of certain individuals: there were warmongers on both sides.[2] 'I myself', he states shortly afterwards, once more writing to Tiro, 'as soon as I arrived before the city, directed all my thoughts, words and actions to preserving the peace, but it was not only wicked individuals who had been seized by a strange madness, but also those who were reckoned to be men of sound principles. They were determined to fight at all costs, although I cried out that nothing was more disastrous than a civil war.' Cicero was prepared for the worst, for famine, pillage and destruction. He once went so far as to state that an unjust peace was preferable to a war, however just, that was waged on one's fellow-citizens.

Understandably, he regarded Caesar as the person mainly responsible. 'You can surely see what sort of a war it is', he writes to Atticus, 'it's a civil war, but it has not been provoked by any dissension between citizens, but rather by the sheer wilfulness of a single depraved individual.'[3] Caesar seems to him like a second Hannibal:

> This insensate wretch who has never glimpsed even the shadow of the beautiful and the good! And he is doing all this for the sake of his dignity. But where is dignity if it is not matched by honour? Is it honourable, then, to maintain an army without the authority of the government, to seize free cities in order to force an entry into one's homeland, to encompass the remission of debts, the recall of exiles, and a thousand other vicious crimes, 'to achieve the supreme divinity, tyranny?' He is welcome to his happy lot! Truly, I prefer a stroll in the sunshine with you to all the kingdoms of this sort![4]

But it is not only Caesar whom Cicero judges by the standards of a strict political morality: Pompey is also taken severely to task. Quoting a passage from his essay *On the State*, to the effect that the welfare of the citizens is the aim of the true statesman, Cicero says: 'Such ideas have never entered the head of our Gnaeus, least of all in the present conflict. Everyone is seeking power for himself alone, rather than the honest welfare of the citizenry.... What Pompey has long been aspiring to is Sulla's kind of despotic regime, and there are many around him who want the same thing.'[5] Since the issue is merely who is to be sole ruler, Cicero believes, Rome faces the prospect of a *malorum* Ἰλιας, an Iliad of disasters.

From the very beginning Cicero reckoned that the Senate party's chances of victory were very slight. 'Caesar should have been resisted while he was still weak', he writes, 'that would have been easy. But now he has eleven legions, as much cavalry as he needs, the population beyond the Po, the city mob, numerous people's tribunes, our incorrigible young folk – and he has all this as a highly respected and intrepid commander.'[6] From Caesar's formidable resources and the rapidity of his advance, Pompey drew the conclusion that Italy could not be held; such troops as he could hurriedly muster he shipped from Brundisium across the Adriatic. Cicero, who had reckoned with a plan of this kind from an early stage, now criticized it severely – unjustifiably so, from a strategic point of view. Here, too, he was inclined to apply moral criteria: 'For heaven's sake, what do you think of Pompey's move – I mean the fact that he has abandoned Rome? I don't know what to think – what could be more absurd? You abandon the city – would you do, the same, if the Gauls were on the way?'[7] Pompey was an ἀστρατήγητος, a non-general, Cicero remarks on one occasion, referring to the retreat from Italy; no one could be more pusillanimous, more panicky than him.[8] 'But our Gnaeus', we read elsewhere, 'it's a crying shame, it's unbelievable how down and out he is! There's no spirit, no plan, no forces, no judgement.'[9]

The letter to Atticus numbered 8, 8 is more or less a general summing-up of events. Pompey had allowed Caesar to grow too powerful and had subsequently disapproved of every offer of a peaceful settlement, but without preparing for war. He then abandoned Rome and Central Italy and set off for Greece. Once, Cicero says, when Caesar came up against resistance on the part of Lucius Domitius Ahenobarbus in Corfinium, about 60 miles east of Rome, Pompey should have had a radiant vision of the καλόν, the beautiful and the honourable. But Pompey had bidden the καλόν farewell, he had left Domitius in the lurch and continued on his way to Brundisium.

In spite of his criticism of Pompey's tactics, Cicero still thought that he was one of the boni, the conservative members of the Senate party or, to be more precise, one of the few boni who were left. For, if one looked round for *ordines*, various groups of conservatives, it turned out that they no longer existed, there were only a few individuals of that persuasion left. 'What do you mean to do, then?' he asks himself through the mouth of Atticus. 'What cattle do when they are stampeded', is the answer, 'run after their own kind. Like a bullock following the other bullocks, I'll run after the conservatives, or those to whom I give that name, even if they fall into a ditch.'[10] With these words Cicero predicted exactly what later happened. 'Don't be surprised', he says a few days later, 'that I am reluctant to join the party that has exerted itself neither for peace nor for victory, but has always thought only in terms of a shameful and disastrous flight. I must be prepared, all the same, to share the fate and fortunes of those who are called conservatives, rather than not be counted among their number.'[11]

Cicero was indeed obliged to avoid this impression. He was not simply an ordinary former consul, but an official with authority (imperium) and a function, which he did not even attempt to carry out. Besides, he was still maintaining friendly relations with Caesar and his accomplices. He wanted to remain neutral, as far as possible, so that he might appear to both parties as a suitable mediator. Trebatius, a supporter of Caesar, appealed to him on his master's behalf to remain close to the city. He had replied, Cicero reports to Atticus, that it was difficult for him to comply at the time, but he was, after all, staying on his estates and taking no part in recruiting troops or in any other martial activities.[12] 'I shall stand by this, as long as there is still a hope of peace', he goes on to tell Atticus, 'but if war does break out, I shall do whatever is required of me by my duty and my position.' At the end of January 49, when Cicero wrote this, negotiations were still in progress between Caesar and Pompey. Shortly afterwards, it became known that he had addressed a letter to Caesar; he was criticized and felt it necessary to justify himself. Caesar thought that he was useful and was wooing him with flattering words. A letter which Balbus, a supporter of Caesar, wrote to him at the beginning of March assured him of Caesar's warmest gratitude. In a letter to Caesar himself in the middle of March Cicero stressed for the last time the part he might play as mediator in achieving a peaceful settlement.[13] He had not so far taken part in military operations, and hence was more suitable than anyone else to participate in negotiations 'de otio, de pace, de concordia civium' – 'on peace and quiet and harmonious relations between citizens'.

In the meantime Caesar had been pursuing military operations with the greatest vigour; by the middle of March, after Pompey had quitted Brundisium with the last of his troops, the whole of Italy was in Caesar's grasp. Even Cicero could no longer ignore the fact that, for the time being, any hope of peace had vanished. He had long been wondering apprehensively what he should do if Pompey abandoned Italy: whether he might remain, or whether he would have to follow suit. As

early as the middle of February a letter to Atticus sums up in a long list
the reasons which seem to him to favour one or the other alternative,
and in letter 9, 4 – writing in Greek – he deduces all sorts of philosophical problems from his personal situation.[14] Whether it was in
order to employ any possible means to eliminate tyranny, even supposing the state should perish in the process; or whether we should beware
of the individual who, having put an end to tyranny, himself rises too
high; or whether, if one's fatherland was ruled by a tyrant, one should
assist by awaiting a favourable moment, by wise counsel, or by war,
and so on.

At the time Cicero was posing these questions, the balance was
inclining more and more towards a decision to escape into the camp of
the Senate party. 'Cautior est mansio, honestior existimatur traiectio' –
'It is safer to stay, but it is deemed more honourable to cross the sea', he
said to himself. It was not the talk of the so-called right-thinking men,
rather his bond with Pompey which governed his decision, he claimed
on another occasion.[15] When he heard the news that Pompey and the
consuls had embarked for Greece, he was beside himself with remorse
at not being there among the boni.[16] Even though he was reassured
by letters from Atticus, who had advised him time and time again to
stay put, he was overwhelmed with distress and αἰσχροῦ φαντασία, a
nightmare of ignominy. In his violent remorse he even went so far as to
draw his metaphors from the sexual sphere:

> What shall I say? I felt as one does when one is in love: just as we are put
> off by women who are slatternly, silly or tactless, so his unseemly flight
> and his negligence caused my love for Pompey to cool. For he did nothing
> that merited my joining him in his flight. Now my love is returning, now
> my longing is insufferable, books don't help me now, nor do studies or
> philosophy. So I gaze out to sea day and night, like that bird, and long to
> fly away.[17]

'That bird' is an allusion to Plato, who had written of Dionysius
imprisoned in Syracuse: 'I look out and long to fly away, like a bird.'[18]
But Cicero had first of all to undergo a severe ordeal: a meeting with
Caesar. A Senate meeting was scheduled for 1 April, and a man like
Cicero, among all the supporters of Caesar who would be present,
might add a little more lustre to the occasion. This was why the great
man not only approached him by letter (which has survived), but also
called on him in Formiae on 28 March as he was hastening from
Brundisium to Rome.[19] Cicero looked forward to the occasion with

some misgivings. But, soon afterwards, when he had survived it, he informed his friend that he had remained firm: 'in eo mansimus, ne ad urbem', – 'I insisted that I would not come to Rome.'[20] Cicero ought to deliver a speech on peace, Caesar suggested. Cicero retorted that he would appeal to the Senate to veto Caesar's moving into Spain or Greece – which Caesar would not accept. He had asked Cicero to think the matter over, and so they had parted. 'I don't think he was pleased with me', Cicero writes, 'but I am – and that hasn't happened for a long time.'

Cicero had evidently now decided to take up an unequivocal attitude, and the ordeal of the meeting with Caesar had confirmed in his own mind how resolute his stand was. True, he occasionally considered making his way to some neutral place of refuge, to Malta perhaps, and his letters from the spring of 49 do repeat his sharply critical view of Caesar's – and Pompey's – domineering ways. By and large, however, Cicero had made up his mind, and he was now mainly concerned as to how he might safely effect his escape. Curio, who visited him in April, assured him that, if Cicero reached his province of Sicily, he would help him make the crossing to Greece. But at the beginning of May, Antony, Caesar's adjutant in Italy, let him know that he had instructions to allow no one leave the country. Cicero discovered that the coast was in fact being closely watched. This in no way affected his decision. The last letter[21] addressed to Atticus from Italy was written about 20 May: he was being hindered more by the absence of wind than by the presence of sentries and Atticus should expect no more letters from him until he had reached his destination.

On 7 June he embarked in Caieta, near Formiae, together with his son, his nephew and his lictors. From there he sent greetings to Terentia.[22] He now felt recovered from his indisposition after vomiting clear bile during the night. He recommended Terentia and Tullia to the care of their many friends, although he was not at all apprehensive. The women should take up their abode as far away from the military as possible; if the cost of living should rise, then it would be best to go to the farm at Arpinum. It had by no means been a foregone conclusion that Cicero's nephew would join the party. He had written to Caesar and even visited him – much to the dismay of his father and his uncle. Cicero regarded his nephew as an unprincipled young man, and in this he was not far wrong.

In the spring of 49 the situation was not as unfavourable for the Senate party as Cicero believed. Caesar's successes in Italy had earned him the evil reputation of a rebel, and one of his ablest officers,

Labienus, had deserted to the Senate party for this reason. Caesar sought to win friends by his lenient policy, which he implemented for the first time following his victory at Corfinium. But this '*insidiosa clementia*', as Cicero called it,[23] his calculated magnanimity, did not produce any notable success to begin with. In Rome Caesar was forced to violate the immunity of the people's tribune in order to gain possession of the treasury. And the session of the Caesarian Senate on 1 April, which Cicero had refused to attend, turned out to be a failure. Caesar stood more or less on his own. Not only the eastern provinces with their well-nigh inexhaustible resources, but also Spain and Africa were securely held by the Senate party, while the Adriatic was dominated by naval forces under the command of Pompey. After adequate preparations, Italy was to be reconquered from the East, and Sulla offered a precedent for this.

Cicero, it seemed, never bothered to make a sober assessment of the military prospects of the party which he had decided to join in the end. It is to his credit that he took this decision simply and solely because he felt himself under an obligation to Pompey, and because he did not wish to appear ungrateful. On the other hand, the absence of any political or military calculation indicates how out of touch he was with the powerful forces that were about to be unleashed. While Pompey was arming his forces, Caesar used the summer of 49 to secure his rear. With a risky campaign that was rendered even more hazardous by the resistance of Massilia he succeeded in gaining control of Spain, whereas a similar operation in Africa under Curio's leadership ended in defeat.

When the second year of the war began, the issue was still entirely open. The Senate party still had the greater resources at its disposal, and hence the better chances of success. During the winter Caesar succeeded in transporting troops across the Adriatic and establishing a bridgehead near Apollonia (south of Dyrrhachium, in present Albania). And now the two armies lay facing each other for months on end near Dyrrhachium. Caesar wished to force Pompey to a rapid and decisive battle by encircling him, but instead paid for this attempt with a grievous setback. The Senate party were so elated by their victory that Pompey was induced to abandon his original tactics of attrition and to risk a decisive battle at Pharsalus in Thessaly. His army, which outnumbered Caesar's by almost two to one, was defeated and scattered. Pompey himself attempted to take refuge in Egypt and was killed there at the behest of King Ptolemy XIII, a teenage boy, and his advisers.

During these events – from the hostilities in the summer of 49 down to the battle at Pharsalus in the summer of 48 – Cicero had remained on territory controlled by the Senate party. He was at first probably in Thessalonica, where the legitimate Senate had established itself; then in Pompey's camp, subsequently in Dyrrhachium; and finally in Patrae on the Gulf of Corinth. We know only in outline what Cicero was thinking, saying and doing at this time. A rapid sequence of letters, especially those to Atticus, provides detailed and graphic evidence of Cicero's thoughts and feelings during the months of inner conflict, but this sequence came to an abrupt end with his escape from Italy. Not a single letter has survived from the second half of 49, while only five letters to Atticus and a number of other items have come down to us from the remaining period preceding his return to Italy. This dearth of sources is due mainly to the fact that Cicero could not – or dared not – write to friends or relations who had stayed behind in Italy. Even those few letters which do exist are couched in casual and allusive terms and deal for the most part with private, and especially with financial, matters. They manifest concern for Cicero's daughter on various counts. Cicero was having difficulty in finding the money to pay an instalment of her dowry that was now due, and the marriage with Dolabella was already in serious trouble. Besides, Atticus had written that Tullia was distressed, and Cicero asked him to go to her aid.

The sparse evidence from Cicero himself and from others relating to his time with Pompey suggests that he was of no great service to his Senate party. He disapproved of everything that was going on around him and refused to accept any appointment. He was acting in accordance with a slogan which he had coined in March: 'Ego ... quem fugiam habeo, quem sequar non habeo' – 'I know whom to avoid, but not whom to follow'.[24] Later, in his *Second Philippic*, he claimed that he had remained on friendly terms with Pompey, in spite of his constant exhortations to make peace.[25] It is more likely, however, that he got on Pompey's nerves and annoyed the Senate leaders. He obviously liked playing the untimely part of the onlooker who always knows best, who makes sour jokes by way of commentary on events. Later writers have in fact preserved a few examples for our benefit. Nevertheless, in spite of his own shortage of money, he assisted Pompey with a substantial loan.

In the early summer of 48 illness forced Cicero to move to Dyrrhachium for a period. It was at this time that he received an extremely cordial letter from his son-in-law Dolabella, who was in Caesar's camp.[26] Pompey, he claimed, had lost the war (a bold claim, before Pharsalus); Cicero should now think of himself and should retire to some place outside the immediate theatre of operations – Athens, perhaps.

Cicero was still in Dyrrhachium, where Cato was in command of a garrison of fifteen cohorts, when the news of the disaster at Pharsalus arrived. Cato set sail for Corfu to join the Senate party's fleet and urged Cicero to take command. When Cicero, who believed the Senate's cause to be already lost, refused to do so, Gnaeus, Pompey's eldest son, tried to attack him with his drawn sword. Cato intervened, however, and allowed Cicero to travel to Patrae, together with his brother. A pretty violent quarrel then arose between Cicero and Quintus, for the latter now regretted that he had been talked into joining the Senate party by his brother.

In the meantime Cicero had once again received a letter from Dolabella in which he was urged to return to Italy as quickly as possible.[27] Thereupon he crossed over to Brundisium in the middle of October 48. He was still escorted by his lictors, the mark of his authority, but when they entered the city, he ordered them to exchange their bundles of rods for staves. He feared they might provoke the anger of Caesar's soldiers who formed the garrison.

'Totally worn out by a burden of serious worries' – 'confectus iam cruciatu maximorum dolorum':[28] this phrase, which opens a letter to Atticus, is typical for the wretched year that Cicero had to spend in Brundisium waiting for Caesar's pardon. In the score or so letters to Atticus that have been preserved from this period no word recurs as frequently as '*dolor*', 'worry, grief'. It soon turned out that Cicero had placed himself in an awkward and embarrassing position by his precipitate crossing to Brundisium. For Mark Antony, Caesar's supreme representative in Italy, gave him to understand that no member of Pompey's party might set foot in Italy until Caesar had reviewed his case. Cicero referred him to Dolabella's letter, which had been sent to him at Caesar's suggestion. Antony then exempted Cicero – along with Decimus Laelius, who had been Pompey's admiral – from Caesar's ban, so that Cicero was publicly singled out as an exception. This circumstance became more and more irksome the longer he had to wait for Caesar, with whose return Cicero had reckoned immediately after the battle at Pharsalus. For one thing, the civil war was taking a course quite different from what Cicero had anticipated; for another, his family troubles and vexations were multiplying.

Immediately after the battle at Pharsalus Caesar took up the pursuit of Pompey and proceeded via Asia to Egypt, where Ptolemy XIII had the murdered Pompey's head and signet ring carried out to meet him. Caesar then became involved in the dynastic disputes which prevailed there, and by favouring Cleopatra, Ptolemy's sister, precipitated the Alexandrine War, which kept him in Alexandria from the autumn of 48 until the spring of 47. The most deplorable consequence of this irresponsible venture was the destruction by fire of the celebrated library there.

Caesar's prolonged absence gave the remnants of the Senate party a chance to recover: they turned the province of Africa into a bulwark of the Republic. All the same, Caesar turned to Asia Minor, where Pharnaces, the ruler of the Bosphorus empire in the Crimea, had set out on a campaign of conquest. In the late summer of 47, after his 'veni-vidi-vici' victory over Pharnaces, he set out for Rome, where none other than Cicero's son-in-law had begun to pursue a radical policy aimed at the cancellation of all debts. This culminated in street fighting between him and his antagonist, Trebellius. Antony was unable to cope with the situation, and order was not restored until after Caesar's return.

Cicero had assumed that the battle at Pharsalus would at once be followed by general pacification, but month after month passed and nothing was settled. Caesar seemed to have vanished from the face of the earth, while his enemies were beginning to rally in Africa. Cicero started to regret that he had returned to Italy and to reproach himself with this move, as he invariably did when he had miscalculated. He had done likewise during his exile and after the outbreak of the civil war. Might he not have done better, he thought, to have gone to Africa or, at least, to some neutral territory as, for instance, Servius Sulpicius Rufus had done?[29] (Sulpicius Rufus was standing by on Samos, waiting to see how matters turned out.) Cicero found it extremely embarrassing that he had cut himself off from any return to the Senate party. This consideration weighed all the more with him in that no one else had chosen to follow this wrong path – apart from Laelius, who didn't count for anything. He even began to fear the victory of his erstwhile allies, and their vengeance, seeing in his mind's eye, perhaps, that scene in Corfu. 'I can see how everything has changed in the long intervening period', he writes in March 47, 'that things are now going well where they ought to go well, and that I shall have to pay dearly for my folly'.[30] And a few days later we read: 'Of all the insufferable ills that plague me, the worst is that I have evidently landed myself in a situation where I have to regard as being in my interest all those things that I used to deplore.'[31]

Following their violent quarrel, Cicero had parted from his brother in Patrae. He did write a letter, however, exonerating Quintus when he heard that Caesar was holding him rather than Cicero responsible for their defection to Pompey's party. Then, in December 48, he heard the distressing news that Quintus had sent his son to Caesar: 'non solem sui deprecatorem, sed etiam accusatorem mei' – 'not just to seek a pardon for himself, but also to accuse me'.[32] Soon afterwards, on his fifty-ninth birthday, Cicero discovered that Quintus himself had embarked on a campaign of correspondence designed to blacken his name. It was reported to him from Ephesus that one of Quintus's sons had turned up there with a speech attacking Cicero which he proposed to deliver before Caesar. And thus it went on. Caesar, it is true, was so little impressed by Quintus's unseemly behaviour that he passed on to Cicero all the libellous letters he received from Quintus.

The worry that Cicero's beloved daughter Tullia was causing him was of a graver kind. In May 49, just prior to Cicero's departure for Greece, she had given birth prematurely; the child was sickly and died soon afterwards. Towards the end of the succeeding year Tullia was ill and in a weak state. Cicero's main worries, however, were, as they had been in Pompey's camp, shortage of cash and Tullia's unhappy marriage to Dolabella. Cicero's ne'er-do-well son-in-law, people's tribune at the time, had provoked serious unrest by an arbitrary policy that ran counter to all Cicero's convictions. Dolabella's private life was characterized by an affair with Metella, Lentulus Spinther's wife, a notorious courtesan. Cicero suffered all the more from this predicament since he was in a precarious situation and could hardly ask Caesar's supporters to return his daughter to him. A visit which Tullia paid him in the summer of 47 did little to comfort him, but merely made it more obvious what harm he had done her.

As if this were not enough, after thirty years Cicero's own marriage was now entering a crisis which ended in divorce shortly after his pardon. Little is known of what happened or what the cause might have been; Cicero was extremely discreet, even in his letters to Atticus. Terentia had been guilty of very irresponsible conduct, he says at one point, 'scelerate quaedam facere'.[33] Elsewhere, Cicero waxes indignant because she had sent him 2,000 sesterces less than his due, according to what Atticus had told him.[34] The letters he sent to his wife from Brundisium (more than a dozen have survived) are extremely terse and cool, not to say icily matter-of-fact. The last of the series, which Cicero, now pardoned, had despatched from the Venusia area on 1 October 47, reads as follows:

Cicero to his Terentia. I think I shall arrive in Tusculanum on the seventh,
or the day after. See that everything is got ready there: I shall probably
arrive with several companions and will probably stay for some time. If
there is not a tub in the bathroom, get one, as well as anything else
needed for our comfort. Farewell.[35]

Cicero had increasingly suffered under the sultry, oppressive climate of
the port, but at the end of September the long trial of his patience was
at last over. When the dictator, who had landed first in Tarentum,
arrived in Brundisium, Cicero went out to meet him, far in advance of
the rest of the welcoming crowd. As soon as Caesar caught sight of
Cicero, he dismounted, greeted him and walked beside him for a considerable distance, conversing amicably. Cicero returned to Rome via
his Tusculum. There he finally laid to rest his ambition to celebrate a
triumph. He dismissed the lictors, who had accompanied him constantly from Cilicia via Rome, Greece and Brundisium, and hence
formally renounced his status as a general, his imperium.

15

The Philosopher under Caesar's Dictatorship

The civil war had not been decided, much less concluded, by Caesar's return from the East. It was like a fire smouldering under the surface: as soon as it was extinguished at one point, it flared up at another. Caesar stayed barely two months in Rome; before the end of 47 he had landed in Hadrumetum on the African coast. The Republicans had far superior forces at their disposal there. The leaders were Metellus Scipio, Pompey's erstwhile father-in-law, Pompey's sons, Gnaeus and Sextus, together with Cato, the heart and soul of the resistance to Caesar. The issue was not settled in the African theatre of operations until 6 April 46, at the battle at Thapsus, after numerous contingents of Republican troops had deserted to Caesar. Cato committed suicide – not wishing to be beholden to the tyrant for his life. This event made a profound impression on all those who had not totally committed themselves to Caesar's cause. Cato quickly became a symbol of Republican freedom.

Caesar did not return to Rome until the end of July. He celebrated a fourfold triumph over his foreign foes (victories in the civil war did not count): over Gaul, Egypt, Pharnaces and the Numidian King Juba, who had joined the Republicans. During the three months he was present in Rome he busied himself with internal affairs, among other things with the reform of the calendar, for which he sought the Senate's advice. At the beginning of November a resumption of hostilities by Pompey's sons called him away to Spain. Here, too, he succeeded in gaining a victory with a numerically inferior force. The battle at Munda (17 March 45) decided the final phase of the civil war between Caesar and Pompey. In September Caesar was back in Rome, where he remained until his death on the Ides of March 44, the longest period he had spent there since his departure for Gaul in 58.

During the winter of 47–46 peace reigned in Rome – the peace of a dictatorship. Commissioners appointed by Caesar, notably Gaius Oppius and Balbus, were responsible for maintaining order. For the moment there was no chance of Cicero, the orator and politician, playing any kind of active part, as he well knew. Nevertheless, he stayed in Rome throughout the winter, so as not to incur the suspicion that he meant to escape from the city again. It was not until news of the battle at Thapsus arrived that he saw a chance of being employed once more: 'Let it be agreed between us', he wrote at the end of April 46 to the scholar and scientist, Varro, 'that we will apply ourselves together to the studies that were once our pastime but are now our refuge; supposing, however, that anyone should wish to employ us on the reconstruction of the state – even if it is only as artisans rather than as architects – then we shall not be found wanting, indeed, we shall hasten forward joyfully.'[1] Cicero was evidently hoping that Caesar would continue the policy of clementia, which he himself had once found suspect, and that he would have recourse even to former adversaries in an attempt to establish a new order in the Republic that had now collapsed. He was not mistaken in this assumption. Caesar knew that he had not achieved his goal simply by his victory in the war; he knew also that he would need capable people. He therefore treated the defeated members of the Senate party in a consistently lenient and conciliatory manner, without being diverted from this policy by disappointments he experienced. As far as Cicero was concerned, these endeavours opened up a limited area for political collaboration soon after Caesar's return. Since his return was delayed, however, Cicero ventured to withdraw to his Tusculanum in the early summer. At this time he was engaged in close correspondence, exchanging ideas with Marcus Iunius Brutus – who later assassinated Caesar – a man twenty-five years his junior. Possibly he regarded this versatile individual as his intellectual heir, who would inherit his culture, his rhetoric and his political convictions. After all, Brutus had made his name as an orator, had written philosophical treatises and had also tried his hand as a poet. He had initially been on Pompey's side but had gone over to Caesar following Pharsalus. The fact that Cicero had to curb his young friend's excessive lust for profit four years previously in Cilicia was evidently no obstacle.

At that point Brutus wanted him to produce a eulogy of Cato, and Cicero used his leisure hours in his Tusculanum to carry out this perilous project, although he knew he was unlikely to endear himself to Caesar and his followers by praising *constantia*, Cato's fidelity to his political principles. His panegyric encouraged a number of other eulogies, so that the opposing side felt obliged to intervene in this literary campaign with similar methods. A refutation from the pen of the Caesarian protagonist, Aulus Hirtius, was followed by the *Anticatones* which Caesar himself composed a year later, after the battle at Munda. The feud demonstrated that at that stage there was no question of forcibly suppressing the candid expression of dissident political opinions, as was the practice in the Imperial period from Tiberius onwards.

After Caesar's return Cicero once again took part in Senate meetings, although he remained silent to begin with, since the Senate no longer possessed any real powers of decision. On the other hand, he was an active supporter of Caesar's policy of reconciliation. His house was a meeting-place, not only for former opponents, but also for adherents of Caesar. Both here and in personal representations to Caesar – which Cicero was not too proud to undertake on behalf of his like-minded associates – there were opportunities to solicit the pardon of members of the Senate party who were still living in exile. Cicero was guided here by the consideration that the forces of the opposition would have all the more influence, the more strongly they were represented in the Senate. Besides, he had not yet given up hope that Caesar was seriously thinking of restoring the res publica, the traditional Republican order, as it had once been restored by Sulla. He was no more able than most of his contemporaries to accustom himself to the thought that the old Republic might have gone for good.

A fortunate chance has preserved documents relating to his activities as mediator that offer impressive evidence, both of his humanitarian feelings and his skills as a negotiator. In books 4 and 6 of the *Ad Familiares* collection there is an abundance of letters in which Cicero tries to console exiles, reporting on his efforts to have them pardoned and predicting their imminent return home. His strenuous efforts are totally devoid of any suggestion of complacency and were in fact quite frequently crowned with success, as in the case of the former praetor, Titus Ampius Balbus, and the knight, Trebianus. Other exiles, again, appear to have died abroad, for example Aulus Caecina, the son of a former client of Cicero, who had put himself at risk by lampooning Caesar, and Publius Nigidius Figulus, a devotee of esoteric learning.

The most celebrated case in this connection is that of Marcus Claudius Marcellus, consul for the year 51. Cicero was obliged to effect his return, not only through negotiations with Caesar, but also with Marcellus, who was reluctant to accept a favour from Caesar. Several letters have survived in which Cicero tries to prevail on him with sound arguments, being careful at the same time not to wound his pride.[2]

There was nowhere Marcellus could go, he argues, that was beyond Caesar's reach, even Mytilene on Lesbos was not safe, and if Pompey had won, then the venerable res publica would in any case be in the same deplorable state as it was after Caesar's victory.

Marcellus had probably not had a chance to respond to these arguments when, in the middle of September, an incident took place in the Senate that prompted Cicero to break the silence he had hitherto maintained and to pay a warm tribute to the dictator. He gave an exact account of the affair to his friend Sulpicius Rufus, who was governor in Greece at the time.[3] Lucius, Caesar's father-in-law, had raised the issue of Marcus Marcellus and what was to be done about him. Gaius Marcellus, Marcus's cousin, had prostrated himself at Caesar's feet, whereupon the whole Senate had risen to plead for Marcus. To begin with, Caesar had spoken of his adversary's harsh manner, but then had suddenly declared that he would not deny the Senate's request, in spite of his misgivings. The former consuls then addressed a vote of thanks to Caesar which Cicero elaborated into a brief speech – the address or, rather, the vote of thanks on behalf of Marcellus that has come down to us. The subject of Caesar's pardon, who informed Cicero that he had been convinced by his arguments, was nevertheless not fated to see Rome again. On his way back to the city he was the victim of an apparently unmotivated murder.

Shortly afterwards Cicero once more had a chance to use his gifts as an orator on behalf of another former supporter of Pompey – Quintus Ligarius, who had been little more than a fellow-traveller. Together with the exiled man's brothers, Cicero had arranged an audience with the dictator, and a pardon seemed imminent, when a charge of high treason in collusion with the Numidian King Juba foiled Cicero's efforts. In the trial which then took place in the forum with Caesar as presiding judge, one of Caesar's adherents, Gaius Vibius Pansa spoke first for the defence, followed by Cicero. As Plutarch reports, Caesar is said to have remarked before the trial, 'What's to stop us listening to Cicero again. After all, it's long since been obvious that Ligarius is a scoundrel and our enemy.'[4] But when Cicero started to speak, the dictator had been unable to conceal his agitation, until finally, when the battle at Pharsalus was mentioned, he had begun to tremble all over, so that some papers he was holding fell to the ground. He thus saw himself obliged to exonerate the accused. The anecdote no doubt tries to convey an excessively naive impression of Cicero's eloquence. In fact it was almost certainly political factors which tilted the balance, as far as Caesar was concerned. Cicero had sought to hold the dictator to his policy of leniency, just as he had previously done in his vote of thanks on behalf of Marcellus. Moreover, he was probably hoping to promote the case for restoring the ruined res publica.

Caesar's departure for Spain frustrated any such expectations for the time being, however. Cicero was once more reduced to the role of a mere spectator – this time for a whole year. He was no doubt taking less interest in politics anyway, for personal reasons. He was plagued by grave domestic worries, especially the sudden death of his beloved Tullia, and he immersed himself with incredible zeal in his writing – the great philosophical encyclopaedia. And, indeed, it did not seem to matter much how far he was prepared to become involved. He occasionally found his name appended to Senate resolutions he had never heard of – so far had the Senate at that stage been reduced to the function of a rubber stamp.

Towards the end of 45 Cicero had the chance to deliver the third and last of his so-called Caesar speeches – a plea in defence of the vassal King Deiotarus of Asia Minor, who had allegedly been implicated in all manner of treasonable dealings in opposition to Caesar. The king was represented in his absence by a delegation, the sole judge was once again the dictator himself, and the proceedings were conducted behind closed doors in his own home – an arrangement criticized by Cicero with uncompromising candour.[5]

In December 45 Cicero had two experiences which drastically illustrated the radical transformation that had taken place; his letters give a graphic account of the two events in question. On 19 December the dictator was a guest on the Cumanum estate.[6] Cicero was extremely upset: Caesar was said to have turned up with no fewer than two thousand troops. Fortunately, an officer was able to prevent the host's villa from being overrun and the troops were served in the open air. The illustrious guest and his retinue made themselves at home in several rooms, and there was no lack of succulent dishes and witty conversation, which was confined, however, to literary topics, with no mention of politics. 'What else?' writes Cicero. 'I held my own. But my guest was not one of those to whom you say, "I shall be glad to see you soon again." Once is enough.'

The second event took place in Rome on 31 December.[7] The consul Quintus Fabius Maximus had died suddenly, and Caesar proceeded to play a cynical game with the constitution, which had been reduced to a pure formality. He arranged for another consul to be elected specially for the last few hours of the year, a consul under whose rule, as Cicero remarks with grim humour, no one had ever broken his fast. 'During his consulate', he goes on, 'not a single evil deed was committed. The fellow was so much on the alert that he never once closed an eye throughout his period in office. That may strike you as funny', Cicero writes to his friend and host Curius in Patrae, 'the point is, you weren't there. If you had to watch, you wouldn't be able to keep back your tears.'

The final months of Caesar's dictatorship were governed by preparations for the advent of a monarchy – a theocracy, in fact. A multitude of honours was designed to open the path to this goal, one of which has persisted to the present day: the month of Quinctilis was renamed Iulius. Cicero cooperated, but tried to exercise some restraining influence. It is not known whether he was present at the feast during which Antony offered the dictator the diadem, the insignia of monarchy, but the detailed description in his *Second Philippic* suggests that he was in fact an eyewitness.[8]

Caesar's dictatorship imposed strict limitations on Cicero's activities in the political field, and his abounding energies could scarcely be absorbed, even in his courtroom practice. One obvious consequence of this was that he tended more than ever to seek refuge from the inevitable frustrations of public life in leisure and in social intercourse with cultured friends; there is plentiful evidence of this in letters from the period. There were few men quicker to appreciate a joke, a witticism, an *aperçu* or a subtle point. He had made himself thoroughly familiar with the theoretical aspect of the subject, as is proved by the long digression on the joke, *iocus*, and *facetiae* which he introduced into the second book of his *De Oratore*.[9] But he was also himself a great exponent of all forms of intellectual wit, a master of ironically humorous description and caustic sarcasm, and he positively overflowed with inspired witticisms when he was in the right mood.

Already in the 50s many of his witticisms were going the rounds. In a letter that he wrote from Cilicia in 50 BC to Publius Volumnius Eutrapelus – the cognomen means 'jocular' or 'urbane' – he complained that all sorts of trite phrases and excruciating puns were being attributed to him, although he should really be given credit only for what was elegant, apposite and original.[10] Even Caesar himself, as appears from a letter to Lucius Papirius Paetus, had Cicero's witticisms reported to him and had such infallible judgement that he was able to distinguish unerringly between the authentic and the spurious items.[11] Gaius Trebonius, a very able officer in Caesar's service, collected an anthology of Cicero's *bons mots* and sent it to the author, who thanked him profusely.[12] After Cicero's death Tiro issued three books with jokes and puns by his master and patron, and an anthology from the late Classical period has preserved a number of them.

Cicero often gave free rein to his talent for witty puns and turns of phrase, even in court. Now, under Caesar, he had ample opportunity to exercise it within the circle of his cultured friends and acquaintances. They were for the most part disciples of Epicurus, in whose cheerful company he sought relief from the pressure of political circumstances. This was no mere accident, because the Epicureans abstained from politics and cultivated friendship, polite manners and an urbane style of life in which the witty joke was not the least important ingredient.

The number of Epicurus's disciples had increased significantly in Rome during the first century BC. Civic disorder with its attendant atrocities deterred many – and by no means the worst of men – from engaging in politics. In particular, knights like Atticus steered clear of conflict and confrontation and concentrated on preserving and augmenting their private fortunes. There were also Epicurean writers, above all the brilliant poet Lucretius, who gave an account of Epicurean physics in a didactic poem that has survived in its entirety. Cicero knew this work and thought highly of it. Indeed, he is even said to have published it, since its author was prevented from doing so by his early death.

The doctrine of Epicurus in itself he found uncongenial, and he wrote in very disparaging terms about it, especially in his attack on Piso. The Epicureans' main ethical concept, the pleasure principle, *voluptas*, offered him a convenient pretext. This principle was misinterpreted by many as a licence to indulge in gross sensuality and unbridled debauchery, so that the entire doctrine of Epicurus and his disciples fell into disrepute. Under Caesar, it was only by way of a joke that Cicero linked the cult of pleasure with the Epicureans – and his own association with them. His attitude henceforth anticipated what Horace subsequently incorporated in his life and poetry as Epicureanism: it was cheerful and not without an element of self-irony.

In the letters to Atticus, the most prominent of his friends who were inclined towards Epicureanism, relatively little is reflected of Cicero's new, casually ambivalent affirmation of Epicurean urbanity and Epicurean hedonism. As far as Cicero was concerned, his association with Atticus served a more important purpose. He was Cicero's 'alter ego', the person to whom he might confide all his thoughts, his cares and troubles, towards whom he was always himself, and with whom he never wore the mask of some role or other. Thus, the minatory question which he once put to his friend – whether it is only the man who strives after pleasure who truly lives – is certainly meant in an ironic sense, and is prompted by the lavish architectural ambitions of Caesar's hench-man, Balbus.[13] But perhaps there is a grain of self-confession in the statement that follows, 'If you ask me what I think: I'm in favour of indulgence.'

As far as Epicurean jocularity and sensual pleasure were concerned, Cicero's most important correspondent was Paetus. 'I have cast aside all my concern for the state', Cicero once wrote to him in a positively programmatic vein, 'all my cogitation on views expressed in the Senate, all my preparations for court cases, and have deserted to the camp of my adversary, Epicurus' – 'in Epicuri nos, adversari nostri, castra coniecimus'.[14] He, a brave man and a philosopher into the bargain, remarked on another occasion, not without a tinge of bitter self-irony, that he reckoned life to be the supreme value. So he, Cicero, could not help being beholden to Caesar, to whom he owed his life.[15] He was making progress as a gourmet, he confesses to Paetus. Hirtius and Dolabella were his pupils in the art of declamation, but his masters in eating, so that he could no longer be satisfied with humble fare, as he once had been.[16] Cicero expresses himself no less jocularly, but more in the sense of a true Epicurean in a note announcing that he proposes to dine with Paetus.[17] He had heard that his friend was confined to bed with gout, and he writes as follows: 'I am very sorry to hear it, as is only proper, but I am determined to come and see you all the same and to dine with you. For I trust that your cook hasn't got the gout as well. So count on a guest who is no glutton and who is also an enemy of lavish repasts.'

There is a letter to Paetus which is particularly revealing as regards Cicero's frame of mind, in which despair is overlaid with humour.[18] It was written during a banquet at the home of the aforementioned Volumnius Eutrapelus, no doubt also an Epicurean:

It is now about nine o'clock as, reclining at table, I scribble this note on my writing-tablet. You ask, 'Where?' At the home of Volumnius Eutra-pelus, and beside me on one side lies Atticus, and on the other Verrius, your friends. You are surprised that our servitude is so pleasurable? What am I to do? I ask you, who go and listen to a philosopher every day. Should I be dejected, chastise myself? What would I achieve, what would be the outcome? 'Live with your books', you say. Do you think I do otherwise and that I could live, if I did not live with my books? But there, too, there is, if not satiety, at least a certain measure; if I turned my back on my books, I don't know what I should do before I go to bed. Now, listen to this! Beside Eutrapelus lies Cytheris. 'What', you cry, 'at such a banquet the celebrated Cicero is present, 'upon whose countenance the Greeks themselves did fix their gaze?'

By my troth, I had no idea that Cytheris [an actress, later mistress of Antony] would be present.... Incidentally, no one ever excited me so much, even in my youth, never mind now, when I am old. I delight in this conviviality; I talk, as they say, twenty to the dozen, and turn my sighs into belly-laughs.... This is now my mode of life: every day I read or write something; then, so as not to lose touch with my friends, I dine with them, no more than the law permits (if there is any such thing as laws these days), but less, a good deal less, in fact. Have no fear, then, of my coming: you will have in me a guest who eats little and laughs a lot.

Farewell.

There were other friends who profited from Cicero's propensity for Epicurean witticisms. Cassius, for example, who had successfully defended Syria against the Parthians, and who was later to be one of Caesar's assassins. He, too, subscribed to the doctrine of Epicurus. Cicero delighted him, for instance, with a satire on the Epicurean theory of perception, the doctrine of the εἴδωλα, the images which detach themselves from things so that they may impinge on the eye.[19] In other letters there are grimly ironic references to that Sulla whom Cicero had successfully defended in 62. Sulla had been an officer in the civil war and a follower of Caesar; he had enriched himself handsomely on the property of proscribed political opponents. 'Just to let you know something of what is happening in these parts', Cicero reports to Cassius, 'the death has occurred of Publius Sulla; he is said to have been the victim of robbers or, as some claim, of an indigestion – people didn't bother to ask many more questions: after all, his body had been cremated. Philosopher that you are, you will bear this fateful blow with equanimity.'[20] And, as an addendum to a number of aphorisms about the various philosophical doctrines on the supreme Good in human existence, Cicero writes: 'When Sulla, whose judgement we are bound to respect, observed how divided the philosophers were among themselves as to what the Good was, he simply bought up all the goods he could. Upon my word, I have borne his death bravely.'[21]

There is something forced, histrionic and stereotyped about these jokes exchanged with Epicurean friends. Somewhat similar is the jocularly jovial note which Cicero occasionally strikes with Dolabella, his former son-in-law. (The marriage with Tullia had been dissolved in November 46.) His relationship with Marcus Terentius Varro, on the other hand, evidently went beyond mere conventional sociability. The brief sequence of letters in the ninth book of the *Ad Familiares* collection, most of them from the first half of 46, includes, besides caustic jokes, serious observations like that which we have quoted concerning Cicero's readiness to collaborate in rebuilding the state. There are signs, too, of cordial affection. Varro, a versatile and extremely productive writer, especially in the field of cultural history, had been on Pompey's side during the civil war and had made his peace with Caesar after Pharsalus, so that he shared Cicero's views.

There is a strain of black humour in a letter which Cicero wrote to Varro after hearing of the murder of Lucius Caesar, who had been Cato's right-hand man (the deed had probably been committed without the dictator's knowledge). 'When I heard what had happened to young Lucius Caesar, I said to myself (in the words of Terence): "What, then, will he do to me, the old man?" And so I'm for ever at the table of those who are now our masters. What is to be done? I have to move with the times! But enough of these jokes, especially as we have nothing to joke about: "Africa still trembles, shaken by the horrors of war." '[22] In the following year Cicero dedicated to his learned friend the first essay in his philosophical encyclopaedia, the revised version of the *Academica*, in which the dialogue is conducted by Varro, Cicero and Atticus. In the letter which accompanied the dedication copy, Cicero points out that this kind of fiction is a feature of the genre, adding: 'But in future, dear Varro, we shall converse as often as we can, if you agree – perhaps it is rather late, but, after all, it may have been the fate of our country that governed our past, now we are on our own.'[23]

Cicero was possibly trying to overcome by this hectic social life the distress that the breakdown of his marriage with Terentia caused him. It was he himself who sued for divorce in 46. We learn nothing of the grounds for the divorce, but probably financial considerations played a major part. The atmosphere which prevailed between the two parties is reflected in something that Cicero said to Plancius, one of his clients fron 54 BC. Plancius had congratulated him on his second marriage, and Cicero was constrained to reply in the following terms:

> I wouldn't have thought of making any change during these wretched times, had I not discovered on my return that my household was in as deplorable a state as our political situation. Those who owe me so infinitely much, and to whom nothing should be of more concern than my welfare and my fortune, had brought matters, as I saw, to such a pass that I found nothing in my own home secure and safe from secret machinations. Then I thought it best to arm myself through the loyalty of new ties against the disloyalty of the old.[24]

Six months after the divorce Cicero brought home his new bride, a very young girl by the name of Publilia. Money was certainly the major factor in his choice, as it had been in the divorce from Terentia. Cicero was deeply in debt, the girl's fortune was already being handled by him and through the marriage he gained the power to use it as he pleased. To the outcry which this union quite rightly provoked, Cicero is said to have responded with an aphorism: 'When they reproached him, a man of sixty, with having married Publilia, a mere girl, he said, "Tomorrow she will be a woman."'[25]

In the middle of February 45 Cicero suffered a fateful blow which caused him profounder sorrow than any other misfortune, whether of a domestic or of a political nature: his daughter Tullia died in childbirth. Totally devastated, he first sought refuge with Atticus in Rome. But, unable to stand the crowds of people, he went to ground in a remote villa which he owned near Astura, on the shores of the Tyrrhenian Sea. 'I am living in this silence and seeing no one', he writes to Atticus, 'and when I set off in the morning into the dense and trackless woods, then I do not emerge again until the evening. Apart from yourself, nothing is dearer to me than solitude, in which my books are my sole distraction.'[26]

However overwhelmed Cicero was with grief, and however much he succumbed to it, he did try to master it. He wrote to Atticus that he was working on a *Consolatio*, the first man, he says, to comfort himself through such a work. The work itself is lost. A remark in the *Tusculanorum* suggests that Cicero had there assembled all the arguments he could glean from the literature offering comfort to the bereaved that had been current since the Hellenistic period.[27] He proposed to erect a memorial to his daughter, a sanctuary that would perpetuate her memory, and he constantly reverts to this intention in letters from these months. He was, however, undecided as to where the sanctuary should be located, and so the plan seems never to have been carried out.

Cicero received various expressions of condolence from those around him, from Caesar, for instance.[28] One letter of condolence has been preserved: it is from the pen of Sulpicius Rufus, a former consul of Republican sentiments, like Cicero himself. Writing from Athens, Sulpicius remarks that, after losing his homeland, his status and the chance to influence the destiny of the state, Cicero must by now be so inured to misfortune as to endure the death of his daughter. He should bear in mind that she, too, had been affected by the change in her father's fortunes, and that she would have had an unhappy life to look forward to, had she not died. Sulpicius goes on to depict a panorama illustrating the transience of everything on this earth. During a voyage across the Saronian Gulf he had seen the once flourishing, but now deserted cities of Aegina, Megara, Piraeus and Corinth, and had reflected how idle it was to make so much ado about the loss of a single individual, when one was confronted with the mortal remains of so many cities.

While Cicero was seeking solace in the woods of Astura and in other rural retreats (he did not appear again in Rome until mid-summer), poor Publilia was living alone in his grand city residence. At the end of March she enquired humbly – as Cicero himself reports – whether she might join him, together with her mother. Cicero at once replied with an obdurate refusal, and in order to be safe from a surprise visit he went into hiding on one of Atticus's estates.[29] The marriage was thus dissolved, and Cicero had difficulty in repaying the dowry.

His son Marcus and his nephew Quintus were both giving cause for concern and irritation. Quintus was serving under Caesar in the campaign against Pompey's sons in Spain. He had spoken harshly, it was said, of his father and his uncle and maintained that both of them were sworn enemies of Caesar, and had otherwise – in his uncle's view – behaved in an insolent and aggressive manner. Marcus would have liked to follow his cousin to Spain, but Cicero objected. It was enough that they had abandoned the Republican cause, they didn't actually have to fight against it. His son obeyed, and so he was packed off to study in Athens where, in fact, he soon began to live on a rather too lavish scale.

Political misfortune and personal sorrow did not only prompt Cicero to seek distraction in the society of cultured friends. This aspect of his life was merely a symptom, his main preoccupation was intellectual, his philosophical writing. Towards the end of 47 a period of literary productivity began which lasted for about two and a half years and culminated in 45. It is from this period that most of Cicero's rhetorical and philosophical works came. He was encouraged by Brutus, who had written from Asia to console him in his troubles, as well as by Atticus. To begin with, in 46 BC, apart from the lost panegyric on Cato (a political work that also owed its inception to Brutus), three shorter works dedicated to Brutus were also completed: the dialogue on the history of rhetoric in Rome which bears the name of the man to whom it was dedicated; the *Paradoxa Stoicorum*; and the *Orator* (not to be confused with the long dialogue *De Oratore*).

Brutus and the *Orator* are closely related in their subject-matter: *Brutus* deals with oratorical practice in a historical context; the *Orator* is mainly concerned with an important area of rhetorical theory, the doctrine of modes of expression, *elocutio*. But the two works are also linked by their tenor: Cicero deplores the fate of the res publica, and, in the *Orator*, coins the phrase, 'tempora inimica virtuti', 'the times that are hostile to virtue'[30] – a phrase which Tacitus adopted in his *Agricola*.[31] Cicero is particularly sorry for his young friend Brutus, who will be denied a political career commensurate with his wealth of talent. Of himself he says that, considering there is no room for forensic skills or political initiative, he proposes to devote himself to writing rather than lapse into idleness and gloom.[32] Both works suggest an ageing author who is inclined to hark back to his memories and to the past in general. *Brutus* concludes, as already mentioned, with an autobiographical sketch of Cicero's own career as an orator, while in the *Orator* the author reflects on his speeches and quotes examples from them to illustrate his stylistic precepts.

The *Paradoxa Stoicorum* are little more than a formal *jeu d'esprit*. The paradoxes, that is the strict principles of Stoic ethics, which ran counter to the generally prevalent view, are shown to be correct by the use of rhetorical clichés. In earlier times the Romans had been able to live up to the ideal of the Stoic sages, whereas in recent times there had been problems. It is possible that Cicero did not make public this work, with its criticism of contemporary morality, which he had apparently dashed off very rapidly.

Tullia's death in February 45 changed the direction of his writing. This fateful blow impelled him to concern himself more seriously with philosophy, to seek a refuge in it and to give his life a new footing and a new substance through it. This is how, at any rate, he himself represented this change of direction.[33] During the period of his political activity he simply revived his philosophical knowledge and read works of philosophy in seclusion as often as he found the leisure to do so. Now that fate had inflicted this grievous wound on him, however, and now that he was relieved of his political responsibilities, he was seeking a cure for his suffering in philosophy – 'nunc vero et fortunae gravissimo percussus vulnere et administratione rei publicae liberatus doloris medicinam a philosophia peto.' Paradoxically, it was the loss of his daughter that gave Cicero the composure and the strength to immerse himself in philosophical writing.

The first two works, which were produced in rapid succession at this time, are especially clearly marked by the frame of mind in which Cicero found himself in the spring of 45. These are the *Consolatio*, already referred to, and the dialogue *Hortensius*, a revivalist or admonitory tract, i.e. a work that attempted to convert its readers to philosophy as the sole guide to fulfilment in human life. The most celebrated model for this kind of thing was derived from Aristotle, but numerous other philosophers had similarly sought to demonstrate the value of their profession by way of tracts, letters or dialogues. It was a genre that dealt with basic issues, with the question of the correct mode of life and the correct attitude to things. Up to a point it was a question of the soul's salvation, only, in the case of the ancient philosophers, it was a matter of salvation in this life, which was limited to the life span that nature allotted to each individual. The individual was, however, exhorted to remain as independent as possible of mere worldly goods. Anyone who wrote a *protreptikos* of this kind – like any preacher – did all he could to mount an emotional appeal matching the importance of his subject.

Cicero's *Hortensius* has not come down to us, for the vagaries of literary tradition have left us with a gap that is almost as vexatious as in the case of *De Republica*. But quotations from later grammarians, and especially from Lactantius and Augustine, give us an idea of the outline of the work – a dialogue in which the the main protagonists are the title figure and Cicero. The argument deals with the usual question of the uses of philosophy. Hortensius declares it to be utterly useless, while Cicero attempts to explain that it is in fact more necessary to a man than anything else, since happiness in life depends on the insights it has to offer. In antiquity *Hortensius* found many grateful readers, and it was still being used in the fourth century as an introduction to philosophy. The work made a profound impact, above all, on the young St Augustine. He tells us in the *Confessions* that it had brought about the transition from illusion to truth in his case and had opened up the path that was to lead to God.[34]

It was probably during the writing of *Hortensius* that Cicero conceived the firm intention of presenting his contemporaries in Rome with the whole body of Greek philosophy in a series of volumes – the logic, physics and ethics of the four main schools. At any rate, the first work that was to constitute this philosophical encyclopaedia, the *Academica*, announces the undertaking as something which had already been decided. 'I have begun to set forth in Latin the ancient philosophy that was brought into being by Socrates.'[35] Cicero had reverted, then, to the occupation that had afforded him the keenest satisfaction, even before the civil war, under the rule of the triumvirate. Only he was now pursuing quite different aims with his philosophical writings than he had once done with *De Oratore* and *De Republica*. He could no longer attempt to pursue political aims by other means and affect the course of events by appeals to his contemporaries' sense of responsibility. Given Caesar's firmly established dictatorship, any such move would have appeared impossible, even to Cicero. The works comprising the philosophical encyclopaedia, then, were, among other things, the product of his total retreat from politics. They had, as one might say in Cicero's sense, literary, cultural and ethical aims. For Cicero now wished to produce a philosophical literature in Latin that would match its Greek model. On the other hand, he was trying, through discussion of issues that had a bearing on the well-being and happiness of the individual, to open up for his Roman readers the rich Greek sources of practical wisdom.

The sense of the enterprise was not beyond question, even for Cicero himself, much less for his contemporaries: it had to be explained and defended. Cicero did not fail to do this, repeatedly using the introduction to the *Academica* and to the other later treatises to dispel doubts and reservations to which his endeavours might seem to give rise. It was relatively simple to dispose of the objection that it was unbecoming for a senator and former consul to dabble in philosophy. Should Roman aristocrats not be permitted, then, to crack jokes in their leisure hours, he asks sarcastically on one occasion.[36] Philosophy would be just as seemly a topic, provided that they did not neglect their public obligations. He himself was forced by political circumstances to lead a retired life, and he was trying to use his enforced idleness to instruct his fellow-citizens, rather than lapsing into dismal brooding.

Cicero did not waste much time, either, on those who still thought that Greek literature and culture should be rejected lock, stock and barrel. Such backwoodsmen were certainly long since no more than a tiny minority who might be ignored. The case was different, however, with two arguments that Cicero puts into the mouth of his Varro, undoubtedly a man with expert knowledge. Anyone who cared for Greek philosophy, said Varro, preferred the Greek originals, but someone who wasn't interested anyway would not bother with Latin versions either.[37] Besides, Latin lacked the terminology necessary for the discussion of philosophical problems. In the arguments that Cicero advances to counter these objections he seems to be precisely paraphrasing the motives which prompted him to compile a philosophical encyclopaedia in the first place. Latin poetry, he explains, was also dependent on Greek models, but it still found readers. Attempts made hitherto to render philosophical topics into Latin could not be regarded as a standard. (Cicero was referring to various hack writers, not, for instance, to the didactic poem of Lucretius.) Latin was not, as many

thought, poorer than Greek, but in fact richer. Cicero proposed, therefore, to make good for philosophy what he believed had already been
achieved for literature. He wished to produce something that would
stand comparison with its Greek models. In this ambition he was
trusting that the resources of the Latin language, combined with his
own linguistic skills, would enable him to master the problems of
philosophical terminology – and in this he was not mistaken.

Nothing was further from Cicero's mind than to offer his readers
philosophical observations of his own; he had no ambition to be an
original thinker. What he intended to do was to put the most important
teachings of the Greek schools into lucid and readable Latin – how
could he otherwise have handled such a mass of material and have
produced such an impressive number of treatises in the space of a year
and a half. He himself spoke in very definite terms about the essential
nature of his philosophical writing in the preface to De Finibus. He was
not content simply to act as a translator, but was trying to reproduce
precisely the gist of his subject, using his own judgement and his own
style of writing. Nowadays we would say that he had adapted his
models. This would be claiming neither too little nor too much.

All the works in this course of philosophy take the form of a dialogue
discussing in general terms the dogmas of various schools or trends.
Cicero has his figures explore the pros and cons of the views advanced
in each case. His own sceptical point of view emerges in the sense that
the representative of academic scepticism invariably has the last word.
When he assigned a speech to an Epicurean Cicero obviously drew on
an Epicurean source, when it was the turn of a Stoic, he used a Stoic
authority. The arguments refuting these views were customarily drawn
from relevant works of the academic school. It seems, then, that Cicero
could not locate in his Greek sources a ready-made arrangement of
dogma and sceptical response that was suitable for his purpose. He was
thus obliged to match the two sets of arguments himself as best he
could. There are cases where assertions are not refuted, or arguments
are refuted which have not been advanced. Lapses of this kind are
certainly occasioned mainly by the rapidity with which Cicero turned
out one work after the other. Further evidence of the positively hectic
pace of production is to be found in the fact that he is forced to make
do with an absolute minimum in the way of background description
and dialogue conventions. There is no parallel to the charming intro-
ductory conversation in the fifth book of De finibus, which has Cicero
and his fellow-students enthusing about those sites in Athens that remind them of the philosophers and other notable men.

'In the absence of any major obstacle I was in a position to make sure that no area of philosophy was left which was not accessible via the Latin tongue.'[38] Thus Cicero wrote in the balance which he drew up after a major obstacle had in fact appeared unexpectedly following Caesar's assassination. He thought it incumbent on him to devote himself once again to the service of the state. The grand plan for a philosophical encyclopaedia, therefore, could not be entirely fulfilled. In particular, physics, the philosophical analysis of nature was not treated. That Cicero meant to include this subject is shown by fragments that have survived from his translation of the *Timaios*, Plato's major scientific work. These were clearly meant to be incorporated in a dialogue on the subject.

Otherwise, the primary goal had been achieved by the time the Ides of March 44 changed the course of Cicero's life. By then the Roman public had access to works that dealt in adequate detail with epistemology, ethics and religion. In the summary mentioned above, which is incorporated into the preface of the second book of *De Divinatione* (*On Soothsaying*), we read the following:

> In the book entitled *Hortensius* I have advised my readers to the best of my ability to occupy themselves with philosophy – and in the four books of the *Academica* I have suggested to which philosophical method I attribute an especially large measure of circumspection, consistency and elegance. Then, in *De Finibus Bonorum et Malorum* [*On the Highest Good and the Worst of Evils*] I have discussed the fundamental problems of philosophy and have dealt with this whole area in detail in five books, so that it may be seen what arguments may be advanced for and against every philosophical system. There then followed a similar number of books with *Conversations in Tusculum*, which expounded what it is most important for us to bear in mind in our search for a happy life. For the first book deals with indifference to death, the second with how to bear pain, the third with solace in times of trouble, and the fourth with other distractions affecting our peace of mind; the fifth book, finally, is concerned with the subject that is best calculated to clarify the nature of philosophy: it demonstrates that moral worth alone is adequate to ensure a happy life. After that, three books *De Natura Deorum* [*On the Nature of the Gods*] were completed, which enter into all the relevant issues. After this entire area had been adequately covered, I began to compose the present book *De Divinatione*: when I have added, as is my intention, a further work *De Fato* [*On Destiny*], then the entire subject will have been satisfactorily covered.[39]

The *Academica* are particularly ambitious on account of the difficult epistomelogical subject-matter. They deal with a domestic dispute in

Plato's school: Philon and Antiochos had spoken in different terms about the basic thesis of the Sceptics, namely, that irrefutable truths were impossible. We may think it positively miraculous that Cicero in the thoroughly dispirited mood in which he was at that time was able to express himself so lucidly on such an intractable topic. He revised the work a number of times, and by sheer chance parts of the first and of the third and final versions have been preserved. They include the second half of the first version, which consists of two books under the title *Lucullus*, and the first book of the final version, with the dedication to Varro. This version is divided into four books.

The two great ethical dialogues, on the other hand, have survived the ages intact. No other part of the philosophical encyclopaedia is capable of appealing so directly to the present-day reader. The issues discussed there concerning the correct mode of life and the correct attitude to things have scarcely lost any of their significance in the intervening period. *De Finibus* brings together three conversations which differ in time, in place and in Cicero's interlocutor. The first two books deal with Epicurean ethics, where 'pleasure' is the highest good and 'pain' the greatest evil. A disciple of Epicurus commits himself unreservedly to this doctrine, whereupon Cicero contradicts him. The second couple of books deal in the same way with the rigorous doctrine of the Stoa, which wished moral worth to be regarded as the good, and moral depravity to be seen as evil: a positive account of this theory is followed by Cicero's criticism. Finally, the last book deals with the ethics of Peripatos, according to which the welfare or the perdition of men depend on mental and moral factors on the one hand and on physical and material factors on the other. In the case of this doctrine, Cicero's argument is limited to a few incidental remarks.

The *Conversations in Tusculum*, a work of an especially charming essayistic character, unlike *De Finibus* and the subsequent dialogues on the philosophy of religion, is not about the disputes of philosophical schools. Cicero discusses the topics that have been mentioned, but essentially follows the Stoic doctrine. The dialectical principle epitomized in the dialogue form is radically reduced in this case. A pupil advances a provocative proposition (for example, death is an evil, so is physical pain, and so on), which is then refuted by Cicero in a disquisition that is only rarely interrupted by objections. Whereas *De Finibus* discussed the basis on which man's well-being and salvation are founded, the *Conversations in Tusculum* attempt to represent as groundless all those disruptive forces (fear of death, pain, and so on) which might possibly threaten man's autarky, his self-determination.

The conversations do not simply depict an ideal, but also give instructions as to how this ideal may be approached. The ideal is that of the sage who appraises everything in terms of its true value.

The ethics is followed by the philosophy of religion. Cicero did what he said he would do, and added to the two major works a further monograph on *fatum* (destiny). The subject was for the most part somewhat alien to him, and is even more so to us today. The philosophical systems of the ancients attempted in various ways, by interpretation or rejection, to come to terms with polytheism, which they encountered as the prevailing religion. Cicero evidently could not avoid taking some account of these debates in his philosophical encyclopaedia. *De Natura Deorum*, the third and final book of which has come down to us in an incomplete form, explains how the Epicureans and the Stoics visualized the nature of the gods: the dogmatic arguments are followed by criticism on the well-tried pattern. *De Divinatione* and *De Fato*, for their part, are reserved for two favourite concepts of the Stoic school to which Cicero was strictly opposed: manticism, i.e. the belief in god-sent omens and the art of detecting them; and fate, the conviction that the entire course of events in the world was ineluctably determined.

On one occasion only did Cicero interrupt his labours on his philosophical course of instruction, which certainly demanded a high degree of dedication, and, as though by way of respite, wrote the brief dialogue *Cato Maior de Senectute* (*The Elder Cato on Old Age*). Here he was at liberty to select whatever he pleased and whatever suited him from Hellenistic literature and from the wealth of his own knowledge, in order to elucidate this practical problem in every man's life. He was all the more inclined to do this, in that both he and Atticus, the recipient of the work, had recently crossed the threshold of their seventh decade. Cato, the gnarled figure from the time of the Punic Wars, was designed to serve as a kind of exemplary aged Roman, on whom the writer could model himself. The title figure, self-confident and somewhat grumpy, considers himself in a position to dismiss as inconsequential all those things commonly regarded as the infirmities of old age.

16

The Ides of March

Caesar's assassination brought about yet another turning-point in Cicero's life – the last, for the consequences of this event led him, too, to a violent death. Having returned from Spain in September 45 after his victory over Pompey's sons, Caesar attempted during the succeeding months to legitimize his power on a constitutional as well as on a religious basis. He aspired to a form of sovereignty which would combine the charisma of a Hellenistic theocratic ruler with the ancient Roman monarchy.

These efforts merely led all the more rapidly to disaster. Dictatorship and monarchy were anathema to the aristocracy who had hitherto ruled and were now deposed. This was true, not only for uncompromising Optimates, but also for many aristocrats who had been won over by Caesar's conciliatory policy and who had been prepared to collaborate with him. After all, the traditional image of the Roman kings was not altogether negative. Romulus and his successors were regarded as the founders of the Roman state and many of its institutions. But the reputed end of the monarchy under Tarquinius Superbus overshadowed everything else: *rex* was, and remained, a synonym for tyrant. Moreover, the unlimited power of a rex served as a contrast, against which the liberal constitution of the res publica shone out all the more brilliantly.

And so Caesar made scant progress in his attempts to find an enduring form for the power which he possessed de facto, and to establish it generally in the awareness of the citizenry. Indeed, an oppressive atmosphere of hostility and opposition developed which found an outlet in pamphlets and overt criticism. Caesar tried to escape from this impasse by linking his domestic political problem with an appeal to Roman patriotism. He began preparations for a campaign against the Parthians which would erase the memory of the shameful defeat at Carrhae. It was in this context that he proposed to solve the problem of establishing his authority. He would claim the title of king for the subject territories only, and no more than a dictatorship of unlimited duration for Rome and Italy.

Caesar meant to join his troops on 18 March; on 15 March the Senate was to adopt a resolution relating to the monarchy outside Italy. This never came about. As the Senate meeting began, Caesar was struck down by several members of a conspiracy in which some sixty individuals had banded together. Cicero was not among those who were privy to the secret, although no one could be in any doubt about his view. He did, however, witness the deed, and Brutus, one of the ringleaders, holding a blood-stained dagger aloft, called out Cicero's name and congratulated him on the restoration of liberty. Cicero evidently enjoyed a high moral standing with members of the conspiracy, and was regarded by them as the principal representative of everything that the res publica signified for them. On the other hand, it was assumed – and certainly not without good reason – that he was not cut out to be a participant in the actual deed, since he lacked the necessary courage and determination.

The origins of the conspiracy are obscure: the initiative seems to have been taken by Gaius Cassius Longinus, while Brutus, Cassius's brother-in-law, was not recruited until later. On account of his name, however, he rapidly advanced to become the leader of the conspiracy. Brutus and some of the other conspirators had studied in Athens; there they had seen in the market-place the statues of Harmodius and Aristogiton. These two men – according to the official legend – had paved the way for the restoration of freedom for the citizens of Athens by their plot to overthrow the tyrannical rule of the Peisistratides. There were also Roman legends telling of the justified assassination of tyrants. Thus, about the middle of the fifth century BC, Servilius Ahala, an accomplice of the dictator Cincinnatus, was said to have killed Spurius Maelius, because the latter was trying to set himself up as a monarch. The most celebrated tale of this kind was linked to the name of Brutus. In 509 BC, so it was said, a Lucius Iunius Brutus had driven out Tarquinius Superbus, the last Roman king, whose rule had degenerated into tyranny. Iunius Brutus had thus founded the Republic.

In Classical times legends of this sort had the binding power of moral imperatives. In states not ruled by monarchs, above all in Athens and Rome, they contributed more than mere abstract principles to the conviction that the assassination of a usurper was not merely permissible, but a positive moral obligation. Accordingly, the conspirators plotting against Caesar believed that they were serving a righteous cause. In fact, they really ought not to have been called 'conspirators' at all, since they were at pains to avoid any appearance of a clandestine subversive association – so utterly convinced were they that they were acting in self-defence. Brutus later attempted to justify the deed on these grounds, delivering a speech on the Capitol which he subsequently made public. Cicero, too, thought of defending the legality of tyrannicide, and for a while he had a plan in mind to write a dialogue entitled *De Interito Caesaris, On Caesar's End*.

The circle of conspirators was by no means of one mind. Resolute opponents of Caesar rubbed shoulders with former supporters and with men who had so far refrained from adopting any firm stance. Brutus and Cassius had taken part in the civil war on Pompey's side; after Pharsalus they had been pardoned by Caesar and had attained the office of praetor in 44 BC. Brutus, who had made up his mind to join the conspiracy only after a severe inner struggle, owed his standing above all to his antecedents and to his personal culture. His mother Servilia, a half-sister of Cato Uticensis and for a number of years Caesar's mistress, was numbered among the most influential women of her time. After the early death of Brutus's father, his uncle Cato had seen to it that he was thoroughly well educated. For Brutus, the path to freedom that Cato had chosen was a legacy and a compelling duty. Apart from the two main protagonists, other prominent figures from Caesar's entourage joined the conspiracy, largely, it would seem, from idealistic motives – Decimus Iunius Brutus, who had fought under Caesar's command in Gaul and who had been acting as governor of Upper Italy since 44, and Gaius Trebonius, who had distinguished himself during the civil war at the siege of Marsilia, as well as a number of others.

Caesar had evidently reckoned for some considerable time with the chances of assassination. He could not fail to have noticed the hostile atmosphere he encountered in pursuing a constitutional policy that aimed at legitimizing monarchy, and he had also received specific warnings. He did nothing, however, to ensure his own safety. Indeed, he dismissed his bodyguard of Spanish soldiers and had no thought of replacing it. Various statements he is alleged to have made regarding the risk of a violent death suggest a mixture of indifference and resignation. One, in particular, is noteworthy. He is reported to have said that it was not so important for him to remain alive for his own sake as for the sake of the country.[1] He had gained more than enough in terms of power and reputation, but if anything should happen to him, then the state would find no peace and would be bound to undergo civil strife that would be worse than ever before.

The members of the resistance movement, however, showed themselves to be much less perspicuous than their opponent and victim, and so his prophetic pronouncement came true in every detail. Basically they thought in stereotyped and apolitical terms. They were obsessed with the need to assassinate the tyrant and were so peculiarly blind to realities that they imagined the old res publica would be restored, once Caesar had been removed. They ignored Caesar's supporters and his potential power and failed to see that the consequence of their deed would merely be a monarchy without a monarch. Nothing would have been gained except a renewed struggle for the dominant place in the power structure.

Cicero, it is true, soon realized that events were heading towards a new civil war, but even he was incapable of grasping the true state of affairs. He clung to a superficial view that was far too dependent on day-to-day politics. To begin with, however, he was simply elated at the death of Caesar. On 15 March, or shortly afterwards, he addressed a famous, indeed notorious, letter to the conspirator Lucius Minucius Basilus: 'I wish you good fortune and cannot forbear from rejoicing; you have my love and I am concerned to defend your interests. I would like you to love me in return, and I would like to know what you mean to do, and what the general purpose is.'[2] Cicero repeatedly asserted that, in his initial elation, he had made no secret of his satisfaction. Caesar had, after all, been a tyrant, and his regime, in Cicero's eyes, cancelled out everything he had possessed in the way of talents, and all he had achieved. This is, at any rate, the overall impression given by the character sketch he devoted to Caesar in his *Second Philippic*:

> He possessed genius, perspicacity, a good memory, culture, prudence, mental discipline and judgement; he performed great feats of arms which were important, although they had a pernicious effect on the state; fired for many years by the ambition to be sole ruler of his country, he had gained his goal by strenuous efforts and in the face of great dangers; he had enticed the ignorant masses by games, buildings, gifts and public banquets and had bound his friends to him by largesse, his foes by the semblance of leniency – in short, he had contrived to inculcate in our free people the habits of servility, in part by intimidation, in part by the dulling of their senses.[3]

Cicero's joy did not long remain unalloyed. The murder of Caesar had left an ominous vacuum. Neither on the Republican, nor on the

Caesarean side were there forces making for integration, men whose authority would have guided the citizens, who seemed as though stunned by the event. Even Cicero and Brutus were in no position to help the senatorial aristocracy, who had been hard hit by the civil war. Caesar's party was similarly confused and had no idea of a common policy. Caesar's devoted lieutenants, men like Balbus and Oppius, however efficient they might be, had little or no standing. Those senators who had once been inclined to support him, if they had not actually joined in the conspiracy, had observed Caesar's aspirations to monarchy with severe disapproval, so that they tended to regard the assassins' deed as justified. Above all, there seemed to be no one, at first anyway, who dared avenge Caesar's death and lay claim to his authority. No one except the Roman mob and Caesar's soldiers and veterans demonstrated their loyalty to his cause. But these forces did in fact represent a potential which lacked only effective leadership.

The liberators suffered from the great disadvantage that the one consul who then existed (Caesar had been the other) was not on their side, namely Mark Antony. This at once became obvious when Cicero, who was no more able than his contemporaries to command a view of the confused situation, tentatively tried to encourage the Republicans to take some positive action. On 15 March he took part in a discussion to which he had been invited by the liberators. He believed that an understanding with Antony was not feasible, and thought that the praetors, Brutus and Cassius, should seize the initiative and convoke the Senate. This suggestion was dismissed for sound reasons, and it was decided to negotiate with Antony. It is questionable whether Cicero had already arrived at the conclusion which he expressed some weeks later to Atticus, and subsequently to a number of other people: namely, that the liberators had acted in a childish manner, that they should not have left Antony alive.[4] At any rate, he must have had misgivings even on the night of 15 March, for Antony's death would have made the praetors the highest appointed officers of the state, and Brutus and Cassius would automatically have gained the freedom of action which they so urgently needed.

Subsequent developments were not calculated to allay Cicero's fears. Increasingly obvious signs suggested that none other than the consul Antony was aiming to assume Caesar's mantle. He intervened wherever he could, and was nevertheless astute enough not to fall out with anyone, so that within a matter of months he had brought together a respectable following which enabled him to play a leading part in Rome and *vis-à-vis* the Senate. He managed to gain possession of Caesar's posthumous papers as well as his financial resources, an inestimable advantage as it turned out. For the Senate meeting of 17 March, which he had convened, led to a resolution which appeared to confirm the restoration of the Republic, but which recognized at the same time the position of the Caesarean party. Caesar's assassins were granted immunity, while all the legislation enacted by Caesar was declared legal and valid. Cicero played a leading part in arriving at this compromise. In claiming immunity for the conspirators he cited the precedent of the amnesty that the Athenian democrats had granted to the members of the deposed oligarchy after their victory in 403 BC.[5] He later professed that he had assented to the reciprocal deal involving the recognition of the *acta Caesaris* only because he had no choice when faced by the armed veterans assembled by Antony. It is also possible, however, that he did not at once detect the hidden snag in this agreement. As Caesar's executor, Antony was in a position to invoke not only decrees promulgated by Caesar, but also all sorts of unpublished measures. In fact, he did not scruple to invent orders that had allegedly been drafted by Caesar before his death.

On the following day, 18 March, in the course of a further session of the Senate, Antony succeeded in pushing through a motion that Caesar should be accorded a public funeral. Cicero presumably had to stomach this as best he could, but Atticus at once pointed out to him that the liberators' cause was totally lost from that moment on.[6] In keeping with ancient custom, Antony delivered a speech in praise of the deceased at the funeral, which did in fact degenerate into a violent riot. The infuriated mob cremated Caesar's body in the centre of the forum and then set off with the intention of burning down the homes of Caesar's foes. It was possible to repel the attack, because it had been anticipated, but Brutus and Cassius were forced to leave Rome in the interests of their safety. Cicero did not long remain in the city either. In spite of various concessions on the part of Antony, he had come to the conclusion that he was not in a position to change the course of events, which had taken a generally inauspicious turn, so he chose a way out that had served him well in the past. He avoided taking part in meetings of the Senate by retreating to his country estates.

Cicero was absent from Rome from the beginning of April until the end of August. Fifty-eight letters to Atticus have been preserved from this period, fifty-seven of them fairly evenly spaced throughout the months from April to July. We can thus see precisely how Cicero acted the part of onlooker, with which, by and large, he now had to be content. He never spent more than a few days in any one place, moving first to his estates on the Bay of Naples, at Cumae, Puteoli and Pompeii. He then moved back towards Rome, to Tusculum and Antium. Finally, on 1 July, he set off from Tusculum on the journey that was meant to take him to Greece, but which in fact never got beyond Syracuse, because of an unforeseen turn of events.

The letters of the first few months revolve round the Ides of March. Cicero was unable to adopt the view of Gaius Matius, a friend of his and also an admirer of Caesar, but it did impress him. Caesar's murder, Matius maintained, had left things in an unholy muddle.[7] Cicero interpreted the current state of affairs as a paradox which he once summed up in the phrase, 'Vivit tyrannis, tyrannus occidit' – 'Tyranny lives, only the tyrant is dead'.[8] Nothing could be as absurd, he writes elsewhere, as to praise the tyrannicides to the skies and, on the other hand, to support the measures the tyrant had ordained.[9] The elation of the Ides had been short-lived, since the tyrant's former henchmen were now in power:[10] 'Interfecto rege liberi non sumus' – 'We have killed the king, but still we are not free'.[11] At times Cicero is inclined to regard this outcome as inevitable: 'Our heroes', he says at one point, 'have done in the most glorious manner possible all that it was in their power to do; what remains to be done needs money and troops, and these we do not possess.'[12] At another point he states: 'You defend Brutus and Cassius, as if I were criticizing them – in fact, I cannot praise them too highly. I was speaking of errors which are in the nature of things, not in individuals.'[13] For the most part, however, he finds fault with what had been left undone, especially with the fact that the job had been only half completed – Antony had been spared. He also suggests at one point that the Republican cause might still have been saved if his advice had been followed and the praetors had convened the Senate immediately after the deed. 'Oh, ye immortal gods, what might we not have achieved at that moment, when all the conservatives and even our half-hearted supporters were jubilant, whereas the gangsters had utterly lost heart?'[14]

With his letter of 26 April Cicero's fears become more acute: the nightmare of a renewed war was raising its ugly head.[15] In that case, Cicero says, no one will be at liberty to remain neutral, as in Caesar's time, for the party of the scoundrels would consider as their enemy anyone they thought had rejoiced at Caesar's death, so that it would all end in a dreadful bloodbath. Only once did Cicero believe in a reversal of fortune, which would be brought about by none other than his erstwhile son-in-law, Dolabella. Caesar had envisaged that Dolabella would act as his successor during the period he was absent from Rome.

After Caesar's murder, however, Dolabella had gone over to the Republicans and had persuaded them to confirm him in his consulship. When he then proceeded to give short shrift to all kinds of allegedly Caesarean riff-raff without consulting his colleague Antony, Cicero got the impression that he had decided to throw in his lot with the Republicans for good and sent him an effusively flattering letter.[16] His joy was short-lived, and the scepticism that Atticus had expressed right at the beginning soon turned out to be totally justified. Dolabella was an unprincipled time-server, and in May he came to terms with Antony.

Cicero once again saw the threat of a ruthless civil war – especially when it was reported to him that Antony was recruiting Caesar's veterans. He came to the conclusion that Caesar's party feared nothing as much as peace and stability. At the end of May Cicero learned of a plan by Antony to strengthen his position through an exchange of provinces, a plan that he was subsequently able to put into practice with the aid of the popular assembly, which he controlled. Decimus Brutus was to cede his province of Cisalpine Gaul (Upper Italy) to Antony, taking over Macedonia instead – but without the legions that were stationed there. Cicero now believed civil war to be inevitable and even confessed reluctantly that the Ides of March had merely made matters worse, since Caesar would have been a more indulgent monarch.[17]

For some time Cicero had been thinking of leaving Italy and going to visit his son, who was studying in Athens. For this purpose he proposed to acquire an appointment as legate, i.e. chief adjutant to a provincial governor, which would have secured him all the privileges of a Roman official without burdening him with too much in the way of duties. At first he hesitated, hoping that clearly defined positions would emerge; he would then depart only if it was certain that he was not needed and that he could do nothing for the Republican cause. At the end of May, when Antony was undisputed master of the situation in Rome, Cicero began to regard the position there as hopeless. He now went ahead and applied to both consuls for a post as legate. The response was prompt: Dolabella, who had just been appointed governor of Syria for the next five years, nominated Cicero as his legate for the entire duration of his office, without stipulating any particular location.

But Cicero hesitated once again, as was his wont. At heart he would have preferred to stay in Italy, but if he went, then he intended to return for 1 January. He was still obsessed with notions of legitimacy and was hoping for a new policy from the new consuls. In his gloomiest moments he was capable of writing that his departure would be a consequence of *desperatio* rather than of *legatio*.[18] He wanted to get out of Antony's fish-trap, not in order to make good his escape, but in order to die in dignity. However, he then hesitated once more – 'I torment myself in an odd way, although I feel no pain' – because reasons for and against kept crowding in on him.[19] Moreover, he was receiving any number of letters which offered contradictory advice.

It was probably the end of June when Cicero wrote a cordial farewell letter to the worthy Oppius, one of Caesar's supporters, committing his property to the latter's care.[20] On 1 July he set out from his Tusculanum. By 7 July he had got as far as Puteoli, but at that point the choice of route called for a certain amount of careful thought. Brundisium seemed too risky, because the troops Antony had ordered from Macedonia were expected to disembark there. Consequently, Cicero thought of the minor port of Hydrus, which was situated further to the south. For a while he tried to join Brutus, who was staying on a small island nearby, intending to travel on to the East from there. As Brutus was delayed, Cicero set out with three boats on 17 July, from his Pompeianum. He left Atticus in no doubt about his frame of mind, writing as follows:

> Now that I am on the point of departure, my heart is heavy for a number of reasons – but most of all, by God, because of parting from you. The trials of the voyage also depress me, for it is unfitting both to my years and my social position – which is also true of the peculiar time of my departure. For we are leaving the country in peacetime in order to return in wartime, and the time I might have spent on my finely tended and charmingly situated country estates I am spending instead on my travels. This is my one consolation: I shall be able to foster my son's progress, or at least to observe what can be made of him. Besides, you will soon be joining me, as I hope and as you promise. Then everything will be better.[21]

Cicero is here summing up everything that weighed on his mind at the time. The sense that he was growing old was what inspired him to write *Cato* ('ad senem senex de senectute' – 'As an old man to an old man, about old age', he wittily remarked).[22] Now, faced with the unpromising political situation, he felt the urge to read it over and over again: 'Old age is making me cantankerous; I get worked up about everything. After all, my life is behind me, let the young people see what they can do!'[23] The painful death of his doctor Alexio prompted him to reflect that he no longer needed a new doctor, and in the same letter he asked the question, 'Isn't the mask of old age sufficiently ugly?'[24]

On the other hand, he now seems to be particularly responsive to the charms of the countryside surrounding his villas; he experiences them by way of contrast to the gloominess of the political situation, and questions the justification for his journey. 'You ask me and you assume that I myself do not know the answer', he writes in April, 'whether I enjoy distant views from the hills more than walks by the seaside. It is indeed as you say: both kinds of landscape are so agreeable that I am uncertain which I should prefer.'[25] And at the end of July, still clinging to his plan to travel to Greece, he remarks to Atticus: 'Why am I not with you? Why can't I see the jewels of Italy, my villas?'[26]

His son Marcus had gone to study in Athens in 45 BC. His nephew Quintus had served under Caesar in Spain and then joined Antony after Caesar's death in order to rid himself of his crushing debts. Marcus at least did not cause Cicero any trouble in a political respect. All the same, the young man's mode of life did not seem to be altogether impeccable. The reports of his Greek mentors were at times not unqualified in their praise, so that there was good reason for Cicero's wish to visit his son and supervise his studies. However, no less a person than Gaius Trebonius, substitute consul for 45 BC and a convinced Republican, sent a letter which was unsparing in its praises: Marcus was devoting himself diligently to his philosophical studies and was reputed to be very modest – he wasn't writing this, Trebonius says, simply because it was what the boy's father wanted to hear.[27] He would be able to bring Marcus over to Asia Minor as soon as he took up his governorship there, and the philosopher Cratippus could accompany the young man, so that his studies need not be interrupted. Marcus had evidently done his best to make an agreeable impression on Trebonius, and in a long letter to Tiro he also tries to show himself in as favourable a light as possible.[28] He had renounced his youthful aberrations, he claims, was constantly in the company of Cratippus and was also at pains not to neglect his rhetoric.

Cicero cruised with his three boats at a leisurely – not to say sluggish – pace along the coast of the Tyrrhenian Sea towards Sicily. The voyage cannot have been all that arduous and Cicero was doubtless at peace with the world, otherwise he would hardly have occupied himself with his philosophical writings. In doing so, he stumbled upon an amusing blunder. On 17 July, shortly before leaving his Pompeianum, he had sent Atticus the revised manuscript of the essay *On Fame*, which he had just completed. Now he discovered that he had preceded it with a preface which he had already used – at the beginning of the third book of the *Academici Libri*.[29] He had a whole stock of such prefaces embroidered with recurrent themes, so that, given the large number of works he had committed to paper in rapid succession at that time, it could happen that he had picked out the same version twice. During the voyage he read the *Academici Libri*, which he had written about eighteen months previously, and thus discovered the duplication. He immediately wrote a new preface and asked Atticus to paste it into the fair copy which he had been sent. The text of the duplicated preface is not extant, nor is the substituted version. No more than scanty fragments of the essay *On Fame* and of books 2–4 of the *Academici Libri* (in the final version) have survived.

We do have a brief rhetorical treatise which Cicero says he also wrote during this voyage in the summer of 44 – the *Topica*, a guide to the methodical search for rhetorical arguments that took its title from an Aristotelian model. The work lists 'sources' (τόποι, *loci*), from which arguments might be deduced for the resolution of any given dispute: the whole, the parts, definition, relations such as etymology, genre, manner, analogy, difference, and so on. Aristotle's *Topica* has obviously not been used, but Cicero would not have depended solely on his memory and would have consulted various notes – possibly taken from lectures on rhetoric by Philon or Antiochus. The treatise is dedicated to the lawyer Trebatius, who had just visited Cicero in his Tusculanum. There Trebatius had come across Aristotle's *Topica* and had wished to have it explained to him. On his journey to Elea – the home of the famous 'Eleatic' school of philosophers – Cicero had stayed on an estate belonging to Trebatius, who was absent at the time, and had felt the need to reply to his friend's request.[30] Thus, the *Topica* had been written on his way to Rhegium. From there he sent a copy to Trebatius. For the recipient's benefit he had included various legal illustrations. Nevertheless, in his accompanying letter he expresses the fear that Trebatius may come across obscure passages here and there.[31] In that case he should bear in mind that no art can be learned simply from books, not even civil law, and that a teacher and a certain amount of practice are also necessary.

On 1 August Cicero arrived in Syracuse, meaning to cross from there to Greece. Adverse southerly winds held him up, so that he was stuck on Cape Leucopetra at the south-western tip of Italy. While waiting for more favourable weather he was making himself at home in a villa belonging to his companion Publius Valerius when news suddenly reached him which forced him to interrupt his journey and return to Rome.

17

The Final Battle for the Republic

Some citizens of Rhegium had brought important tidings from Rome.
Brutus and Cassius had issued an edict protesting against certain actions
taken by Antony, and a meeting of the Senate had been convened for 1
August at which as many former consuls and praetors as possible were
to be present. There was a chance that Antony would back down, and
Cicero would be sorely missed. Atticus wrote to the same effect. Indeed,
he now took Cicero to task for having left Rome at all: an Epicurean
might behave like that, but not Cicero. Cicero had already turned back
of his own accord, without the need of any such admonition, and in his
reply he defended himself vigorously against his friend's sudden change
of mind.[1] He did admit, however, that his return had delighted Brutus,
whom he had met in Velia in the middle of August, and that by
returning he had escaped severe criticism. His conversation with Brutus
had made him aware of certain new facts which considerably dampened
his expectations, although they did not make him hesitate in his decision to return to Rome. Antony had reacted in a manner that was
anything but conciliatory: he had issued a counter-edict and was
threatening to use force. And at the Senate meeting on 1 August only
one member had dared to raise his voice against Antony: no other than
Lucius Piso, the individual – how embarrassing! – whom Cicero reckoned to be the principal agent of his exile and who had grossly slan-
dered him in a vicious lampoon.

Before he had a chance to emulate Piso and express his opinion of
the Republic's enemy, with whatever success, Cicero received a visit in
Tusculanum from Trebatius. He had initiated a memorable exchange
of ideas in correspondence between Cicero and Matius, an admirer of
Caesar to whom we have already referred. It seems that Cicero had
spoken in critical terms to third parties about the political position and
actions of Matius; at any rate, rumours to that effect had reached the

ears of Matius. Two accusations in particular had evidently played an important part. Matius had voted for a law favouring the Caesarean party, and he had helped to sponsor games commemorating Caesar's victories. Matius, for his part, had complained to Trebatius that this kind of criticism was not in keeping with the friendly relations existing between himself and Cicero.

Cicero, informed by Trebatius of Matius's annoyance, at once composed a letter that was obviously meant to prove that Matius's complaints were groundless, and to restore their former relationship – in spite of their political differences of opinion.[2] He begins by reviewing the history of their friendship and proceeds extremely cautiously. He emphasizes what Matius had done for him, especially in relation to Caesar, and asks repeatedly whether Matius imagined that he had forgotten those services and benefits. 'Why these expostulations', Cicero goes on, 'which have turned out to be lengthier than I thought they would be? It's because I was astonished that you – who should have known all this – imagined I had done something not in keeping with our friendship.' Only then does Cicero turn to the alleged accusations. It had seemed to him unlikely that Matius had voted for that law; had he done so, however, Cicero would have assumed that he had had good reasons. As a rule, he responded to malicious gossip in two ways: he refuted the allegation, as in the case of the alleged vote, or he adduced honourable motives, as in the sponsoring of the games. Admittedly, Cicero adds, if Caesar had been a dictator, opinions might differ about the service that Matius wished to render his memory. One might, as Cicero did, emphasize his loyalty and piety, but one might also, as some others did, argue that the country's liberty should be more highly esteemed than the life of one's friend.

Cicero stands by his guns at this point, but at the same time he respects Matius's point of view. However, for the sake of good relations he is no doubt expressing a more tolerant view of the latter's actions than he held in private. (To Atticus, for instance, he had remarked bluntly that he did not care for Matius as a sponsor of games.)[3] His association with Atticus and his experience in the civil war had evidently taught Cicero that political allegiance as the sole test of good personal relations led, when rigorously applied, to questionable results. The political game was too perilous to permit any individual to dispense with personal connections across the gulf dividing the parties. In any case, one would have been the poorer through the loss of a good many fine individuals from one's circle of friends. And Cicero was well aware of how much Matius was worth to him: 'All your qualities please me, but above all your steadfast loyalty in friendship, your perspicacity, your seriousness, your resolute stance, your subtle mind, taste and culture.'

In his reply Matius did his best to accept in more than a purely formal sense Cicero's conciliatory approach, which was pitched on more than one level.[4] However, he does not seem to have entirely succeeded. The friendly phrases with which his reply begins and ends are clearly drowned out by the swingeing central passage – a heated self-justification which largely misses the point of Cicero's painstaking attempts to draw fine distinctions. Matius deals instead in a one-sided fashion with the point of view which Cicero had said was not his own, but rather that of the uncompromising Republican. Matius attempts to refute five separate allegations: that he had been outraged by the death of Caesar, a man whom he had loved; that he had disapproved of the liberators' deed; that he had behaved in a way that was detrimental to the interests of the state by giving his vote; that he had sponsored games in honour of Caesar's victories; and that he now frequently visited Antony's home in the morning in order to pay his respects. This rather too vehement letter, which very clearly betrays the writer's injured pride, manifests an unusual attitude to Caesar – and its value consists mainly in this fact. On the one hand, Matius was positively devoted to Caesar, indeed, he seems to have assigned to the latter's influence as a statesman something like a historical necessity. On the other hand, as distinct from the average Caesarean partisan, he definitely dissociated himself from Caesar in a number of essential respects. He explains that he had not approved of the civil war or of the occasion for it, and he had done everything he could to stop it breaking out. Following Caesar's victory he had accepted neither high office nor money and had pleaded for leniency towards the conquered as if he were pleading for his own life.

On 31 August Cicero arrived in Rome. Antony had called a meeting of the Senate in the Temple of Harmony for the following day. He had arranged for a formidable number of his armed followers to be present, and was proposing to force through a resolution to the effect that a day in honour of Caesar should be added to all thanksgiving festivals dedicated to the gods. Such was now the plight of the Republic. Antony ruled the roost, suppressing every free expression of opinion and elevating Caesar to a divine guarantor of the state and a universally binding religious authority. Cicero, who was informed of Antony's intention, avoided the embarrassment of being forced to give his consent, pleading the rigours of his journey and absenting himself from the meeting.

Antony, infuriated by this move, swore that he would force Cicero to appear by tearing his house down – although he did not in fact carry out this monstrous threat.

On 2 September the Senate met again in the same place. This time Antony was absent and his colleague Dolabella chaired the meeting. The debate was meant to deal with the res publica and the political situation in general. Cicero turned up well prepared and delivered a speech which he published shortly afterwards. It was incorporated as the first item in the final phase of Cicero's rhetorical works and was the first in a series of fourteen addresses which really ought to be called 'Speeches in opposition to Antony', but which have come down to us as *Philippics*. This symbolic title harks back to the battle which Demosthenes, the greatest of all Athenian orators, had fought in the middle of the fourth century BC against the Macedonian King Philip II, a fiercely impassioned fight for power and for the freedom of Athens to which four of the *Philippics* literally bear witness. The title of Cicero's addresses was evidently suggested by Cicero himself. Brutus, by that time commander-in-chief of considerable Republican forces in Greece, wrote to Cicero on 1 April 43: 'I have read two speeches by you.... Now you will certainly expect me to praise them. I don't know what deserves more praise – your political views or your talent; I absolutely agree that they should be called *Philippics*, as you yourself once suggested jokingly in one of your letters.'[5] This letter has not in fact been preserved, but another one has, in which Cicero himself uses the term *Philippicae*.

What did Cicero mean to say when he used this term? Certainly there is a formal implication. Cicero, who had wished to awaken associations with Plato through his philosophical works, *On the State* and *On Laws*, was now suggesting that he would be willing to stand comparison with Demosthenes as orator. Like many other statements by Classical Roman authors, from Lucretius down to the Augustan poets, the title indicates that they were striving to produce works to match the finest achievements of the Greeks. In the case of the *Philippicae*, it is true, Cicero was probably thinking more of the similarity of theme and of political situation. Like Demosthenes in his time, he felt called upon to fight a relentless battle against an enemy who was threatening the freedom of the state. In each case it was a matter of encouraging one's own divided forces to sink their differences and to arm themselves adequately in preparation for war as the only way out of the situation. Cicero took less account, however, of a further common feature which could be obvious only to someone who was acquainted with the outcome of the dramatic conflict. Namely that both the Greek and the

Roman orator were championing a lost cause: they were pursuing a policy that could no longer succeed and were doomed to fail.

In fact, the *First Philippic* does not carry on the battle with all its subsequent ferocity: it still attempts – in its form, at least – to avoid an irrevocable break. Nevertheless, it met with no more success than the initiative undertaken a month previously by Piso: the response of the leading senators, the former consuls, was an embarrassed silence. Only Publius Servilius Isauricus, formerly a moderate member of Caesar's party who was now inclined – like Piso – to pursue a policy aimed at the restoration of the Republic, dared to second Cicero's criticism of the measures taken by the consuls in office. Circumstances, it seemed, did not favour this kind of initiative.

At the beginning of his speech Cicero explained the reasons for his departure and subsequent return. To stay longer would have been pointless, he said, in view of the illegal actions that Antony, after a promising start, had found it expedient to take from 1 June onwards. He had meant to stay away until 1 January, when the new consuls would take up office. However, when he heard along the way that Antony had had a change of heart, he at once turned back. The threats of the previous day, Cicero went on, had been out of all proportion to the importance of the agenda. Antony should really have been glad that Cicero was not present. Under no circumstances would he have been prepared to consent to a combination of divine service and funeral rites for a deceased mortal – Caesar. After these preliminaries Cicero sharply criticized the laws that Antony had imposed since 1 June – without ever once mentioning the latter's name. He tried to demonstrate that this manner of legislating was a gross infringement of the generally accepted 'acta Caesaris', which formed the basis of the state's internal political stability. Cicero concluded with an appeal addressed to the consuls. They should not take the speaker's plain words amiss, but rather revert to the promising policy they had pursued immediately following Caesar's death.

Antony was well aware that Cicero's relatively mild form of words implied a devastating judgement on his policies, and he was outraged. Cicero believed that Antony was capable of seeking his death even at that stage. But the time was not yet ripe, and Antony, who at that time ruled no more than the city of Rome, could not feel entirely secure. He attempted, then, to defeat Cicero with his own weapon – the word. He retired to his country estates, and there, with the aid of his teacher of rhetoric, Sextus Clodius, he worked out a reply. This speech, which he addressed to the Senate during its meeting on 19 September in Cicero's absence and subsequently published, was intended to revoke the 'friendly relationship' which had hitherto existed between the two men. Its content may be deduced from Cicero's response in the *Second Philippic*. Antony justified this official breaking-off of relations by a kind of general settling of scores, a devastating criticism of Cicero's overall political activity. He claimed that Cicero, as consul, had engineered the death penalty for the Catalarinians with the assistance of gangs of armed slaves; that he had instigated the murder of Clodius; that he had caused the quarrel between Caesar and Pompey, and hence the civil war; that in Pompey's camp he had made himself unpopular as the man who always knew best, and, what was more, he was morally responsible for the murder of Caesar.

There is no evidence that Antony's attempt to isolate Cicero by making him the chief culprit in a series of disastrous events would have altered the situation in any essential way. The confusing multitude of conflicting political forces persisted – Caesareans, Republicans, and those who were still prudently holding back and waiting for their chance. In particular, the two consuls for the succeeding year, Hirtius and Pansa, still refused to have anything to do with Antony, and so it was important to limit his influence pending the expected change of leadership on 1 January. Cicero appears to have conducted a lively correspondence with this purpose in mind. A number of letters – to Cassius, Lucius Munatius Plancus, the governor of Gaul, and Quintus Cornificius, the governor of Africa Vetus – give graphic accounts of Antony's tyranny and urge the recipients to take patriotic action. Apart from Piso, Servilius and Cicero himself, one letter to Cassius states that no one dares to raise his voice against Antony: anyone who has not been lured away by Antony steers clear of the Senate, or is prevented by illness or absence from Rome from attending.[6] 'There you have the spokesmen of the council of state', Cicero goes on, 'if their number was insignificant even in auspicious times, how do you rate them now, in this catastrophic situation?' Cicero draws the conclusion that the only hope for the Republic lies in the governors and the military commanders outside Rome. If they had plans in mind befitting their good name, then the state would soon regain its constitutional rights.

Cicero had realized, then, that he had returned prematurely to Rome. The situation was not affected by Antony's departure to fetch a contingent of troops from Brundisium – the Macedonian legions assigned to him in consequence of the exchange of provinces with Decimus Brutus. Cicero, however, did not set off again on his journey to Greece, he simply withdrew to his country estates and did not return to Rome until

9 December. Having realized that there was no point in remaining in the capital, he was already engaged in committing the *Second Philippic* to paper. It is presented to the reader as if it had been delivered on 19 September, immediately following the attack by Antony. In fact, like the *Second Speech against Verres*, it is a pamphlet that was composed some time after the event. It was completed on 24 October. Cicero sent it immediately to Atticus, remarking, 'Enclosed is the speech; it's up to you whether you keep it dark, or publish it. When do you think the day will come when you consent to its publication?'[7] Atticus no doubt advised his friend not to publish, for the *Second Philippic* was certainly not made public until after Cicero's death.

Its vehemence sets it apart, not only from the *First Philippic*, but also from all the subsequent accusations levelled at Antony. The possibility that the work might have to be kept secret, with which Cicero had reckoned from the start, once more gave him the chance to parade his supreme skill in the handling of words via a masterly piece of invective that contrives to represent his adversary as the very epitome of vice and depravity. The general line of attack is laid down right at the start. Antony was carrying on in a way that was worse than any Cataline or Clodius – Cicero's black and white portraiture starts off miles away from political reality.

To begin with, the points made by Antony in his attack on Cicero are refuted successively; his one-sided assault provokes a defence that is no less one-sided. The counter-attack then follows, with Cicero reviewing his adversary's life in chronological sequence. This section is more entertaining: derision, wit and sarcasm alternate with sentiment and indignation in a torrent of brilliantly phrased vituperation. Antony's alleged political misdemeanours are mingled indiscriminately with notorious incidents from scandaleus gossip concerning Antony's private life.

His youth: debts and prostitution; the earliest phase of his political career down to his appointment as quaestor: violence, defiance of the divine will, and so on. In the passage dealing with Antony's consulate Cicero hurls back at him the charge of having started the civil war. The indictment reaches its climax in a swingeing attack, reminiscent of the *Second Speech against Verres*, with Cicero mercilessly scourging Antony's outrageous behaviour in every part of Italy. Following Pharsalus: immorality, greed, then drunken debauchery (with the famous – indeed, notorious – account of vomiting in public) and – during a period of enforced inactivity – the squandering of Pompey's fortune. So one scene follows another until we come to the most brilliant episodes in the sequence: the attempt to crown Caesar king and, following the Ides of March, the traffic in forged Caesarean edicts.

It was probably at the end of November that Cicero completed a counterpart to *Cato on Old Age*, the little dialogue entitled *Laelius on Friendship*. The subject had always attracted a good deal of attention among philosophers – as befitted its great practical significance, not only in the private, but also in the public life of the Greeks and Romans. Of what has survived, pride of place is taken by Aristotle's *Nicomachean Ethics*: books 8 and 9 offer a great variety of observations and reflections on the subject of friendship. Following Aristotle, we do not encounter a similar body of work which has survived the passage of time until we come to the teachings of Epicurus, in whose theory and practice friendship plays a similarly large part. Their survival is due in large part to Cicero, who has the Epicurean Lucius Manlius give a detailed account of his doctrine in the first book of *De Finibus*.[8] Subjects of particular controversy were the nature of true friendship and the hierarchy of the motives giving rise to friendship. Does one form friendships for one's own profit or for security, in short, from purely utilitarian considerations, or is man predestined by the nature of his being to form friendships? There were even voices which called in question the fundamental value of friendship. The more perfect someone was, the less he needed friends; besides, one was liable to jeopardize one's peace of mind by forming bonds with others.

Cicero's essay reflects this rich tradition of thought on the subject of friendship in a felicitous synthesis that was sustained by his own experience. A later author claims that Cicero had closely followed a work by Theophrastus on the same subject.[9] There, indeed, we find in a rather more precisely circumscribed version the rather tricky maxim of *Laelius*, namely, that one might occasionally depart from the straight and narrow path in order to help a friend. Apart from this work by Theophrastus, Cicero may also have consulted the main source for his *De Officiis*, the doctrine of duty proposed by Panaetius.

Like *Cato*, *Laelius* is distinguished by its ethical complexion and the palpable sincerity of its author. The figure who gives the work its title is once again an apt choice. Laelius, from whose son-in-law, Quintus Mucius Scaevola the Augur, Cicero had once received instruction in the law, was best known to posterity through his lifelong friendship with the younger Scipio. And Cicero himself had for more than four decades been the intimate friend of the work's recipient, Atticus. 'Just as I recently wrote, as an old man, to an old man, on old age, so I have now composed the present work as his best friend, for my friend, on the subject of friendship': thus Cicero writes in the introduction to *Laelius*, alluding to the analogous situation in *Cato*.

But the twin dialogues differ from each other in mood. *Laelius* deals with a more ambitious subject; the style is more restrained and solemn, and the character of the work is dictated by philosophical proofs and moral reflections rather than by a slightly forced genial candour. There is ecstatic praise for friendship, but the speakers are almost more keenly aware of the risks arising from the bond with another person than of the expected gain. For here, in fact, it is not simply a matter of the individual's subjective attitude: the condition of friendship is dependent on all those involved, and also on the circumstances. True friendship is at risk precisely because it knows no boundaries, and a conflict between loyalty to a friend and loyalty to the state may present a particularly delicate problem. Hence, there is nothing that Laelius stresses more emphatically than the need to choose one's friends with care. In this connection we must seek some way out of the vicious circle: namely, the necessity for a friend to be trustworthy before we put our trust in him, and, on the other hand, the need to trust him in order to discover whether he is trustworthy.

The sequence of ideas is not very clear, particularly in the central section, and suggests that Cicero wrote the work in great haste. Besides, he was obliged to insert into the argument of his models a personal passage which obviously concerned him deeply.[10] This was the extract about a collision between the claims of friendship and one's loyalty to the state. This had been suggested to him by his experiences with followers of Caesar, with people like Matius, who, it seemed to him, went much too far in their loyalty to a friend.

The weeks of enforced idleness in the autumn of 44 brought a further major philosophical work: 'Exstabit opera peregrinationis' – 'This journey will leave a memorial behind it', Cicero wrote to Atticus at the end of October.[11] He was referring to *De Officiis*, which, unlike all of Cicero's other philosophical works, is not a dialogue, but is written in the straightforward form of a treatise. On 5 November Cicero was able to report that the first two of the three books had been completed. He had adhered to the Περὶ τοῦ καθήκοντος of Panaetius, his treatise *On Propriety and Seemliness*, hence, *On duty*. But only two problems were dealt with there, the moral and the utilitarian, together with their opposites, while a third point, the problem of an (apparent) conflict between morality and utility, was not discussed. Cicero hoped to gain insight into this issue from a work by Poseidonius, and he asked the philosopher Athenodorus Calvus to send him extracts from it.

Poseidonius had little to offer, as it turned out, and so Cicero was obliged to compile the third book 'nullis adminiculis', 'without aids', and from his own resources.[12]

The work is dedicated to Cicero's son, who was studying in Athens. It is addressed, therefore – as its predecessor by Panaetius certainly was – to the younger generation within a certain class, to those young people who would eventually take over the political leadership. It might be of practical assistance, but only to the Roman aristocracy. Cicero is not concerned with the common citizens. The trades practised by craftsmen and small shopkeepers he reckoned to be 'dirty', and professions like medicine or architecture were 'honourable' only in the case of those to whose lowly status they were appropriate.

The first book, which deals with *honestum*, the honourable, is clearly constructed, articulated in terms of the various types of moral duties which are deduced from the nature of man. The intellectual duty to recognize the truth, on which Cicero bestows the briefest of glances, is followed by the concept of social morality, arranged according to the basic notions of justice and benevolence. Third place is occupied by 'magnitudo animi', a quality which embraces both a contempt for all worldly goods and bold and vigorous action. Cicero is here expounding subjects which had always been important to him: the superiority of a life devoted to governing the state over the philosopher's secluded existence, the reasons why the activity of the statesman often brings more benefit than that of the general. The final section is devoted to *decorum*, what is fitting and proper. By this Cicero understands the phenomenon of morality, that aspect of it which is turned towards our fellow-men, decency or propriety. What is proper in any given case is assessed in terms of human nature, which is characterized particularly by the ascendancy accorded to reason over instincts and emotions. It is here that Cicero introduces the celebrated metaphor of the masks which everyone wears. He is putting forward a theory of role-playing in order to elucidate what nature prescribes for man as a species and as a type involving an infinite variety of dispositions. In conclusion Cicero establishes that Panaetius had ignored the problem of conflicting *honesta*, the clash of two duties. He adds some considerations of his own indicating that 'vita activa' was more important than 'vita contemplativa', and that duties to the community took precedence over any kind of pure cognition.

In the second book Cicero proceeds from the notion of utility, arguing strenuously against the widespread opinion that seeks to separate the useful from the honourable and is incapable of realizing that true utility is always identical with what is honourable. The theme of this book is stated as: 'quonam modo hominum studia ad utilitates nostras allicere atque excitare possimus' – 'how one may win people over, how to acquire power and influence'.[13] It is therefore not a matter of 'utilitarian duties' (Cicero would only have shaken his head over this absurd combination proposed by a modern scholar.), but of matters similar to those that Cicero's brother Quintus had once dealt with in his *Commentariolum Petitionis*: how can an ambitious politician achieve success without infringing honestum? Cicero is concerned mainly with fame and with the means conducive to fame: military competence, jurisprudence, eloquence, donations. At the end of the work the duties of the statesman towards the populace as a whole are discussed. Here Cicero advances what seems to him the correct disposition of property rights – with the retention of private ownership as the supreme principle.

There then follows – at the beginning of Cicero's personal contribution, the third book – a renewed discussion of the relationship between the honourable and true utility. The remainder of the book is concerned with special cases. Cicero quotes particular instances where it seems doubtful whether the seemingly useful end could be reconciled with the demands of honour. He has arranged these cases in terms of the four cardinal virtues, but they are otherwise only loosely linked. There is a good deal of entertaining anecdotal detail in these episodes which are taken partly from Greek literature and partly from the contemporary judicial practice of Rome. For instance, the case of someone who hastily sells to an unsuspecting purchaser a house that is subject to an official demolition order, but is then required by the court to repay the difference in value – on the basis of the newly introduced principle which requires the seller to inform the purchaser of known defects. A good deal of this special pleading might be reviewed from an angle which Cicero does not discuss – that is, whether a moral duty has been infringed only or whether a legal obligation subject to the jurisdiction of a court is also involved.

Cicero has transferred the doctrines of Panaetius to Roman circumstances and to the relevant social and historical conditions. The material from Greek sources is augmented with numerous Roman examples, and the discussion repeatedly revolves round the sphere of the politically active Roman aristocrat, his aims and the means he uses to achieve them. A good many problems and various symptoms of decay associated with the great political crisis that had persisted since the time of the Gracchi are also reflected in the work. In particular, Cicero's experiences with Caesar and his image of Caesar have left a deep impression here (mainly in the first book). Cicero was incapable of seeing in his great contemporary anything other than a destructive force – a man who had ruined the Republic by his unbridled lust for power and fame, – recognizing Caesar's genius but repudiating it because of its pernicious effects. In the passage on justice he writes, for example:

> Many men are misguided and ignore the claims of justice on account of their lust for dominion, honour and fame. For what Ennius said, namely, 'There is no sacred community or loyalty in monarchy', has far-reaching significance. If something is so constituted that a number of individuals cannot achieve eminence, then such discord generally arises that it is extremely difficult to preserve the hallowed community. This was recently demonstrated by the unscrupulous behaviour of Gaius Caesar, who cast aside all divine and human law for the sake of the pre-eminence on which he had deludedly set his heart. As far as this phenomenon is concerned, it is an aggravating circumstance that it is precisely the greatest minds and the most illustrious talents who are most susceptible to the craving for honour, authority, power and fame.[14]

The great man's unbridled lust for power is also referred to in the section on 'magnitudo animi', and, although Caesar's name is not actually mentioned, it is obvious that his behaviour played no small part in guiding Cicero's pen:

> It is unfortunate that obsession and the intemperate lust for eminence should arise in conjunction with this sublimity and greatness of soul ... The more a man is distinguished by the greatness of his soul, the more he will wish to be the first among all others, to be unique, in fact. But if a man seeks to outstrip all others, then it is hard to respect equality, the most important feature of justice. So it happens that men of this ilk brook no restraint by way of discussion or public and legal process, and that they appear on the scene as spendthrift party leaders, because they wish to acquire as much power as possible and would sooner be superior by dint of force than equal by virtue of justice.[15]

While Cicero was still deeply immersed in his work on *De Officiis* a new political development began to arouse feelings in him that fluctuated between hope and apprehension. Octavian was importuning him with letters: he had troops, he wished to march against Antony and was seeking the support of the Senate. Cicero saw this as a splendid chance for the Republic. On the other hand, he wondered whether Octavian was powerful enough to stand up to Antony and, if he was, whether he could be trusted to form a sound alliance with Caesar's assassins.

There were a great many arguments against this conjecture. Gaius Octavius – the young man who was just beginning to play a decisive part in Roman politics in the autumn of 44, at the early age of nineteen – was descended from a wealthy, but not particularly aristocratic family. His mother, Atia, it is true, was the daughter of Julia, a sister of Caesar; his father, the first of the Octavians, had pursued a political career leading to the office of praetor and a governorship. Everything else followed from the family connections with the Julian household. The childless Caesar cared for his grand-nephew and in his will made him not only his principal heir, but also his adopted son. The news of his great-uncle's murder reached him in Apollonia on the Adriatic coast of Albania where he had gone on in advance, meaning to take part in the campaign against the Parthians. He resolved, in spite of all the warnings he received, to claim his inheritance, and proceeded to Rome. Here he presented himself at a popular meeting as Caesar's heir and also had his adoption confirmed in a public record. In this way, however, a conflict was bound to arise with Antony, who had taken possession of Caesar's estate and who was seeking to become his political successor. The young man, who henceforth called himself Gaius Iulius Caesar after his adoptive father (with the addition of Octavianus to denote his descent), was playing an exceedingly hazardous game, for he lacked connections, followers and authority. He proceeded with extreme caution, and, in particular, he left the Republicans in the dark concerning his true aims. On the one hand, there was no lack of evidence that he intended to avenge his adoptive father and take over his position. On the other hand, his youth and his insignificance furnished him with an extremely effective mask: he was not taken seriously.

This was more or less how things stood in the spring of 44 when Cicero first heard of Octavian and began to take an interest in him. 'The advent of Octavian: are people rallying to him; can we count on a radical change?'[16] 'What is happening about Octavian is all the same to me.'[17] These are the first two references to Octavian in correspondence with Atticus. Even two weeks later, following a first meeting on Cicero's Cumanum estate, he simply states that Octavian meant to claim his inheritance and that there would be trouble with Antony.[18] A few days later Octavian was 'quite submissive' at another meeting with Cicero, behaving in a 'very respectful and friendly manner' towards him.[19] At this point, however, certain misgivings are voiced: Octavian's entourage addressed him as 'Caesar', which Cicero cannot bring himself to do. In the middle of May he made the statement already referred to: that he did not care for the games which Matius and others were organizing – on behalf of Octavian, as Cicero well knew.[20] In the middle of June he attempted an asessment in some detail of Octavian's somewhat enigmatic character:

> In Octavian there is a great deal of talent and valour, and he seemed so disposed towards our heroes as we would wish him to be. But we must give serious thought to what may be expected of his years, his heritage and his counsellors ... We must at any rate devote careful attention to him and, above all, separate him from Antony.[21]

Here, for the first time, we have an indication of the policy to which Cicero applied himself from the end of 44 onwards, and which led to his downfall: the pact which the Republicans concluded with Octavian with the aim of forming a common front against Antony.

In November it looked as if the time was ripe for an alliance of this kind. At the beginning of October the strained relations between Antony and Octavian had led to an open quarrel. Both men had then left Rome: Antony, as already mentioned, had made his way to Brundisium, to the four legions he had had despatched from Macedonia; Octavian went to the Campania to enlist troops among his adoptive father's veterans. It was from here that Cicero was urged in a series of letters to join in a common action. He should commit himself to the cause, come to Capua and save the state a second time – and in any case hasten to Rome. Octavian seems to have been well aware of the kind of language he must use in order to win Cicero over.

Cicero was once more trapped in a well-high insoluble dilemma. No one would risk breaking away from Antony in such a precarious situation.[22] Besides, this would merely be a matter of getting out of the frying-pan into the fire, for Octavian would terrorize the state just as much as Antony, if he once got the upper hand.[23] Finally, Octavian had raised claims to a statue of Caesar at a public meeting and had sworn to regain the honours accorded to his adoptive father, as far as this might be permitted him – 'I wouldn't care to be rescued by someone of that kind', was Cicero's comment.[24] On the other hand, Brutus was letting a glorious opportunity slip away![25] If Cicero did not go to Rome, then a great deed might be performed without him being present![26] So he intended to arrive there on 12 November, he suggested. But then he hesitated once more.[27] Finally he wrote on 28 November that he meant to venture into the heart of the political conflagration –

without concealing the fact that he was being constrained to do so less by political considerations than by tiresome financial problems.[28] As already mentioned, he was not back in Rome until 9 December.

Both Octavian and Antony were absent at the time. Octavian had addressed the populace at the beginning of November (on which occasion he had sworn the oath that so upset Cicero), and had then retreated before Antony. Antony had marched his Macedonian legions to Ariminum. (The governor there, Decimus Brutus, seemed disinclined to acknowledge the exchange of provinces that had been decreed by law.) Antony then made his appearance in Rome with great military pomp and circumstance, no doubt with the aim of intimidating the Senate. He was on the point of having Octavian declared an enemy of the state, when he received news that his rival had succeeded in persuading two of the Macedonian legions to change sides. He had to be content with a hurried Senate meeting at which the praetorian provinces were assigned by lot, before departing for Upper Italy during the night of 28/9 November.

Matters were then advanced by developments in Upper Italy, the province of Gallia Cisalpina. Immediately after his arrival in Rome Cicero had called on Pansa, one of the consuls for the following year, from whom he heard, to his satisfaction, that Decimus Brutus was refusing to hand his province over to Antony. He tried to encourage Decimus Brutus in his stand by writing him a letter: all hopes of restoring liberty now rested with him; they would be frustrated if Antony seized possession of Upper Italy.[29] At the same time letters were despatched to Plancus, the governor of Cisalpine Gaul, with whom Cicero had always enjoyed good relations: it was imperative for him to join in the battle for the Republic.[30] The new people's tribunes (they had, as usual, assumed office on 10 December) convened a meeting of the Senate for 20 December: it was to debate security measures for 1 January, when the new consuls would assume office. Shortly before the meeting began, a communication arrived from Decimus Brutus: he was placing his province at the disposal of the Senate and the Roman people. Cicero, who had originally meant to wait until the beginning of the new year, decided that the moment to strike had come. He hastened to the Senate and delivered a speech before the crowded meeting – the *Third Philippic* – in which he exhorted the senators to adopt measures preparing the way for his policy: an alliance with Octavian and a declaration of war on Antony.

The speech begins with the urgency of the situation: no more delay! Cicero then went on at once to explain what the real issue was. The private moves on which the campaign against Antony had hitherto been based (and which, as it turned out, boldly anticipated a distant goal) must be confirmed by the Senate. Octavian, here referred to officially as Gaius Caesar, had raised an army, and his action ought to be endorsed. Two legions had deserted Antony and had gone over to Octavian: their action had to be approved. And now Decimus Brutus's declaration of loyalty – that, too, was a move by a private individual, since a law forced through by Antony had virtually deprived Decimus Brutus of his Upper Italian governorship: thus, this act, too, had to be endorsed by the Senate. Cicero then proceeded to launch a witty and scathing attack on the latest measures taken by Antony. A renewed appeal to the Senate to declare its support for Octavian and Decimus in the name of freedom was then followed by a motion in these terms: (1) Brutus and his province deserved praise and gratitude; (2) the allocation of provinces promulgated by Antony on 28 November was null and void; (3) the new consuls should report as soon as possible on proposals in favour of Octavian and the legions which had gone over to his side. The Senate approved this motion, which was actually of a provisional nature only, and Cicero communicated the result to a public meeting on the afternoon of 20 December – not without placing his own interpretation on it (the *Fourth Philippic*).

Cicero certainly considered 20 December as a further climax in a life that was full of such turning-points. This is indicated by the fact that he once more addressed the Senate and then the assembled people and that he declared his commitment to the constitution in twin speeches – as he had done on 7 and 8 November 63 in the battle against the Catalinarian conspiracy, and on 5 September 57, following his return from exile.

Even a few weeks earlier he had been expressing nothing but gloom and despair. In particular, the introductions to books 2 and 3 of '*De Officiis*' declare in a tone of profound resignation that the state is doomed, that the Senate and the courts no longer exist, and that consequently he could see no possibility of political action or political writing. His philosophical writing was the only substitute for all this that he could possibly consider. Letters to various official personalities at the time were scarcely more optimistic in tone: 'We are all suppressed, the conservatives have no leader and the tyrannicides are scattered throughout the wide world.'[31]

Now, however, his despair was transformed into an elation that bordered on certainty. For what Cicero had identified only shortly before as the sole dim glimmer of hope now seemed to be imminent:

'that the Roman people would some time or other prove to be worthy of their ancestors'.[32] This at any rate is what is proclaimed in the *Fourth Philippic*, which urges his hearers to aspire to the *virtus* of their forefathers.

> Cling to this, I beg you, oh, Quirities: your forefathers bequeathed you valour as a kind of legacy: everything else is fallacious and uncertain, fragile and unstable – valour alone has deep roots; no force on earth can shake it or shift it from its place. With its aid your ancestors began by conquering the whole of Italy, then they destroyed Carthage, annihilated Numantia and made the mightiest kings and warlike peoples subject to our rule.[33]

The part which Cicero assigned to himself in this new departure – the revival of the ancient Republican political sentiment – is outlined in the concluding sentence of the *Fourth Philippic*: 'Hodierno die primum ... longo intervallo me auctore et principe ad spem libertatis exarsimus' – 'This very day is the first occasion in a long time that we have been inspired with the hope of freedom at my instigation and under my leadership.'

1 January was drawing near, and with it the Senate meeting customarily held on that day under the chairmanship of the new consuls. In the meantime hostilities had begun. Antony was besieging Decimus Brutus in Mutina (Modena), and Octavian was marching his troops to the theatre of operations in Upper Italy. Hence Cicero had every reason to believe, following the *Third Philippic*, that he was not far from his goal. The Senate would not only approve the initiatives taken by the military leaders, Decimus Brutus and Octavian, but would also declare Antony an enemy of the state.

Things turned out quite differently. Apparently Cicero had taken Antony's supporters by surprise on 20 December. Either they had not been prepared for such vigorous action or they had not taken sufficient notice of the meeting on 20 December, which, it was assumed, would recommend no more than provisional measures. Hence, they were not in a position to counter Cicero's move effectively. Now, on 1 January, the formal requirements for more far-reaching decisions had been established. The consuls were chairing the meeting, and the agenda specified – apart from the sacrifices customarily ordained for the new year – the question of honours and rewards for those who had rendered services to the state (i.e. for Decimus Brutus and for Octavian and his troops), as well as a debate on the general political situation.

On this occasion, when it really mattered, the opponents of Cicero's warlike policy turned up well prepared and in a determined mood. The consuls exercised restraint, as was only proper. Both of them had served under Caesar since the campaign in Gaul and they had been rewarded by him with the highest offices in the state. Now, as stalwart soldierly characters, they stood loyally by the Republic – initially, no doubt, in the sense that they regarded Cicero's belligerent policy as too precipitate and were more inclined to favour negotiations with Antony and an amicable settlement of the dispute. Accordingly, in the debate that ensued, Pansa did not call on Cicero to speak first, but chose another former consul, his father-in-law, Quintus Fufius Calenus. He was a relatively insignificant member of the Caesarean party and a declared friend of Antony; he now became the spokesman of all those who recommended the Senate to come to an understanding with Antony. On 1 January he claimed that Antony wanted peace and proposed to the Senate that they should send a deputation to request him and his adversaries to cease hostilities forthwith. Cicero's policy was thus called into question, and a conflict between the two opposing views in the Senate began which was to last for months: a radical view that called for war at once, and a moderate view that preferred negotiations and delaying tactics.

Cicero attempted to counter this unexpected resistance by the speech which he published under the title of the Fifth Philippic. Fufius Calenus's proposal, he argued, was pernicious, absurd in fact. One could not come to an understanding with Antony, who had been guilty of all manner of breaches of the law and of acts of violence, as one could with an external enemy, with Hannibal, for example. There could be no turning back for the Senate, which had in effect already declared Antony to be an enemy of the state on 20 December. Cicero therefore wanted a state of emergency proclaimed: the consuls should do everything in their power to shield the Republic from harm.

He then turned to the second item on the agenda: the matter of honours. He proposed five motions to the Senate, beginning with Decimus Brutus, the defender of Mutina, whose action should be endorsed. He then moved on to a man who had not been mentioned on 20 December, Marcus Aemilius Lepidus – a brother-in-law of Marcus Brutus and an utterly undistinguished member of the Caesarean party who should be honoured by a gilded equestrian statue for services in the province he had once governed, Hispania Citerior. He had come to an understanding with Pompey's recalcitrant son Sextus. Cicero evidently thought that he could win over the devious Lepidus to the Republican cause in this way. The proposal should be seen in the context of his attempts to win over the governors of the western provinces, of which we also have evidence in his letters. In the third place, he turned his attention to Octavian, putting his case convincingly and at great length and seeking the powers of command of a *propraetor* for Octavian, along with various other special powers. In order to dispel manifest misgivings about this highly dubious proposal, Cicero pointed out forcefully that Octavian, as distinct from his adoptive father, had been guided exclusively in his actions by the approval of the Senate, the knights and the Roman people. Than came the final two proposals, dealing with the quaestor Egnatuleius, who had led one of the two Macedonian legions over to Octavian's side, and with Octavian's troops.

The debate on 1 January was inconclusive. On the following day it seemed as if Cicero's proposal to impose a state of emergency would achieve majority support, but a people's tribune demanded that the vote should be postponed. All the same, Cicero's proposals on the bestowal of honours went through; his proposal regarding Octavian was approved in even more favourable terms. Whereas on 3 January the debate on whether to send a delegation or to declare war had ended inconclusively, on the following day a compromise put forward by the lawyer Servius Sulpicius Rufus was approved. A delegation would require Antony to raise the siege of Mutina, evacuate Upper Italy and retire to quarters on the near bank of the River Rubicon, which marked the frontier, at least 200 miles from Rome. Otherwise a state of war would be declared.

Cicero was by no means satisfied with this outcome. The decision to send a delegation had momentarily blocked the main purpose of his policy – war against Antony. Besides, it had become obvious that not even staunch Republicans like Sulpicius Rufus were prepared to back him unconditionally, because they had good grounds for doubting the durability of an alliance with Octavian. The *Sixth Philippic*, delivered before a popular assembly just prior to the decision on 4 January, attempted to extract as much as possible from the existing situation. The dispatch of a delegation was tantamount to a declaration of war, since Antony would in no circumstances yield to demands in the form of an ultimatum. Nevertheless, Decimus Brutus deserved to be relieved more rapidly. At any rate, after the delegation's return, everyone would have to admit that war was inevitable.

So the tug-of-war continued. Cicero was tirelessly active, and so were his opponents. Thus, in the middle of January, it was decided, in line with Cicero's idea, that one of the consuls (Hirtius was chosen by lot) should assume command of the troops in Italy, while the other raised recruits throughout the country. At the same time, Antony's supporters were trying to gain public backing for their cause by spreading all kinds of conjectures about Antony's readiness to come to an understanding and by denigrating Cicero as a rabble-rouser and warmonger. This campaign provoked the *Seventh Philippic* in which Cicero used a routine meeting of the Senate to air his views, trying to show that there was no alternative to his war policy. He deplored the initial situation, the feeble and foolish speeches of those who called themselves consulars, or former consuls. He is here reverting to a point which he made on a number of occasions in his letters at this time.[34] It was precisely the senior senators, the former consuls, who behaved in a scandalous fashion, as opposed to the other, energetic senators – they were either pusillanimous or malicious. The complaints which he had expressed to Cassius in the autumn of 44 continued, but he had not the least intention of letting this opposition on the part of most leading members of the Senate cast doubt on the feasibility of his intentions.[35] On the contrary, in the *Seventh Philippic* he goes to great lengths to make clear to his listeners, with the aid of a scheme taken from the academic rhetorical tradition, that a peace with Antony would be shameful, risky and totally out of the question.

The delegation returned on 1 February. It had consisted of the former consuls Sulpicius Rufus, Piso and Marcius Philippus. One of its members, Sulpicius Rufus, had succumbed to illness *en route*. As Cicero had predicted, Antony had not accepted the Senate's proposals, but had put forward proposals of his own. The Senate proceeded to debate these on 2 February, with Lucius Varius Cotyla present as Antony's intermediary. Fufius Calenus recommended that negotiations should be continued through a second delegation. Cicero demanded that the Senate should declare war on Antony and ban any communication with him. Neither of these proposals was accepted. In keeping with the devious tactics it had followed hitherto, the Senate adopted a proposal by Lucius Iulius Caesar, an uncle of Antony. It stated that an insurrection was in progress and the decision was taken to assume military attire from that point onward.

The debate was continued on the following day and provoked Cicero's *Eighth Philippic*. Disappointed by the course events had taken, the speaker was even more outspoken in his denunciation of those forces who were opposing his policies so stubbornly: the consul Pansa, Fufius Calenus, his most dedicated opponents, and finally the remaining former consuls. He concluded with a proposed motion which scarcely called for the elaborate criticism of the opposition that had preceded it. Anyone who deserted Antony before 15 March should be let off scot-free, and anyone who henceforth joined him should be regarded as an enemy of the state. This discrepancy between the speech and the concluding proposal suggests that Cicero had essentially composed the speech for its own sake. Like the *Seventh Philippic*, it was meant to justify and advance his war policy. Cicero's motion was adopted.

After the Senate had drawn from the meagre results of the delegation equally meagre conclusions, it turned – probably on 4 February – to the question of how the deceased member of the delegation, Sulpicius Rufus, should be commemorated. Pansa delivered a speech in praise of the late senator and proposed that a statue should be erected in his memory. The much respected former consul, Publius Servilius Vatia Isauricus, raised an objection to this proposal. Traditionally, the honour of a statue was accorded only to those who had died a violent death while serving as emissaries. This view, in its turn, prompted Cicero to protest – and hence the *Ninth Philippic* was written.

It is a solemn piece which refrains from criticizing his fellow-senators and is otherwise distinguished by the almost total absence of any attack on Antony. Cicero begins by seeking to show, via reference to illustrious precedents, that Sulpicius Rufus had indeed fully deserved the honour of a statue. He then proceeds to present this conscientious and self-sacrificing patriot to his audience, moving on smoothly to a general account of the character and achievements of the distinguished lawyer, with a passing mention of his son's grief. This passage appears to be modelled on the traditional Roman funeral oration, the *laudatio funebris*. Cicero then suggests a bronze statue, unmounted, as being the most fitting tribute to the unassuming personality of the deceased. His proposal also calls for a state funeral, followed by burial in a hereditary tomb on a public site. These remarks, delivered with every sign of sincerity and affection, did not fail to have their effect, and the Senate voted for the proposal. The statue was in fact erected. As Pomponius, a second-century lawyer, confirms, it was sited in his day in front of a grandstand built under Augustus.[36]

With the delegation's failure, events began to stagnate in Italy. But then news which arrived in Rome from the eastern provinces in the second half of February once more set Cicero's policy in motion. In the first place, it was the Greek scene which became the focus of interest. On 28 November Antony had managed to have his brother Gaius, praetor at the time, made governor of Macedonia for the following year. Gaius was to succeed Quintus Hortensius, the son of the famous orator. Although the Senate's resolution of 20 December had revoked the appointment, Gaius hurriedly set off for Macedonia. His plans were foiled by Marcus Brutus, however. Antony had tried to get rid of Brutus in the summer of 44 by relegating him to an insignificant post as governor of Crete. Brutus did set off in the second half of August – not for Crete, however, but for Greece.

In the autumn he began to act on his own initiative. Numerous Republicans joined him, and Cicero's son and the youthful Horace, who were studying in Athens, served as his officers. Hortensius placed himself under Brutus's command, as did the troops stationed in Illyria. Cicero heard of these and other successes at the beginning of February, and the consul Pansa learned of them shortly afterwards. Brutus had raised an army, Gaius Antonius was powerless, Greece, Macedonia and Illyria had placed themselves at the disposal of the Republic. Pansa instantly called a meeting of the Senate, no doubt in order to provide a legal basis for Brutus's unauthorized action.

As on every occasion since 1 January, Fufius Calenus was permitted to speak first. He proposed that the Senate should confirm that Brutus's report was in order, and that Brutus should be prohibited from continuing to command the army. Thereupon Cicero delivered his *Tenth Philippic*. He was naturally concerned to legalize the position which Brutus had created for himself, and so he took a great deal of trouble to dispel any misgivings the Senate might have: that Brutus had acted in an arbitrary manner, that Caesar's veterans might be enraged by any move to recognize Brutus's authority. The first objection he refuted with the argument that Brutus had rescued Greece and the troops stationed there for the state, that he had acted as an agent of the state according to the principle that the troops belonged to the state and should not be employed against the state. The second objection Cicero simply declared to be groundless – in view of the fact that it was only supporters of Caesar's cause who were fighting a war to lift the siege of Decimus Brutus. Cicero was successful: the Senate responded to his appeal and entrusted the defence of Macedonia, Illyria and Greece to Brutus.

A little later it was the provinces to the east of Greece that attracted most attention. Here it was mainly Cassius who was involved. He, too, had been allocated an appointment by Antony which was intended to render him innocuous: as governor of the province of Cyrenaica. However, Cassius made his way to Syria to take over control, as Brutus had done in Macedonia. His opponent was Dolabella, to whom the governorship of Syria had been assigned by a Senate resolution of April 44. The Senate decrees of 28 November and 20 December, which related to the provinces allocated to the praetors, did not affect this ruling, which applied to a consul. Consequently, Dolabella departed for the East at the end of 44 with a legitimate claim to his Syrian command.

For some time nothing definite seems to have been known in Rome about Cassius. Two letters which Cicero sent him at the beginning of February could only report unconfirmed gossip.[37] The earlier letter speaks of a rumour that Cassius was in Syria and had assembled an army there. If everything was true that people said, we read in the second letter, then the Republic rested on firm foundations: 'From the furthest coast of Greece down as far as Egypt we are protected by the high command and by the troops of our best officers.' Cicero no doubt included his friend Trebonius in his wishful thinking. He was the legitimate governor of Asia Minor, with a province that linked the domains of Brutus and Cassius. Trebonius had gone to the East already in the summer of 44 and had sent Cicero flattering reports from Athens concerning his son's studies.

Cicero soon learned that his scheme would not work. When he wrote to Trebonius at the beginning of February to tell him of his success on 20 December and to inform him of the current situation in Italy, he was not yet aware that his friend had suffered a gruesome death.[38] The news arrived in Rome during the second half of February. It was doubly painful for Cicero, because no other than his former son-in-law, Dolabella, had committed the dreadful deed. The *Eleventh Philippic* gives us the following description:

No suspicion of war (who would have supposed such a thing) – extremely friendly conversations between Dolabella and Trebonius followed, there were embraces as deceitful tokens of goodwill amidst ostensible affection. The handshake, customarily a sign of fidelity, was profaned by disloyalty and treachery: in the dead of night an entry was forced into Smyrna, as though it were a hostile city, although it is the home of our oldest and most faithful allies; Trebonius was taken unawares: if the perpetrator entered openly as an enemy, Trebonius was a victim of his own negligence, if the killer was still acting the innocent citizen, then he was the victim of ill-fortune.... After Dolabella had lacerated the worthy man with abuse from his shameless mouth he interrogated him regarding the state treasury for two whole days, during which he was scourged and tortured. Then, after they had broken his neck, he chopped his head off and had it paraded on a spear; the rest of the corpse he flung into the sea.[39]

In those days people were hardened to all sorts of atrocities, and Cicero's account is certainly not devoid of rhetorical elaboration. Nevertheless, such a degree of cruel depravity still roused the Senate to wrathful indignation, and a unanimous motion proposed by Fufius Calenus declared Dolabella to be an enemy of the state.

The debates of the succeeding days were concerned with the search for a suitable candidate who would overthrow Dolabella. One member of the Senate – perhaps Pansa, who was chairing the session – suggested that the officiating consuls should decide between themselves by lot who was to take over Asia Minor, and who would receive Syria and conduct the campaign against Dolabella, as soon as Decimus Brutus had been relieved. A second proposal, put forward by Lucius Iulius Caesar, recommended that Publius Servilius Vatia Isauricus, Trebonius's predecessor in office, should be given command of a special force.

At this point Cicero rose to speak. His elaborate motion, the *Eleventh Philippic*, took account of the fact that Cassius was not in Cyrenaica, but had set out for Syria in order to forestall Dolabella. Assuming that Cassius had managed to gain the upper hand there, as Brutus had done in Macedonia, he proposed that Cassius should be entrusted with the governorship of Syria and should also be given superior powers of command in Asia Minor and Bithynia-Pontos. He rejected the two previous proposals. A special command, he argued, was a dangerous expedient that ran counter to the Senate's principles. (Only a short time previously he himself had contrived to have extraordinary powers of command conferred on the youthful Octavian!) The appointment of the officiating consuls would merely distract their attention from Mutina and also delay the prosecution of Dolabella. What was needed, Cicero goes on to explain, was a commander who was available and who had proved himself; either Brutus or Cassius would qualify, but since Brutus was tied down in Greece, only Cassius was left. Both of them, Cicero continued, had gone to a province which was not their own, both had acted on the principle that anything was legally right and proper which would preserve the state. The Senate was unable to accept the parallel that Cicero had drawn between Brutus and Cassius, since it was by no means certain at that point that Cassius had established his ascendancy in Syria. It resolved to entrust the campaign against Dolabella to the two consuls.

Cicero was not discouraged by this setback. In an address to the people he assured them that Cassius had not waited for a decision by the Senate, nor would he wait: he was perfectly prepared to protect the state according to his own principles. To Cassius himself Cicero wrote with cheerful unconcern that what he should take as the guideline for his actions, even without the Senate's consent, was precisely this: the state and his own fame.[40] As it happened, Cassius had dispatched the following letter to Cicero on the very same day – 7 March:

> Gaius Cassius the Proconsul offers greetings to Marcus Cicero. If you are well, I am glad; I am well. Know that I have arrived in Syria and joined the generals, Lucius Murcus and Quintus Crispus. These valiant men and worthy citizens handed their troops over to me as soon as they were informed of what had happened in Rome and, in agreement with me, they are conducting public affairs with a firm hand. Know, too, that the legion that Quintus Caecilius Bassus led has come over to me, and that the four legions that Aulus Allienus brought up from Egypt have been handed over by him. Now I do not think you need any further encouragement to defend me, in my absence, and to defend the state to the best of your ability. I would like to inform you that you and the Senate do not lack a strong contingent of troops, so that you can set about your defence of the state with high hopes and in good heart. My friend Lucius Carteius will arrange everything else with you. Farewell. Written on 7 March in camp by Tarichea.[41]

From the beginning of March Italy, and the West in general, figured in the forefront of the Senate's negotiations. Cicero's failure to have Cassius appointed governor of Syria encouraged Antony's followers in the city to call for renewed negotiations. It is hardly surprising that Fufius Calenus supported this proposal, while Piso and Pansa were also involved. Thus, a Senate proposal for a second mission to Antony emerged. As members of the delegation five former consuls were appointed who had in the preceding months exerted most influence on the Senate's policy towards Antony: Fufius Calenus, Piso, Servilius Vatia, Lucius Iulius Caesar and Cicero.

This course of events seems to have given rise to some dissatisfaction, so that Pansa was obliged to have the matter discussed again a few days later. Servilius claimed that his friends and relations had criticized him for taking part in the proposed mission; he would have to withdraw his consent. He was followed by Cicero, who declared in his *Twelfth Philippic* that he, too, was not in a position to negotiate with Antony. They had proceeded on false assumptions, he claimed, when they decided on a second mission; they had been misled by the proposers of the motion into thinking that Antony was seriously interested in a peace that would be acceptable to the Senate. Cicero then reverted to arguments which he had deployed in previous speeches opposing negotiations with Antony, and asked to be excused personally on account of the irreconcilable hostility that prevailed between himself and Antony. The Senate abandoned the plan after both Servilius and Cicero had refused to cooperate.

It was probably on 20 March that Pansa set out for Upper Italy early in the morning in order to join his colleague Hirtius as commander of the operations against Antony. On the same day a meeting of the Senate took place under the chairmanship of the city praetor, Marcus Caecilius Cornutus. Official communications from two of the western governors were read out: from Lepidus (Hispania Citerior and Gallia Narbonensis) and Plancus (Gallia Transalpina). Lepidus had remained silent in response to the honour of a golden equestrian statue which had been bestowed on him at the beginning of January on a motion proposed by Cicero. Now he advised the Senate to make peace, at the same time threatening war, if his advice were not followed. This was his reply to a letter which Pansa had circulated to all provincial governors, instructing them to place themselves at the disposal of the Senate. The letter from Plancus contained a similar recommendation for peace, although it did not threaten military reprisals. Cicero thus once again had good reason to believe that his policy was threatened. What was more, after Antony had been informed of the plan for a second mission, he had made a statement about the political situation. Cicero had a copy of this letter which took Hirtius and Octavian severely to task, representing them as defectors from the Caesarean party and tools of Pompey's faction.

Servilius opened the debate, repudiating Lepidus's suggestion. The next speaker was Cicero, who attempted in his *Thirteenth Philippic*, to refute everything that was opposed to his view of the matter. He also dealt at length with the letter from Antony, quoting it sentence by sentence and advancing his own view against his adversary's at each point. In this way Antony's letter has been preserved in its entirety – thanks to Cicero – so that the *Thirteenth Philippic* allows us to observe with exceptional clarity the lines on which the two men were thinking.

As far as Antony was concerned, a Republic, an integral political structure, no longer existed. He could see nothing but *partes*: the parties of Caesar and Pompey. This, he said, was what Hirtius and Octavian should bear in mind, so that a situation should not arise in which defecting troops would take the field against the forces of Antony, i.e. that the supporters of Caesar should not find themselves fighting against each other, as intended by that trainer of gladiators, Cicero. Antony thus wished to be regarded as an out-and-out supporter of the Caesarean party and also committed himself to their 'programme' of revenge for Caesar's murder. Accordingly, at the end of this letter he offered Hirtius and Octavian a kind of amnesty. All offences committed hitherto would be forgotten, if Hirtius and Octavian were prepared to withdraw from their misguided alliance with the party of Pompey.

Cicero, for his part, advanced his faith in the Republic in opposition to Antony's *partes*. Current events were not simply a matter of a conflict between two parties; they concerned a war which the entire state was waging against a traitor. And, as far as the category of 'Pompeians' was concerned, he stated, 'You are not waging war on the Pompeians, but on the state as a whole'.[42] Octavian, he commented in reference to Antony's offer, would not be distracted from his purpose of saving the fatherland. Octavian, like Hirtius and Pansa, was far better qualified than Antony to represent the party of Caesar – if parties were not long since a thing of the past.

Thus, in the quarrel between Antony and Cicero, two opposite and irreconcilable points of view collided head-on. Doubtless, Antony's way of thinking was closer to the actual facts, while Cicero tended to regard as reality his own wishful thinking, which was rooted in the Republic's illustrious past. If Antony nevertheless was unable to convince those to whom he addressed his letter, this was due to the place he assigned to his own person in the Caesarean party. He claimed sole leadership and was not prepared to come to an understanding on an equal footing. As was to appear a few months later, the error in Antony's calculation could be corrected, whereas Cicero's could not.

The Senate adopted the view expressed by Servilius and Cicero, and Cicero addressed himself by letter on the same day to Lepidus and Plancus. Lepidus was sharply rebuked with icy politeness.[43] A peace which would afford a depraved individual absolutely unlimited power to rule left all reasonable beings with only one choice – whether to prefer death to slavery. In Cicero's opinion Lepidus would be better advised if he were not party to a peace settlement which neither the Senate nor the nation nor any self-respecting individual would approve. The letter to Plancus, however, strikes a totally different note. Evidently Cicero believed he could influence him by an appeal to a moral concept of the state which they both shared. 'So believe me, my dear Plancus', he pleaded, 'all the degrees of distinction which you have achieved hitherto (and you have risen to very high honours) will encompass nothing but the outward marks, not the true inward character of worth, if you do not unreservedly take up the cause of the Roman people's liberty and the prestige of the Senate. Tear yourself away at last, I beg you, from those to whom you are bound, not by common conviction, but merely by the bonds of circumstance.'[44]

A few days later Cicero continued his attempt to win Plancus over by means of a second letter.[45] But before these appeals reached him, Plancus had explained in a letter to the Senate that he had hitherto concealed his true allegiance since he needed time to arm and to muster his troops, but now he was prepared to commit himself and his forces on the side of the Republic.[46] At the time, his declaration may have been sincere enough, and Cicero, who was delighted, rewarded it with high praise on behalf of the Senate. But Plancus was much too cautious to follow his words with unambiguous deeds, and so Decimus Brutus remained among the governors of the western provinces as the sole dedicated champion of the Republic.

Cicero's authority had reached its climax at that point, Plutarch reports.[47] Cicero himself stressed more than ever the sense of duty which inspired his utterly tireless battle for the Republic's survival. In February he had assured his friend Paetus that nothing caused him so much anxious concern as the freedom and security of his fellow-citizens; he neglected no opportunity to encourage them to act and to take necessary precautions.[48] At the end of March or the beginning of April the correspondence with Marcus Brutus started; it has only partially been preserved. In what was probably the earliest of these letters Cicero speaks of his situation at that time and of what he had achieved. He gives his correspondent to understand that he was the *princeps*, the leading man who guided the Senate's policy – or, at least, one of the principes:

> I have done everything for the state, Brutus, that a man is obliged to do who has been placed by the judgement of the Senate and the people in the position I occupy, not only what might be deemed sufficient for such a man in other circumstances: loyalty, vigilance, patriotism – these are things to which everyone must be committed, after all. But I believe that a man who chooses to raise his voice among the leaders who take political decisions must also display prudent judgement, for, if I have undertaken the onerous task of steering the ship of state, and give the Senate false or useless advice, then I deserve blame in one case as much as the other.[49]

Finally, in his *Fourteenth Philippic*, Cicero claims that he had stood guard over the Republic ever since 1 January; that his house and his ears had been open day and night to receive suggestions and advice from all and sundry; and that his letters, his emissaries, his words of warning, in whatever context, had called for the Republic to be defended.[50]

The letters which have survived, scarcely more than a small fraction of what Cicero committed to paper in those turbulent months, are ample proof that these claims were not exaggerated. At that time Cicero was in correspondence with almost all those leading figures who were outside the city – with the exception of his arch-enemy, Antony. The collection *Ad Familiares* includes letters to and from Cassius, Decimus Brutus, Plancus and Lepidus; it also includes letters to Cornificius and from Asinius Pollio, the governor of Hispania Ulterior. The correspondence with protagonists on the Italian scene, with Octavian, Hirtus and Pansa (as well as with Marcus Brutus) was collected in separate volumes, but it has all perished, apart from a few quotations.

Cicero is not claiming too much, then, when he writes that all the political threads came together in his hands. During the first half of 43, especially in March and April, he was indeed the focus of events in Rome. The robustness of the homo novus, his business-like methods and tactical skill, the deadly precision of his phrasing: all those qualities which he possessed to an extraordinary degree, and which had once enabled him to put up such a superb performance in the critical circumstances of the fight against Verres or Cataline, once more stood him in good stead in his battle against Antony. At that time he must have maintained a first-class intelligence service, or at least a network of messengers, and his *prudentia* extended to his own security. The city was full of Antony's supporters, so that he dared not venture on to the streets without numerous bodyguards – if he did not simply prefer to stay at home.

Decimus Brutus, who was besieged in Mutina by Antony, was getting into difficulties. The outcome was balanced on a knife-edge, Cicero wrote to Cassius, Brutus was barely able to hold his own.[51] In a letter to Marcus Brutus already referred to, it is true, he added, that he was not particularly worried by the bad news from Mutina that reached Rome by letter or word of mouth.[52] He had confidence in the troops and their leaders; it seemed to him that only foresight and swift action were lacking here and there. Cicero was not to be disappointed. On 14 April, after an initial setback, the combined armies of the consuls and the propraetor Octavian won their first victory at Forum Gallorum, south-east of Mutina.

In Rome great anxiety prevailed until word of this success arrived. A rumour was circulating that Cicero intended to have himself proclaimed dictator on 21 April, the date of the city's foundation. It may be (as Cicero himself claims in the *Fourteenth Philippic*) that friends of Antony had put this tale about as a pretext for opposing the 'tyrant'.[53] On 20 April one of the people's tribunes denied this dangerous talk at a meeting he had convened, and a few hours later news of the victory reached the city. Cicero was then conducted in triumph to the Capitol and from there to the speaker's podium in the forum by a large crowd that had gathered in front of his house. 'I set no store by that', he wrote to Marcus Brutus, 'and, besides, it is not seemly – still: the consensus of all classes of the population ('omnium ordinum consensus'), the expressions of gratitude and the congratulations impress me because it is a splendid thing to be a friend of the people (Popularis) for the benefit of the people.'[54] Once again Cicero mistook an upsurge of enthusiasm on the part of those who were well disposed to him for a broad and viable majority of the Roman people. Once again he thought that his favourite idea of the 'omnium ordinum consensus' had been realized and could be sustained in the long term.

It was not long before the daily grind began to have its sobering effect again, and Cicero sensed at once that black and white were not as clearly divided for his adversaries in the Senate, the 'spineless former consuls', as they were for him. On 21 April the Senate debated the dispatch from the victorious general. Servilius proposed a festival of thanksgiving that would last several days, the first day to be marked by the donning of peaceful, as opposed to martial, garb. Cicero thought these measures were in part inadequate, in part inappropriate: he rose to deliver his last speech, the *Fourteenth Philippic*. He deplored that a festival of thanksgiving had been proposed without Antony having been declared an enemy, although such ceremonies were customary only after victories over enemies, not after victories in civil wars. He called for a festival of thanksgiving over fifty days, the conferment of the title of 'imperator' on the three generals, and a memorial to the dead. He exploited – evidently with success – the mood of the people to the disadvantage of his detractors and the envy of the 'malicious' former consuls. The Senate adopted his proposals.

On 21 April the allied forces at Mutina gained a second victory. The first goal which Cicero had set himself had thus been achieved: Antony was forced to raise the siege and withdraw from Italy, while Decimus Brutus regained his freedom of movement. True, Hirtius had been slain in the battle, and Pansa died soon afterwards from the wounds he had received on 14 April – the state was consequently in a grave crisis, lacking a legitimate head. The Senate was now finally persuaded to declare Antony and his followers enemies of the state on 26 April. The following day various areas of competence in the battle against these enemies were defined: Cassius and Brutus were to see to the overthrow of Dolabella, and Decimus Brutus was to assume the leadership against Antony, with Octavian as his subordinate.

This scheme did not work. Thirteen months after the murder of Caesar, when the liberators might well have thought that the Republic was well on the way to being restored, events took a turn in the opposite direction. Cicero must have become aware that his policy was beginning to dissolve into nothing, like a phantom, from the very day that had brought him one of his greatest triumphs. He did in fact carry on the fight for another few months, but the cycle of *Philippics* was never completed. Cicero interrupted it because he probably sensed that nothing substantial could be effected by words, everything that was to follow would be settled by weapons.

What we do have nevertheless is a unified whole, not simply by virtue of the objective circumstances, particularly Cicero's hostility towards Antony: his acute aesthetic sense contributed a great deal to this measure of inner, indeed dramatic, consistency. In the sequence of these fourteen 'scenes' nothing can be displaced without impairing the whole. One phase issues inevitably from the other, and subjective factors (Cicero's moods and his political assessments at each juncture) are closely interlocked with external influences (the opposition forces in the Senate, reports from the provinces).

The first two speeches more or less constitute the exposition. In them – and through them – the breach between Cicero and Antony came about, so that they furnish, in personal terms, the basic premise of their bitter quarrel. This is in no way affected by the fact that only the first speech, which was relatively mild in tone, seems to have been accessible to the contemporary public. It was in the second speech that Cicero apparently crossed a threshold of hatred that allowed no return. The first two letters are a subjective anticipation of subsequent events. Cicero worked himself up quite needlessly to the point where the clash with Antony was inevitable – at most, he was goaded on by Piso's example, but otherwise it came about of his own free will.

The inner mould was there, it now only needed to be filled by the external situation. It was not long before this situation arose, when Octavian began to arm his forces against Antony, and Decimus Brutus declared his loyalty to the Republic. Cicero seized his chance. With his two speeches on 20 December 44, which constitute the second act of the drama, he intervened forcefully in the intricate mechanism of the debate. This pair of speeches contains the outlines of Cicero's overall concept: the alliance with Octavian was to help bring about the destruction of Antony, the enemy of the state, and restore the free Republican order.

Cicero's policy, which aimed at war, provoked reactions: in the Senate powerful forces began to emerge which were opposed to a breach with Antony. Thus, the proposal for a delegation was placed on the negotiating table, a topic which – like a delaying factor – links the five succeeding speeches that make up, as it were, the third act of the Ciceronian drama. The first scene of that act, the fifth speech, carries on at the breakneck pace of 20 December and seeks to seize his opponent's stronghold in a bold surprise attack. The defeat in the Senate vote adumbrates the more cautious pace of the following scenes. Here Cicero has to content himself largely with oblique tactics, attempting to win over public opinion, in so far as it is not a matter of having specific measures adopted.

Following the failure of the delegation, it was developments in the East that gave a new impulse to events. The tenth and eleventh speeches, a closely linked pair forming the fourth act of the drama, provide evidence of this fresh phase. They reveal once more how Cicero, heartened by initial success, overreached himself at the second attempt. The tenth speech led to total victory, while the eleventh ended with a setback.

The last three speeches, finally, have in common the fact that they deal once more with the western sphere; the basic theme which links them is the elimination of renewed opposition to Cicero's war policy. It is from them, and from the simultaneous millitary operations – the two battles before Mutina and the relief of Decimus Brutus – that the fifth act of the drama issues, a forward-looking statement concerning the conflict embodied in the *Philippics*.

In his last rhetorical work Cicero once more stated in topical terms the basic ideas underlying his political convictions, committing himself to the platform he had proclaimed in his consular speeches and in his defence of Sestius. The battle against Antony seemed to him to be a fight to maintain the res publica, a fight involving all classes of Roman society. He regarded Antony – as was the case earlier with Verres, Cataline and Clodius – as an isolated phenomenon, a criminal bent on nothing but doom and destruction who had to be eliminated by a combined effort under the slogan, 'Respect for the Senate, Liberty of the Roman people, Welfare of the entire state', as proclaimed in the *Thirteenth Philippic*.[55]

The interpretation Cicero laid on events, using his customary categories – the common front of all conservatives on the one hand, the isolated villain on the other – was more questionable than ever. It assumed that the conflict between the supporters of Pompey and those of Caesar had been resolved, as if it were a thing of the past. Cicero certainly did not fail to understand that the situation was different in reality. When he represented aspirations as facts in his speeches, he was attempting to manipulate his hearers and readers in a particular way. Nevertheless, the scheme he envisaged for the conduct of the dispute following Caesar's assassination was not well founded. In this respect Antony's judgement proved to be sounder and more realistic. He went on using the categories 'Pompeians' and 'Caesarians', and regarded the conflict with Octavian as a domestic quarrel that ought to be settled as swiftly as possible.

The case is quite different with the idea of liberty – a second leitmotif of the *Philippics* and their actual ideological foundation. The concept thus sharply defined is novel, reflecting the experience of Caesar's dictatorship and harking back to the conspirators' political programme. It stands for the Republican constitution of the state and cannot be denied a certain justification – if we disregard the question as to whether such a constitutional order was feasible. The concept directly opposed to 'liberty' in the internal affairs of the state goes by the name of 'monarchy' or 'tyranny', and the name which – unlike any other – could guarantee this liberty was 'Brutus': it referred in the first place to the legendary founder of the Republic, but it might also refer to the two conspirators who bore that name. Given certain preconditions, liberty stands in a kind of strained relationship with peace – from this fact Cicero deduces a powerful argument in support of his belligerent policy. For peace, he explains, can mean servitude, so that we should aspire only to that peace which is founded on liberty – a peace in servitude, on the other hand, such as Antony would bring, is worse than death.[56]

18

Defeat and Death

'It is up to you to see to it ... that not a spark of this dreadful war remains.'[1] This is what Cicero wrote on 5 May to Plancus, the governor of Transalpine Gaul. After the twin victories at Mutina it seemed to him that all that was necessary in fact was to put the finishing touches to a successful operation – through the destruction of Antony. The relatively voluminous correspondence with three provincial governors – Plancus, Decimus and Marcus Brutus – that has survived from this period suggests this. It reveals what he expected to happen at that point and how his expectations were gradually disappointed.

The correspondence with Plancus is even and sedate in tenor. On the part of Plancus there is no lack of protestations of his patriotic sentiments and his friendly feelings towards Cicero. At the same time he is apparently not keen to risk his neck either for the Republic or for Cicero; he keeps his distance and limits himself to cautious troop movements and canny probing operations. One of the main topics is Lepidus, the governor of Gallia Narbonensis and Hispania Citerior. Will he remain loyal to the Republic or will he join Antony? A great deal depended on him, because Antony had withdrawn to his province. If anyone, he, who must be regarded for good reasons as an unreliable ally, would have to declare his allegiance.

On 13 May Plancus was able to give a favourable report of him: after tough negotiations he had declared himself ready to help the Republic, and the forces of the two governors would forthwith be combined.[2] But the very next day there was a contradictory statement: Lepidus would not allow Plancus to approach any closer, and his soldiers had shouted that they would not take up arms against anyone after so much blood had been shed.[3] Plancus declared that he would do all he could to defend his province; Cicero should send troops, so that Republicans should not lose sight of their objectives. A few days later Plancus was able to report more encouraging news in two successive letters.[4] Lepidus had twice asked him to come and see him, which he was ready to do in spite of his scruples and grave misgivings. ('I can't help shuddering: is there perhaps an ulcer concealed under the skin?') Lepidus was waiting for him because he needed help against Antony, who was no more than 24 miles away.

In Rome, too, Cicero remarked that one moment they heard from Lepidus what they wished to hear, the next moment they heard the opposite.[5] Was it a fact – as Decimus Brutus claimed to have heard from Plancus – that Antony had not been received by Lepidus? Then Plancus's letter of 13 May arrived. The Senate passed a vote of thanks, and Cicero added to his expression of pleasure a remark to the effect that, under the prevailing critical circumstances, Plancus should not regard the consent of the Senate as crucial in any issue: 'Ipse tibi sis senatus' – 'Be your own Senate'.[6]

On 6 June Plancus composed a letter that reported a *fait accompli*.[7] Lepidus had meant to lure him into a trap, but he had seen through the deception and had kept a distance of 40 miles between them – whereupon the troops of Lepidus and Antony had joined forces. Plancus expressed satisfaction that he had succeeded in marching back to his province without loss. He once more urged Cicero to provide reinforcements: Octavian should come and join him.

Rome was no doubt already informed of Lepidus's defection when this letter arrived – probably by the defector himself. Only a few days earlier Lepidus had assured Cicero that the Senate and the Republic could rely on him. On 30 May, however, he had the effrontery to address a letter to the Senate, the devious wording of which reveals that – unlike Antony, for example – he was not acting from sincere conviction:

> Marcus Lepidus, for the second time Imperator, Pontifex Maximus, offers greetings to the praetors, the people's tribunes, the Senate and the Roman people.
> If you are well, and your children, too, then it is good; I am well. I call upon the gods and upon men, conscript fathers, to bear witness to the sentiments and the attitude I have always cherished towards the state, and to witness that I have deemed nothing more important than the common good and liberty. This I would shortly have proved to you, had not destiny wrested my plan from my hands. For my entire army has adhered to its practice of preserving the lives of our citizens and the general peace by means of a mutiny and, to be frank, has forced me to concern myself with the salvation and the well-being of such a large number of Roman

citizens. So I beg and beseech you, conscript fathers, to desist from private disputes and to bear in mind the general good of the state and not to stigmatize as a crime the compassion felt by us and by our army. If you are concerned with the welfare and the dignity of all, then you will better serve both yourselves and the state.[8]

Henceforth Cicero's urgent appeals and his assertion that all hope rested on Plancus and Decimus Brutus had less effect than ever. Even although only six weeks had passed since the two engagements at Mutina, Antony once more had a respectable force at his disposal.[9] And in his last letter to Cicero – on 26 July – Plancus remained convinced that he could not risk a battle unless he obtained reinforcements.[10]

The correspondence with Decimus Brutus is in much franker terms. From the outset Brutus appears to be hesitant, indeed despondent: perhaps he had been affected by the prolonged siege. At any rate, it soon transpired that he was in no position to deliver a rapid counter-blow. Cicero, for his part, saw Brutus as mainly to blame for the discontinuation of the campaign against Antony (as had been decided by the Senate on 27 April), and when events took an unexpected, indeed a paradoxical, turn he made no secret of his disappointment and indignation. In a letter of 29 April Brutus undertook to drive Antony out of Italy (a modest goal), even then expressing his concern that Lepidus, 'an extremely fickle individual', might join forces with Antony.[11] In the following letter of 5 May there is not a word about measures he himself proposed to take.[12] He reported that Antony, who had been accompanied on his flight by no more than a handful of unarmed soldiers, was now once more at the head of a sufficiently large force. 'If Octavian had listened to me and crossed the Apennines', he went on, 'then I would have cornered Antony so that he would have perished of hunger rather than by the sword – but Octavian won't take orders, and he is incapable of giving orders to his own troops, and both these things are bad.' In the middle of May Cicero showed clearly how dissatisfied he was with the course of events.[13] The war did not seem to have flickered out but to have flared up once again; Antony had not fled, but had simply moved his theatre of operations.

Tempers grew more and more frayed on both sides. A few days later Cicero indignantly repudiated the accusation of cowardice that Brutus had made in a letter to the Senate which has since been lost; for his part, he criticized Brutus for excessively timid behaviour.[14] And so it went on: when Lepidus discarded his mask and joined forces with Antony, Brutus wrote almost triumphantly: 'In my profound concern I at least have the consolation that people may now understand that my fear of what has now happened was not in fact groundless.'[15] There was not much point now in lengthy discussions as to whether troops should be summoned from Africa, Sardinia or Greece.

As Brutus wrote these lines he was already on his way to Gaul to join Plancus, and a week later, about 10 June, the two governors reported from Cularo (Grenoble) that their troops had joined forces – in the best interests of the state, they do not neglect to add.[16] Cicero might well declare to Brutus that all hope rested on him and his colleague Plancus: Italy no longer had a military force under Republican command; Octavian could do exactly as he pleased.[17] At that time, indeed, Cicero had not grasped the situation with anything like this clarity; he still believed (or was determined to believe) that Octavian was executing the will of the Senate, so that on 30 June he managed to have a virtually anachronistic Senate resolution adopted which declared Lepidus to be an enemy of the state.

Cicero, after all, had for years been intimately associated with Marcus Brutus through a common political mentality, through philosophical studies, sympathy and friendship, so that the correspondence with him is hardly less frank than his correspondence with Atticus. Moreover, the issue was not simply Decimus Brutus, Lepidus and other individuals of the second rank, but the central theme of Cicero's policy: the alliance with Octavian. It is certain that Cicero, too, had decided to come to terms with Caesar's adopted son only for purely practical reasons – because he believed that the Republic could not prevail against Antony otherwise. And perhaps he had even had it in mind to drop the young man the moment he no longer needed him. Decimus Brutus, at any rate, claimed to have heard from a third party that Octavian had been struck by something Cicero had said: 'laudandum adolescentem, ornandum, tollendum' – 'the young man should be praised, honoured and then got rid of'.[18] Octavian had added that he would know how to stop himself being got rid of. Cicero denied strenuously that he had ever said any such thing – whether truthfully or not, it is hard to tell. In any case, Marcus Brutus wanted absolutely nothing to do with Octavian: he was consistently of the opinion that the Republican cause had to be defended against all members of the Caesarean faction. If anything, he would have been ready to enter into a tactical alliance with Antony rather than with Octavian.

A prelude to the great dispute points in this direction. Gaius Antonius, who had been appointed governor of Macedonia by his brother at the end of November 44, had fallen into the hands of Brutus. On 13

April two letters were read out in the Senate: one of them from Brutus, the other from Gaius Antonius. Even the superscription of Gaius Antonius's letter caused great astonishment: 'The Proconsul Antonius' – as if he were the legitimate governor of Macedonia! And Brutus seemed to confirm that Antonius bore this title with his consent – the Senate was even more astonished. A friend of Brutus declared that the letter was a fake. Cicero, to whom this way out seemed unacceptable, could not forbear from censuring Brutus's behaviour. The letter which he addressed straight away to Brutus warned him of the danger of misplaced leniency; the state must be defended, not simply from a tyrant (Caesar), but from tyranny itself.[19] Antony's supporters should be treated no differently from Dolabella. Cicero's next letter, written a few days later, reduced their difference of opinion to the following formula: 'But I cannot in any sense approve of your antithesis: you write that it is more important to prevent civil wars than to vent one's ire on the vanquished. Here I differ from you, Brutus. I cannot approve of your leniency. Salutary severity is better than the deceptive appearance of leniency; if we mean to be lenient, then there will be no end of civil wars.'[20]

It is certain that Brutus and Cicero took different views of Octavian from the very beginning. Cicero was aware of this, otherwise he would not have indicated so very clearly in his letter in the middle of April that Brutus had facilitated Antony's rise by his initial passivity, so that Octavian was then the only hope of salvation. After the second victory at Mutina Cicero praised the 'amazing potential ability' he detected in 'the lad' Octavian, adding, however, 'If only we could guide him and hold him in check amid the splendour of honour and prestige as we have done so far! It is going to be rather difficult, but I am very confident all the same.'[21]

Brutus, on the other hand, began to issue dire warnings concerning Octavian as early as May. In view of the honours that had been conferred on the youth, or were to be conferred on him, he wrote: 'Cicero, worthy and capable as you are, and most dear to me, both on my own account and for the sake of the state, you seem to me to put too much trust in your expectations, and the moment anyone performs a notable feat you are prepared to concede and allow anything at all, as if a character corrupted by gifts could not be seduced into evil designs!'[22] When he wrote his next letter he had evidently got wind of efforts to obtain a consulship for Octavian: 'As far as the consulship is concerned, I fear that your Caesar believes he has risen to a greater eminence by virtue of resolutions you have elicited than he would be prepared to forgo once he has achieved the consulate ... Consequently, I shall not commend your good fortune and your foresight until it seems to me quite certain that Caesar is satisfied with the exceptional honour bestowed upon him.'[23]

The rumour of Octavian's aspirations to a consulship was in fact somewhat premature, but it was by no means unfounded. Octavian, who was firmly lodged with his forces in Upper Italy and showing no signs of budging, began to blackmail the Senate. Who was in a position to stop him? He at once demanded his election as consul. At that point Cicero still had enough courage to ensure that this suggestion was refused. He informed Brutus during the course of June that Octavian, who had hitherto allowed himself to be led, had been disgracefully seduced into cherishing all kinds of unrealistic hopes.[24] In response to Cicero's objections the Senate showed great determination. Nevertheless, the citizens were uneasy: 'We have become a plaything, Brutus, the plaything of unruly soldiers and presumptuous generals; everyone demands as much authority in the state as he has power at his command; no principle, no restraint, no law, no tradition, no obligation counts for anything any more, no criticism, no shame in the eyes of posterity.' Cicero concluded on an irresolute and uncertain note. If Octavian would no longer obey him, if he succumbed to evil influences (which, he hoped, would not happen), then the state was defenceless; Brutus should therefore make his way to Italy as rapidly as possible.

The pressure exerted by Octavian mounted, the appeals for assistance that were addressed to Brutus became increasingly frantic, and the dispute over Cicero's policy grew more heated. Octavian made a further bid for the consulship, this time directly and not through intermediaries. He invited Cicero also to stand as a candidate; he would subordinate himself totally to Cicero. Cicero did not reply, and the Senate rejected this second approach. 'Octavian's army, that was a first-class force', Cicero wrote to Brutus on 14 July, 'is now not only of no use to us, but is actually forcing us to call on your army ... So come to our aid, in the name of the gods, as soon as you can, and you may be sure that you did your country no greater service on the Ides of March, when you and your comrades freed it from slavery, than you can do it now, if you come as quickly as possible!'[25] In a long letter written at the same time Cicero tries to refute the accusation that he had bestowed too much in the way of honours on Octavian.[26] Here, too, he ended with the appeal: 'One thing is necessary, Brutus: that you should come to Italy as soon as possible with your troops ... But do make haste in the name of all the gods! You know how much depends on the circumstances of the moment, how much depends on speed!'

What mattered was not saving the state from the tyrant, but saving it from tyranny as such. Cicero had confronted Brutus with this maxim in April, when the issue had been the treatment of Gaius Antonius. Now, in the summer, it was Brutus who had recourse to it as a criterion by which to judge Cicero's actions, and he came to a positively devastating conclusion. He had already sharply criticized Cicero in a letter to Atticus (here, in discussion with a friend he and Cicero had in common, he could speak his mind openly).[27] He did not doubt that Cicero had always acted with the best of intentions; nothing was more renowned than his loyal disposition towards the state. But, intelligent as he was, he had made a number of moves that were either ill-advised or prompted by vanity – so, for the sake of the state, he had imprudently made an enemy of the powerful Antony. What was the good of a war against Antony, if the price asked for the overthrow of one tyrant was his replacement by another, and if the man who liberated us from one evil was the cause of another which had even stronger and deeper roots? Cicero's anxiety brought about the evil he was trying to avoid; he was prepared to come to terms with his servitude as long as Octavian called him 'father' and was kind to him. What good were all the fine words he had found for the freedom of his fatherland, for dignity, death, exile and poverty? Brutus, however, was prepared to come to grips with the issue itself, that is, with tyranny *per se*, with special command appointments, with autocratic rule that deemed itself above the law. And he would not be diverted from this goal by any sort of servitude, however agreeable.

The letter to Atticus, Brutus's only letter to him, was followed by the last surviving letter to Cicero. Brutus had special, and indeed, painful occasion to turn to Cicero. Atticus had passed on to him an excerpt from a letter written by Cicero to Octavian in which Cicero asked for mercy for Caesar's assassins. Brutus wrote:

> This is how you thank him for his services to the state, you put proposals to him in such a humble and servile tone – what shall I write? I am filled with shame for my rank and my position: you are recommending him to spare my life! What death could be more dreadful! You admit quite openly that we have not got rid of tyranny but merely exchanged one tyrant for another. Read your words again and then dare to deny that they are the supplications of a slave before a king. The only thing you ask

of him, you write, is that he should spare those citizens who enjoyed the respect of all right-thinking men and the entire Roman people.[28]

Feeble despair was driving Cicero to beg a young boy for the life of those who had liberated the whole world. If things had come to this pass, why had he fought Antony? Brutus could not be satisfied with a life lacking dignity and freedom; Cicero must never again recommend him to Caesar's mercy, or himself either. His bold attack on Antony would merely gain him a reputation for timidity, if it was bought at the price of pleas addressed to Octavian. People would think he was not concerned to rid himself of a master, but only to serve a more lenient master.

In Cicero's final letter to Brutus on 27 July, the last of his letters to have been preserved, there is not a single word in reply to these grave charges.[29] Evidently Brutus's letter had not reached Rome at the time he was writing. Cicero once more begged Brutus to come instantly to the aid of the state, which was tottering on the brink of collapse. The victorious troops had refused to pursue the fleeing enemy, and a general who was not involved in operations had declared war on the state (the allusion is to Lepidus). 'But what pains me most of all as I write this', Cicero goes on, 'is that I have vouched *vis-à-vis* the state for a young man, hardly more than a boy, and I scarcely believe that I am in a position to keep my promise.' Nevertheless, this admission was at once retracted by Cicero, who, as always, was inclined to adjust reality to suit his own wishes, even shortly before the disaster. He was still hoping, but he had to contend with a great many evil counsellors round Octavian. In fact, there was no foundation whatsoever for the two possibilities on which Cicero was banking at that time. Brutus was battling with the Thracians in faraway Macedonia and was in no position to hasten to Italy. Octavian, on the other hand, had already started to negotiate with Antony and Lepidus.

One of the most muddled chapters in Roman history was drawing to its close. Octavian had concluded his bizarre alliance with the Republicans under Cicero's leadership only in order to force Antony to acknowledge him. This aim had been reached with the battles at Mutina, and Octavian could begin to come to terms with Antony. It soon became apparent that the entire western half of the Empire was lost to the Republican cause. Plancus and Asinius Pollo had gone over to Antony, and during an attempt to fight his way through to Macedonia Decimus Brutus fell into Antony's hands and was killed on his orders. This course of events was dictated in the main by the fact that the mass of soldiers stationed in the West tended to support the Caesarean party, so that there was hesitation and jockeying for position among the military commanders instead of the vigorous intervention that Cicero so ardently desired. This applied both to those who had no particular allegiance, like Lepidus, and to those who felt themselves to be Republicans, like Plancus.

In the summer of 43 Octavian, still ostensibly an ally of the Republicans, went on playing this part for the benefit of the legitimate authority in Rome, the Senate. At the end of July four hundred soldiers turned up as representatives of the army, demanding money they had been promised and seeking the consulship for their commander. They were forced to leave empty-handed, although one captain had said, pointing to his sword, 'If you won't give him the office, then this will do the job!'[30] At that point Cicero is said still to have been bold enough to rejoin ironically: 'If you challenge Octavian in that way, he will certainly take the office!' Octavian then began his advance on Rome with the entire army – the strongest force that was stationed in the West. An attempt to defend the city came to nothing and, as Octavian approached from the north, all and sundry set out to meet him. Cicero is reported to have called on him the following day and was received, it was said, with the ambiguous remark that Cicero was the last of his friends to make his appearance.[31] On 19 August the electoral act was staged; Octavian had picked an insignificant adjutant as his colleague, his cousin Quintus Pedius. Draft legislation was announced which revised the Senate's previous policy: the proscription of Dolabella was to be revoked and a special tribunal was to be set up to try Caesar's assassins. With Octavian's consent Cicero stayed away from the Senate meetings, and a sentence from his letter of thanks is the last statement by him that we have. 'I am doubly pleased that you have granted Philippus and myself leave of absence: you have forgiven what is past and will exercise mercy in the future.'[32]

When Octavian retired northwards again in October, the official story was that the battle against Antony was to be resumed. Soon this pretence, too, was dropped: Pedius forced the Senate to revoke their resolution declaring Antony and Lepidus enemies of the state. At the end of October Octavian, Antony and Lepidus agreed on a triple dictatorship – the triumvirate – on an island in the River Renus north of Bononia (Bologna). According to this agreement the triumvirate were superior to all the regular officers of state; they had the right to promulgate laws as well as to appoint officials and governors. The area which the Caesareans then controlled was divided: Antony was allocated Upper Italy and Gaul, Lepidus was given Spain (together with Gallia Narbonensis), while Octavian got what was left. The worst feature was the proscriptions, the publication of lists containing the names of political opponents, who were thereby outlawed. This horrific practice stemmed from Sulla's time, when the tables with lists of proscribed individuals were meant to set minimal limits to the blind fury of vengeance. The proscriptions of 43 BC differed from the Sullan precedent in that they were imposed for financial as well as for political reasons: the confiscated property was meant to fill the coffers for the war against Caesar's assassins in the East. Apart from this, they were conducted with meticulous regard for legal formalities – and with absolutely perfect efficiency. As soon as the lists of names had been posted, all ports and city gates were closed and homes were forcibly entered everywhere.

Antony demanded that Cicero should be the first victim, as the individual who had headed the opposition to him. Octavian is reported to have resisted this demand for two days, only consenting on the third day – after all, Lepidus had sacrificed a brother and Antony an uncle in this brutal campaign. As it happened, however, these two potential victims were able to escape execution – Lepidus's brother, because the soldiers let him go, and Antony's uncle, because he was reprieved by his nephew. It would no doubt have been possible for Octavian also to give his agreement at the conference and then contrive the escape of the man to whom he owed so much and whom he had only shortly before addressed as 'father'. As a first step a list with a series of prominent names, including Cicero's, was dispatched to Rome. Shortly afterwards the three commanders entered the city and were authorized by a popular assembly to rule without restriction for five years – as 'tresviri rei publicae constituendae', 'a triumvirate for the restoration of the state'. They then published the proscription edict in its entirety, allegedly outlawing 300 senators and 2,000 knights.

Almost nothing is known of the last months of Cicero's life. Asinius Pollio is said to have claimed in the course of a speech that Cicero had been willing to deny that he had been the author of the 'Philippics' but even Livy refused to credit this absurd disclosure.[33] Cicero probably spent the time on his estates, no doubt in a very poor mental and emotional state, constantly seeking, as he did during his exile, to assign the blame for his misfortune – to himself and to others. This would also explain the total absence of letters during the final few months; neither the collection '*Ad Familiares*' nor the correspondence with Brutus extends beyond the end of July. Only the formal letter of thanks to

Octavian, of which a single sentence survives, dates from August. It is conceivable that Atticus and Tiro destroyed the letters that were extant from that period because of their embarrassing contents.

Cicero was on his estate at Tusculum together with his brother when news reached them that they had both been proscribed. They decided – astonishingly, only now, and not months previously – to make their escape to Marcus Brutus in Greece. Their first destination was Cicero's villa in Astura, on the coast, to which they travelled by litter. On the way Quintus turned aside to provide himself with more funds; shortly afterwards he was denounced and killed, along with his son. Cicero reached Astura safely and from there made his way by sea to Circaei. After a certain amount of hesitation he resolved to carry on to his estate at Formiae, in order to embark at the nearby port of Caieta. While he was spending the night in Formiae Antony's hired killers caught up with him. His people tried to get him to Caieta along a woodland path, but he was surrounded and killed when he looked out of his litter. He is said to have died calmly: 'He was incapable of suffering adversity as a man – apart from his death', said Livy.[34] In accordance with instructions the murderer cut off his head and hands and brought them to Antony in Rome, who had them nailed to the speaker's platform in the forum.

On 7 December 43 Cicero suffered the same fate as, a year and nine months earlier, had befallen the only other Roman of his time who, in spite of all the differences between them, equalled him in stature: the fate of a violent death, which had previously struck down Pompey as well as Cato and which was soon to strike Brutus and Cassius – and, finally, thirteen years later, Antony himself. The protracted crisis in Rome, with its ceaseless civil wars, the transition from Republic to autocracy, inexorably snatched the lives of those who had committed themselves to a cause with no thought of retreat. Certainly, none of those we have mentioned had been as deluded as Cicero in the actions which led to their own doom. On the other hand, it was his influence, both political and literary, which stood for something real, for the aristocratic Roman Republic which had evolved in the course of centuries. And so it was no mere coincidence that his life came to an end only ten days after that 27 November when the rule of the triumvirate began, putting an end for ever to the constitution of the ancient res publica. More than the death of a Cato or a Brutus, Cicero's death symbolized the passing of Republican freedom.

Cicero's son Marcus, who had served as a cavalry commander under Marcus Brutus, had come to Rome against his father's wishes in order to stand for the office of Pontifex. He managed to return to Greece when the proscriptions threatened his life along with that of his father, his uncle and his cousin. He also contrived to escape the double battle at Philippi which destroyed Brutus and Cassius and the last Republican army. He then settled in Sicily, and from 39 BC he was back in Rome. He now enjoyed the protection of Octavian, who was trying to compensate the son for what he had done to the father. Marcus did in fact become Pontifex and in 30 BC he was substitute consul for a short time. Finally, he occupied the office of governor on two occasions – first in Syria, and then in Asia Minor.

Epilogue

With Marcus, the undistinguished son of a famous father, our knowledge of the Tullii Cicerones peters out. The family faded once more
into the obscurity from which Cicero's brilliant genius had rescued no
fewer than four generations. At the same time, however, the history
of Cicero's reputation began, a history which was not in the least
impaired by the fact that posterity from the outset found so much to
criticize in his life and his political career. Cicero became a favourite
topic of an art which he himself had practised in masterly fashion,
the art of disputation, of controversy, of the 'in utramque partem
disputare'.

Under the rule of Octavian, who gave himself the title of Augustus
after 27 BC, Roman literature reached a climax with Virgil and Horace.
At that time Cicero, the murdered 'enemy of the state', was still under a
ban of silence: none of the literary figures of the Augustan Age ever
dared to mention him, not even Horace, who was otherwise fairly
outspoken. The Emperor's attitude was not utterly hostile, however – it
was not he, but Antony who had sought Cicero's death, and Antony
had been vanquished in 31 BC in the battle for dominion over the
Roman Empire. Plutarch's biography of Cicero ends with an anecdote
that casts some light on Augustus's ambivalent attitude. The Emperor
had come to visit one of his grandchildren and found him reading a
book by Cicero. The boy was taken aback and hid the book in his
clothes, but Augustus asked to be given the book and recited a passage
from it on the spot. Then he handed the book back, saying, 'He was an
eloquent man, eloquent and patriotic.'

Cicero considered himself to be Rome's greatest orator: the dialogue
Brutus, which tells the story of Roman rhetoric, is designed to show
him as the supreme practitioner of the art. Posterity has agreed with
him. As early as the first century AD he had risen to be a classic of

Roman eloquence – indeed, of Latin prose in general. An impressive body of his speeches was diligently preserved and handed down, whereas the works of his predecessors, contemporaries and successors have all perished – with the single exception of a brilliant address which the younger Pliny, a friend of Tacitus, had once delivered on the Emperor Trajan in 100 AD. And Cicero the orator and stylist was soon joined by Cicero the philosopher. In particular, he became a source for the Church Fathers, and an important point of reference in arguments against the heathen philosophy that were by no means invariably hostile.

Historical developments outside Rome were totally beyond the grasp of the Roman imagination, and so Cicero could never have suspected that he – like Caesar, the founder of autocratic government, and Virgil, the author of the *Aeneid* – would achieve the status of a founding father of Europe through a humane culture that endeavoured to combine philosophical training with competence in the use of words as a public medium. But we cannot, and should not, enter further into this subject here; we should refer the reader rather to two sources in German which trace the history of Cicero's fame, culminating clearly in the age of Italian Humanism and the Age of Enlightenment in Western Europe. These are Zielinski's classic study, *Cicero im Wandel der Jahrhunderte* (*Cicero through the Ages*), Leipzig/Berlin, third printing, 1912, and a work by Bruno Weil, *200 Jahre Cicero* (*200 Years of Cicero*), Zurich/ Stuttgart, 1962.

Notes

Titles cited without an author are Cicero's works.

CHAPTER 1   CICERO'S ANTECEDENTS AND YOUTH

1 Plutarch 2, 1.
2 Livy 9, 44, 16.
3 Plutarch 1, 4.
4 *De Oratore* 2, 265.
5 *Brutus* 168.
6 *De Oratore* 2, 3.
7 *De Legibus* 2, 3.
8 *Ad Familiares* 16, 26, 2.
9 *Pro Archia* 5.
10 Ibid. 1.
11 Plutarch 2, 3.

CHAPTER 2   THE APPRENTICE YEARS

1 *Brutus* 313 f.
2 Homer, *Iliad* 6, 208.
3 *Ad Quintem fratrem* 3, 5, 4.
4 *Laelius de Amicitia* 1.
5 Ibid.
6 *De Oratore* 1, 186 ff.; *Brutus* 152 ff.
7 *De Oratore* 3, 6.
8 *Brutus* 127.
9 *Philippicae* 12, 27.
10 *De Divinatione* 1, 72; 2, 65.
11 *De Officiis* 1, 74 ff.
12 Plutarch, *Mar.* 35 ff.
13 *De Divinatione* 1, 106.

14   *Post Reditum ad Quiritus* 19 f.
15   *Brutus* 310.
16   Sallust, *Invectiva in Ciceronem* 2.
17   *Brutus* 306.
18   *Ad Familiares* 13, 1, 2.
19   *De Inventione* 2, 10.
20   *De Oratore* 1, 5.
21   Jerome, *Chronicles* pr. 1.

CHAPTER 3   FIRST CASES, A CRISIS AND A GRAND TOUR

1   *Pro Sex. Roscio Amerino* 142.
2   Ibid. 136.
3   Ibid. 137.
4   *De Officiis* 2, 27.
5   *Pro Quinctio* 69, 31.
6   *Brutus* 311.
7   *De Officiis* 3, 60.
8   *Brutus* 301 ff.
9   *De Oratore* 3, 228 ff.
10   *Oratoribus* 107.
11   *De Finibus* 5, 1 ff.
12   *Tusculanarum* 2, 34; 5, 77.
13   *De Legibus* 2, 36.
14   *Tusculanarum* 1, 24.
15   *Pro Cluentio* 32.
16   *Brutus* 85 ff.
17   *De Republica* 1, 13.
18   *Brutus* 315 f.
19   Ibid. 316.
20   Ibid. 151 ff.
21   *Ad Familiares* 4, 5.
22   *De Natura Deorum* 1, 6.

CHAPTER 4   QUAESTOR: THE FIRST APPOINTMENT

1   *Brutus* 318.
2   *Verrem* 2, 2, 181.
3   *Pro Caelio* 35.
4   *Ad Familiares* 9, 26, 2.
5   *Pro Caelio* 46.
6   Plutarch 20, 3; 29, 4.
7   *In Pisonem* 2.
8   *Verrem* 2, 2, 138.
9   Ibid. 2, 5, 35.

10 Ibid. 2, 2, 5.
11 Ibid. 2, 4, 74.
12 *Tusculanarum* 5, 64 ff.
13 Plutarch, *Marc.* 17, 12.
14 *Pro Plancio* 64 f.

CHAPTER 5 THE PROSECUTION OF VERRES

1 *Pro Plancio* 66.
2 Plutarch 7, 1 f.
3 *Verrem* 2, 1, 30.
4 Ibid. 1, 32 ff. and especially 53 ff.
5 Plutarch 8, 1.

CHAPTER 6 FROM AEDILE TO PRAETOR

1 *Ad Atticum* 1, 1–11.
2 Ibid. 1, 8, 3; cf. 1, 5, 8.
3 C. M. Wieland, *Cicero's Sämmtliche Briefe übersetzt und erläutert von C. M. Wieland*, vol. 1 (Zurich, 1808), p. 127.
4 *Ad Atticum* 1, 2, 1.
5 Ibid. 1, 5, 2; 1, 10, 5.
6 Ibid. 1, 5, 1; 1, 6, 2.
7 M. L. Clark, *Rhetoric at Rome* (London, 1962), p. 82, 10 f.
8 *Ad Atticum* 1, 5, 7.
9 Ibid. 1, 8, 2; 1, 9, 2; cf. 1, 10, 3.
10 Ibid. 1, 7; 1, 10, 4; 1, 11, 3.
11 Quintus, *Commentariolum Petitionis* 19.
12 I. Puccioni, ed., *Orationum Deperditarum Fragmenta* (Milan, 1963), p. 27, frag. 1.
13 *Verrem* 1, 29.
14 *Pro Cluentio* 139.
15 Quintilianus, *Institutio Oratoria* 2, 17, 21.
16 *De Officiis* 2, 51.
17 Ibid. 2, 59.
18 *Ad Atticum* 1, 10, 6.
19 *Philippicae* 11, 18.

CHAPTER 7 THE BATTLE FOR THE CONSULSHIP

1 Sallust, *Bellum Iugurthinum* 63, 6 f.
2 *Ad Atticum* 1, 1, 2.
3 Ibid. 1, 2, 2.
4 Quintus, *Commentariolum Petitiones* 46.
5 Clark, *Rhetoric at Rome*, pp. 61, 7 ff.

6 *Ad Atticum* 1, 1, 1.
7 Ibid. 1, 2, 1.
8 Plutarch, *Sull.* 32, 3; *Cic.* 10, 3.
9 Quintus, *Commentariolum* 10.
10 *Pro Caelio* 14.
11 Quintus, *Commentariolum* 7 ff.
12 *Contra Rullum* 2, 4; cf. *In Vatinium* 6; *In Pisonem* 3.

CHAPTER 8 THE CONSULSHIP

1 *In Pisonem* 4 f.
2 Puccioni, *Orationum*, p. 71, frag. 1.
3 *Ad Atticum* 2, 1, 3.
4 Ibid.
5 Plutarch 13, 2, ff.
6 Sallust, *Bellum Catalinae* 49, 2.
7 Plutarch, *Cat. min.* 21, 8.
8 *Pro Murena* 22 ff.; 61 ff.
9 *Ad Familiares* 5, 7, 2 f.
10 Ibid. 5, 1 and 5, 2.

CHAPTER 9 THE TURNING-POINT

1 *Pro Sex. Roscio Amerino* 136 ff.
2 *In Caecilium Divinatio* 7 f.
3 *De Imperio Cn. Pompei* 63 ff.
4 *In Caecilium* 70; *Verrem* 1, 36; *Pro Cluentio* 152.
5 *Pro Cluentio* 88 ff.
6 Quintus, *Commentariolum* 5.
7 *De Republica* 1, 10.
8 *Contra Rullum* 123 ff.
9 Ibid. 2, 5 ff.
10 Ibid. 2, 102 f.
11 *In Catilinam* 4, 14 ff.
12 Ibid. 1, 32; *Pro Flacco* 103; *De Domo sua* 94 *passim*.

CHAPTER 10 ON THE DEFENSIVE

1 *Ad Familiares* 5, 6, 2.
2 Aulus Gellius, 12, 12, 2 ff.
3 Sallust, *Invectiva in Ciceronem* 3.
4 *Ad Atticum* 1, 12, 2.
5 Ibid. 1, 12, 1; 1, 13, 6; 1, 14, 7.
6 Ibid. 1, 20, 2; 2, 1, 6.
7 *Pro Sulla* 23.

8   *Ad Atticum* 1, 19, 6; 1, 20, 3.
9   Ibid. 1, 18, 1.
10   Ibid. 1, 19, 10.
11   Ibid. 2, 1, 1 f.
12   *De Divinatione* 1, 17 ff.
13   W. Morel, ed., *Fragmenta Poetarum Latinorum Epicorum et Lyricorum* (Leipzig, 1927), p. 72, frag. 16 f.
14   *In Pisonem* 73.
15   *Ad Atticum* 2, 3, 3 f.
16   Ibid. 2, 7, 4.
17   Ibid. 2, 9, 3.
18   Ibid. 2, 16, 2.
19   Ibid. 1, 12, 3.

CHAPTER 11   EXILE AND RETURN

1   *In Pisonem* 12.
2   *De Divinatione* 1, 59.
3   *Ad Familiares*, 14, 4, 1 and 3; 14, 3, 1; *Ad Atticum* 3, 8, 4; 3, 12, 1; 3, 10, 2.
4   *Ad Atticum* 3, 15, 1.
5   Ibid. 3, 8, 4; 3, 10, 2; 3, 15, 4 ff.; *Ad Quintem fratrem* 1, 4, 1 ff.; *Ad Familiares* 14, 1, 1 f.
6   *Ad Atticum* 3, 15, 7; 3, 19, 3.
7   *Tusculanarum* 5, 106 ff.
8   *Ad Atticum* 4, 1, 4 f.

CHAPTER 12   UNDER THE SWAY OF THE TRIUMVIRATE

1   *Ad Quintem fratrem* 2, 3, 6.
2   *Pro Sestio* 98.
3   *Ad Familiares* 1, 9, 8.
4   *Ad Quintem fratrem* 2, 5, 3.
5   *Pro Balbo* 61.
6   *Ad Familiares* 7, 1, 4.
7   *Pro Plancio* 86 ff.
8   *Ad Atticum* 4, 8A, 4.
9   Ibid. 4, 6, 1 f.
10   *Ad Familiares* 1, 9, 11.
11   Ibid. 1, 9, 21.
12   *Ad Atticum* 2, 16, 3.
13   *Ad Familiares* 1, 9, 23.
14   Ibid. 5, 12.
15   *Ad Atticum* 4, 10, 1.
16   Ibid. 4, 13, 2.
17   *Ad Familiares* 1, 9, 23.

18 *De Divinatione* 2, 4.
19 *De Oratore* 3, 61.
20 *Ad Quintem fratrem* 2, 13, 1.
21 *Ad Atticum* 4, 16, 2.
22 *Ad Quintem fratrem* 3, 5, 1 f.
23 Ibid. 3, 7, 2.
24 *Ad Familiares* 8, 1, 4.
25 *Ad Quintem fratrem* 3, 5, 1.
26 *Ad Atticum* 4, 18, 2.
27 Ibid. 4, 8, 2.
28 *Ad Familiares* 7, 23.
29 Caesar, *De Bello Gallico* 5, 38 f.
30 *Ad Familiares* 7, 10.
31 Ibid. 2, 1–6.
32 Velleius Paterculus, *Historia Romanae* 2, 48, 3.
33 Cassius Dio 40, 53, 2 f.
34 *Ad Familiares* 7, 2, 2.

CHAPTER 13   THE GOVERNORSHIP OF CILICIA

1 *Ad Quintem fratrem* 1, 1, 2, f.
2 *Ad Atticum* 5, 15, 1.
3 *Ad Familiares* 2, 12, 2.
4 *Ad Atticum* 5, 7.
5 Ibid. 5, 10, 5.
6 *Ad Familiares* 13, 1.
7 Ibid. 8, 5, 1.
8 Ibid. 8, 10, 1.
9 *Ad Atticum* 5, 16, 3.
10 Ibid. 5, 15, 1.
11 Ibid. 5, 16, 2.
12 *Ad Familiares* 3, 8, 5.
13 Ibid. 3, 8, 8.
14 Ibid. 3, 9, 1.
15 *Ad Atticum* 6, 1, 2.
16 *Ad Familiares* 9, 25, 1.
17 *Ad Atticum* 5, 20, 5.
18 Ibid. 5, 20, 6.
19 Ibid. 5, 21; 6, 1; 6, 2.
20 Ibid. 5, 1, 3 f.
21 Ibid. 6, 3, 8.
22 Ibid. 6, 7, 1.
23 *Ad Familiares* 16, 1–7 and 9.
24 Ibid. 14, 5.

CHAPTER 14   THE CIVIL WAR

1   *Ad Atticum* 8, 14, 2.
2   *Ad Familiares* 16, 11, 12; 16, 12, 2.
3   *Ad Atticum* 7, 13, 1.
4   Ibid. 7, 11, 1.
5   Ibid. 8, 11, 1 f.
6   Ibid. 7, 7, 6.
7   Ibid. 7, 11, 3.
8   Ibid. 7, 13, 1 f.
9   Ibid. 7, 21, 1.
10   Ibid. 7, 7, 7.
11   Ibid. 8, 1, 3.
12   Ibid. 7, 17, 4.
13   Ibid. 9, 11A.
14   Ibid. 8, 3.
15   Ibid. 8, 15, 2; 9, 1, 4.
16   Ibid. 9, 6, 4 f.
17   Ibid. 9, 10, 2.
18   Plato, *Epistles* 7, 348A.
19   *Ad Atticum* 9, 16
20   Ibid. 9, 18, 1.
21   Ibid. 10, 18.
22   *Ad Familiares* 14, 7.
23   *Ad Atticum* 8, 16, 2.
24   Ibid. 8, 7, 2.
25   *Philippicae* 2, 37 f.
26   *Ad Familiares* 9, 9.
27   *Ad Atticum* 11, 7, 2.
28   Ibid. 11, 11, 1.
29   Ibid. 11, 6, 2; 11, 7, 2 ff.
30   Ibid. 11, 11, 1.
31   Ibid. 11, 13, 1.
32   Ibid. 11, 8, 2.
33   Ibid. 11, 16, 5.
34   Ibid. 11, 24, 3.
35   *Ad Familiares* 14, 20.

CHAPTER 15   THE PHILOSOPHER UNDER CAESAR'S DICTATORSHIP

1   *Ad Familiares* 9, 2, 5.
2   Ibid. 4, 7–9.

3 Ibid. 4, 4.
4 Plutarch 39, 6 f.
5 *Pro Rege Deiotaro* 5 ff.
6 *Ad Atticum* 13, 52.
7 *Ad Familiares* 7, 30, 1 f.
8 *Philippicae* 2, 84 ff.
9 *De Oratore* 2, 216–90.
10 *Ad Familiares* 7, 32, 1 f.
11 Ibid. 9, 16, 3 f.
12 Ibid. 15, 21, 2 f.
13 *Ad Atticum* 12, 2, 2.
14 *Ad Familiares* 9, 20, 1.
15 Ibid. 9, 17, 2.
16 Ibid. 9, 16, 7.
17 Ibid. 9, 23.
18 Ibid. 9, 26.
19 Ibid. 15, 16.
20 Ibid. 15, 17, 2.
21 Ibid. 15, 19, 3.
22 Ibid. 9, 7, 1 f.
23 Ibid. 9, 8, 2.
24 Ibid. 4, 14, 3.
25 Quintilianus, *Institutio Oratoria* 6, 3, 75.
26 *Ad Atticum* 12, 15.
27 *Tusculanarum* 3, 76.
28 *Ad Familiares* 4, 5.
29 *Ad Atticum* 12, 32, 1.
30 *Oratoribus* 35.
31 Tacitus, *Agricola* 1, 4.
32 *Oratoribus* 148.
33 *Academica Posteriora* 1, 11.
34 Augustine, *Confessions* 3, 7 f.
35 *Academica Posteriora* 1, 3.
36 *Lucullus* 6.
37 *Academica Posteriora* 1, 4 ff.
38 *De Divinatione* 2, 4.
39 Ibid. 2, 1 ff.

CHAPTER 16   THE IDES OF MARCH

1 Suetonius, *Iulius* 86.
2 *Ad Familiares* 6, 15.

3 *Philippicae* 2, 116.
4 *Ad Atticum* 14, 21, 3; 15, 4, 2; *Ad Familiares* 12, 4, 1 *passim*.
5 *Philippicae* 1, 1.
6 *Ad Atticum* 14, 10, 1; 14, 14, 3.
7 Ibid. 14, 1, 1.
8 Ibid. 14, 9, 2.
9 Ibid. 14, 6, 2.
10 Ibid. 14, 12, 1 *passim*.
11 Ibid. 14, 11, 1.
12 Ibid. 14, 4, 2.
13 Ibid. 14, 14, 2.
14 Ibid. 14, 10, 1.
15 *Ad Atticum* 14, 13.
16 *Ad Familiares* 9, 14 = *Ad Atticum* 14, 17A.
17 *Ad Atticum* 15, 4, 1 ff.
18 Ibid. 15, 20, 1 f.
19 Ibid. 15, 23, 1.
20 *Ad Familiares* 11, 29.
21 *Ad Atticum* 16, 3, 4.
22 *Laelius de Amicitia* 5.
23 *Ad Atticum* 14, 21, 3.
24 Ibid. 15, 14.
25 Ibid. 14, 13, 1.
26 Ibid. 16, 6, 2.
27 *Ad Familiares* 12, 16, 1 f.
28 Ibid. 16, 21.
29 *Ad Atticum* 16, 6, 4.
30 *Ad Familiares* 7, 19; *Topica* 5.
31 *Ad Familiares* 7, 19.

CHAPTER 17   THE FINAL BATTLE FOR THE REPUBLIC

1 *Ad Atticum* 16, 7, 2 ff.
2 *Ad Familiares* 11, 27.
3 *Ad Atticum* 15, 2, 3.
4 *Ad Familiares* 11, 28.
5 *Ad Brutus* 3, 4; 4, 2.
6 *Ad Familiares* 12, 2.
7 *Ad Atticum* 15, 13, 1.
8 *De Finibus* 1, 65 ff.
9 *Aulus Gellius* 1, 3, 10 ff.
10 *Laelius de Amicitia* 36 ff.
11 *Ad Atticum* 15, 13, 6.
12 *De Officiis* 3, 34.

13   Ibid. 2, 20.
14   Ibid. 1, 26.
15   Ibid. 1, 64.
16   *Ad Atticum* 14, 5, 3.
17   Ibid. 14, 6, 1.
18   Ibid. 14, 10, 3.
19   Ibid. 14, 11, 12 and 14, 12, 2.
20   Ibid. 15, 2, 3.
21   Ibid. 15, 12, 2.
22   Ibid. 16, 11, 6.
23   Ibid. 16, 14, 1.
24   Ibid. 16, 15, 3.
25   Ibid. 16, 8, 2.
26   Ibid. 16, 9.
27   Ibid. 16, 12.
28   Ibid. 16, 15, 6.
29   *Ad Familiares* 11, 5.
30   Ibid. 10, 3 and 5.
31   Ibid. 12, 22, 2.
32   Ibid.
33   *Philippicae* 4, 13.
34   *Ad Familiares* 12, 4, 1; 12, 5, 2; 10, 28, 3.
35   Ibid. 12, 2, 2 f.
36   Justinian, *Digesta* 1, 2, 2, 43.
37   *Ad Familiares* 12, 4 and 5.
38   Ibid. 10, 28.
39   *Philippicae* 11, 5.
40   *Ad Familiares* 12, 7.
41   Ibid. 12, 11.
42   *Philippicae* 13, 45.
43   *Ad Familiares* 10, 27.
44   Ibid. 10, 6.
45   Ibid. 10, 7.
46   Ibid. 10, 8.
47   Plutarch 45, 4.
48   *Ad Familiares* 9, 24, 4.
49   *Ad Brut.* 1, 2.
50   *Philippicae* 14, 20.
51   *Ad Familiares* 12, 6, 2.
52   *Ad Brut.* 1, 1.
53   *Philippicae* 14, 14 f.
54   *Ad Brut.* 9, 2.
55   *Philipiccae* 13, 47.
56   Ibid. 8, 11 f.; 10, 19 f.; 13, 1 ff.

CHAPTER 18   DEFEAT AND DEATH

1 *Ad Familiares* 10, 14, 2.
2 Ibid. 10, 15.
3 Ibid. 10, 21.
4 Ibid. 10, 18 and 17.
5 Ibid. 10, 20.
6 Ibid. 10, 16, 2.
7 Ibid. 10, 23.
8 Ibid. 10, 35.
9 Ibid. 10, 22.
10 Ibid. 10, 24.
11 Ibid. 11, 9.
12 Ibid. 11, 10.
13 Ibid. 11, 12.
14 Ibid. 11, 18.
15 Ibid. 11, 26.
16 Ibid. 11, 13A.
17 Ibid. 11, 25.
18 Ibid. 11, 20, 1.
19 *Ad Brut.* 5.
20 Ibid. 8, 2.
21 Ibid. 9, 1.
22 Ibid. 11, 3.
23 Ibid. 12, 2 f.
24 Ibid. 18, 3 ff.
25 Ibid. 22, 2.
26 Ibid. 23.
27 Ibid. 25.
28 Ibid. 24
29 Ibid. 26
30 Cassius Dio 46, 43, 4.
31 Appian, *Civil War* 3, 382.
32 *Ad Caesarem Iuniorem*, frag 23B Watt.
33 Elder Seneca, *Suasoriae* 6, 15 ff.
34 Ibid. 6, 22.

Appendix 1: Table of Dates (BC)

GENERAL HISTORY		CICERO'S LIFE	
106	Birth of Pompey	106	Birth of Cicero
100	Birth of Caesar	until 82	Education in Rome: Law;
91–89	Social War		Rhetoric; Philosophy
89–85	First Mithridatic War	81–79	Legal practice
88–82	Civil war between Marius and Sulla	79–77	'Grand tour' of Greece and Asia Minor: rhetoric;
82–79	Sulla's dictatorship		philosophy
74–63	Third Mithridatic War	75	Embarks on a senatorial
70	First consulate of Pompey and Crassus	70	career: quaestor Prosecution of Verres
67	Pompey appointed supreme	69	Aedile
	commander in campaign	66	Praetor; first political
	against pirates		speech ('On Pompey, as
60	Coalition of Pompey, Caesar		supreme commander')
	and Crassus (First	63	Consulship; Catalinarian
	Triumvirate)		conspiracy
59	Caesar as consul	62–59	Defence of his consular
58–51	Caesar as governor of Gaul;		policy
	Gallic War	58–57	Exile in Thessalonica and
56	Revival of the Triumvirate		Dyrrachium
55	Second consulate of Pompey	56–52	Policy serving the
	and Crassus		triumvirate; first phase in
53	Campaign against the		his philosophical writing
	Parthians; death of Crassus		(*On the Orator*; *On the*
	at Carrhal		*State*)
52	Pompey sole consul	51–50	Governor of Cilicia
49–45	Civil war between Caesar	49–48	At Pompey's headquarters
	and Pompey	47	Reprieved by Caesar
48	Murder of Pompey	46–44	Second phase of his
48–44	Caesar's dictatorship		philosophical writings

GENERAL HISTORY		CICERO'S LIFE	
44	Assassination of Caesar	45	Death of his daughter Tullia
44–43	War at Mutina	44–43	Campaign against Antony
43	Coalition of Antony, Lepidus and Octavian (Second Triumvirate)		(*Philippics*)
		43	Murder of Cicero

Appendix 2: Family Tree and Maps

Family tree of the Tullii Cicerones

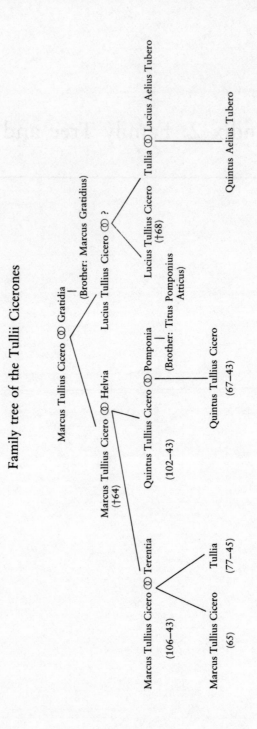

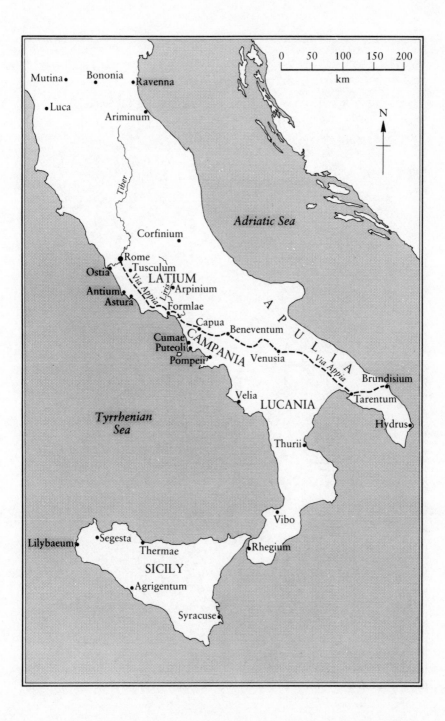

Mutina

Bononia

Ravenna

Luca

Ariminum

Tiber

Adriatic Sea

Corfinium

Rome

Ostia

Tusculum

LATIUM

Via Appia

Liris

Arpinium

Antium

Astura

Formlae

A P U L I A

Capua

Beneventum

Cumae

Puteoli

CAMPANIA

Venusia

Via Appia

Pompeii

Brundisium

Velia

LUCANIA

Tarentum

Tyrrhenian Sea

Hydrus

Thurii

Vibo

Lilybaeum

Segesta

Thermae

Rhegium

SICILY

Agrigentum

Syracuse

0   50   100   150   200

km

N

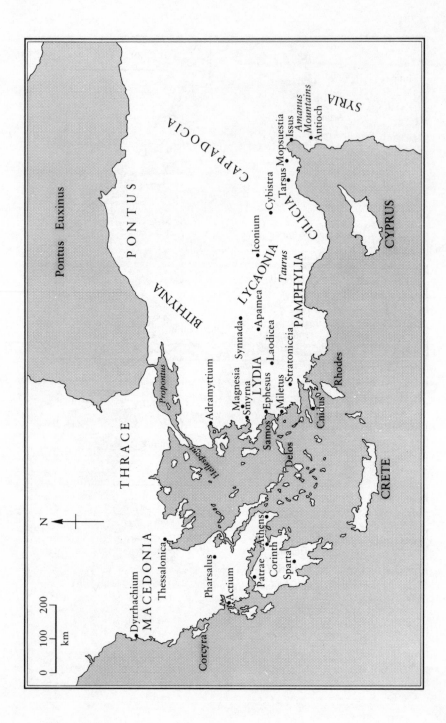

Pontus Euxinus

THRACE

MACEDONIA

PONTUS

BITHYNIA

CAPPADOCIA

SYRIA

Amanus
Mountains
Issus
Antioch
Tarsus Mopsuestia
Cybistra
CILICIA
Iconium
LYCAONIA
Taurus
Apamea
Synnada
PAMPHYLIA
Laodicea
Magnesia
Smyrna
LYDIA
Stratoniceia
Ephesus
Miletus
Samos
Adramyttium
Propontis
Hellespont
Rhodes
Cnidus
Delos

CYPRUS

CRETE

Dyrrhachium
Thessalonica
Pharsalus
Patrae
Athens
Actium
Corinth
Sparta
Corcyra

N

0   100   200
km

Bibliography

BIOGRAPHIES OF CICERO

Boissier, G., *Cicéron et ses amis*, Paris, 1865 (numerous reprints).
Gelzer, M., 'M. Tullius Cicero' (as a politician), in *Paulys Realencyclopädie der classischen Altertumswissenschaft*, VII A, Stuttgart, 1939, 827–1091; also as *Cicero – Ein biographischer Versuch*, Wiesbaden, 1969.
Grimal, P., *Cicéron*, Paris, 1986.
Meier, Chr., 'Cicero – Das erfolgreiche Scheitern des Neulings in der alten Republik', in *Die Ohnmacht des allmächtigen Diktators Caesar*, Frankfurt am Main, 1980, pp. 101–222.
Plasberg, O., *Cicero in seinen Werken und Briefen* (*Das Erbe der Alten, 2nd ser.*, 11), Leipzig, 1926.
Radke, G., ed., *Cicero, ein Mensch seiner Zeit*, Berlin, 1968.
Seel, O., *Cicero: Wort – Staat – Welt*, Stuttgart, 1953.

HISTORICAL BACKGROUND

Bengston, H., *Grundriss der römischen Geschichte*, vol. 1 (*Handbuch der Altertumswissenschaft* 3, 5, 1), Munich, 1967, pp. 153–247.
Bleicken, J., *Die Verfassung der römischen Republik*, 3rd edn, Paderborn, 1982.
Heuss, A., 'Das Zeitalter der Revolution', in *Propyläen Weltgeschichte*', vol. 4, Berlin-Frankfurt-Vienna, 1963, pp. 175–316.
Kroll, W., *Die Kultur der ciceronischen Zeit* (*Das Erbe der Alten, 2nd ser.*, 22–3), Leipzig, 1933.
Meier, Chr., *Res publica amissa – Eine Studie zur Verfassung und Geschichte der späten Republik*, Wiesbaden, 1966.
Meyer, E., *Römischer Staat und Staatsgedanke*, 2nd edn, Zurich, 1961.
Vogt, J., *Römische Geschichte: Die römische Republik*, 4th edn, Basel 1959.

PHILOSOPHY OF THE ANCIENT WORLD

Gigon, O., 'Die Erneuerung der Philosophie in der Zeit Ciceros', in *Recherches sur la tradition platonicienne* (*Entretiens de la Fondation Hardt* 3), Vandoeuvres-Geneva, 1957, pp. 33–61.

Harder, R., 'Die Einbürgerung der Philosophie in Rom', in *Kleine Schriften*, ed. W. Marg, Munich, 1960, pp. 330–53.

Hirzel, R., *Der Dialog*, 2 vols, Leipzig, 1895.

Luck, G., *Der Akademiker Antiochos* (*Noctes Atticae* 7), Bern, 1953.

Polenz, M., *Die Stoa*, 2 vols, 3rd edn, Göttingen, 1978/80.

Praechter, K., *Die Philosophie des Altertums* (*Fr. Ueberwegs Grundriss der Geschichte der Philosophie* 1), 12th edn, Berlin, 1926.

Schmid, W., 'Epikur', in *Reallexikon für Antike und Christentum*, vol. 5, Stuttgart, 1961, pp. 681–819.

Vorländer, K., *Geschichte der Philosophie 1: Philosophie des Altertums*, Reinbek, 1963.

CICERO'S PHILOSOPHICAL WORKS

Becker, E., 'Technik und Szenerie des ciceronischen Dialogs', dissertation Münster, 1938.

Bringmann, K., 'Untersuchungen zum späten Cicero' (*Hypomnemata* 29), Göttingen, 1971.

Burkert, W., 'Cicero als Platoniker und Skeptiker', *Gymnasium* 72, 1965, pp. 175–200.

Görler, W., *Untersuchungen zu Ciceros Philosophie*, Heidelberg, 1974.

Heilmann, W., 'Ethische Reflexion und römische Lebenswirklichkeit in Ciceros Schrift De officiis' (*Palingenesia* 17), Wiesbaden 1982.

Heinze, R., 'Ciceros "Staat" als politische Tendenzschrift', in *Vom Geist des Römertums*, E. Burck, ed., 3rd edn, Darmstadt, 1960, pp. 141–59.

Michel, A., *Rhétorique et philosophie chez Cicéron*, Paris, 1960.

Patzig, G., 'Cicero als Philosoph, am Beispiel der Schrift De finibus', *Gymnasium* 86, 1979, pp. 304–22.

Schmidt, P. L., *Die Abfassungszeit von Ciceros Schrift Ueber die Gesetze*, Rome, 1969.

Süss, W., *Cicero – Eine Einführung in seine philosophischen Schriften*, Akademie der Wissenschaften und der Literatur, Abhandlungen der geistes- und sozialwissenschaftlichen Klasse 1965, 5, Mainz, 1966.

van den Bruwaene, M., *La théologie de Cicéron*, Louvain, 1937.

Weische, A., *Cicero und die Neue Akademie – Untersuchungen zur Entstehung und Geschichte des antiken Skeptizismus* (*Orbis antiquus* 18), Münster, 1961.

RHETORIC IN THE ANCIENT WORLD

Clark, M. L., *Rhetoric at Rome*, 2nd edn, London, 1962.
Kennedy, G., *The Art of Rhetoric in the Roman World 300 B.C.–A.D. 300*, Princeton, 1972.
Kroll, W., 'Rhetorik', in Paulys *Realencyclopäie der classischen Altertumswissenschaft*, Supplementary vol. VII, Stuttgart, 1940, pp. 1039–138.
Marrou, H. I., *Histoire de l'éducation dans l'antiquité*, 3rd edn, Paris, 1960.
Norden, E., *Die antike Kunstprosa*, 2 vols, 4th edn, Leipzig, 1923.

CICERO'S SPEECHES

Barwick, K., *Das rednerische Bildungsideal Ciceros, Abhandlungen der Sächsischen Akademie der Wissenschaften, Philosophisch-historische Klasse 54, 3*, Berlin, 1963.
Berger, D., *Cicero als Erzähler – Forensische und literarische Strategien in den Gerichtsreden*, Frankfurt am Main, 1978.
Costa, E., *Cicerone giureconsulto*, 2 vols, 2nd edn, Bologna, 1927.
Heinze, R., 'Ciceros politische Anfänge', in *Vom Geist des Römertums*, E. Burck, ed., 3rd edn, Darmstadt, 1960, pp. 87–140.
Humbert, J., *Les plaidoyers écrits et les plaidoiries réelles, de Cicéron*, Paris, 1925.
Laurand, L., *Etudes sur le style des discours de Cicéron*, Paris, 1925.
Mack, D., 'Senatsreden und Volksreden bei Cicero', dissertation Kiel, Würzburg, 1937.
Neumeister, Chr., *Grundsätze der forensischen Rhetorik, gezeigt an Gerichtsreden Ciceros*, Munich, 1964.
Schulte, H. K., *Orator – Untersuchungen über das ciceronische Bildungsideal*, Frankfurt am Main, 1935.
Strasburger, H., *Concordia ordinum – Eine Untersuchung zur Politik Ciceros*, Borna, 1931.
Stroh, W., *Taxis und Taktik – Die advokatorische Dispositionskunst in Ciceros Gerichtsreden*, Stuttgart, 1975.
Weische, A., *Ciceros Nachahmung der attischen Redner*, Heidelberg, 1972.

CICERO'S LETTERS

Carcopino, J., *Les secrets de la correspondance de Cicéron*, 2 vols, Paris, 1947.
Jäger, W., *Briefanalysen – Zum Zusammenhang von Realitätserfahrung und Sprache in Briefen Ciceros*, Frankfurt am Main, 1986.
Peter, H., *Der Brief in der römischen Literatur, Abhandlungen der Sächsischen Akademie der Wissenschaften, Philosophisch-historische Klasse 20, 3*, Leipzig, 1901.
Schmidt, O. E., *Der Briefwechsel des M. Tullius Cicero von seinem Prokonsulat in Cilicien bis zu Caesars Ermordung*, Leipzig, 1893.

Index